*This book acknowledges the first people of Australia.*

*This book is dedicated to my immediate and wider family. My rock – my beautiful, spirited wife Sharon, and our wonderful, individual and accomplished young adult children Kate, Tom and Libby – the gift that gives back daily, and my reason for writing - our future. Our generations' greatest obligation is to nurture our families, and foster the social, fiscal, communal and national fabric for future generations.*

*To my parents, Jan and Graeme, who humbly provided me every opportunity to strive for my small slice of the lucky country.*

*Family is the bedrock of life.*

"You can't bargain with the truth,

'Cause whether you're right or you're wrong

We're gonna know what you've done

We're gonna see where you belong in the end …


You can't bargain with the truth,

'Cause whether you're rich or you're poor

You're gonna meet at the same door

You're gonna know the real score in the end."

(from the song 'In the End', by Yusuf Islam (formerly Cat Stevens)

# The Author

Darryl Barber was born in the southern suburbs of Sydney, Australia in 1960. He completed a Bachelor of Arts at Sydney University in 1981, an MBA (Executive) at the Australian Graduate School of Management in 1997, and completed the Australian Institute of Company Directors Diploma. Darryl's 'improvised' career has included a variety of corporate roles across a range of sectors including mining services, transport, and industrial products; he has consulted to a broad range of listed and privately owned companies, including involvement in a number of significant company turnarounds. He has also owned and operated his own manufacturing and supply chain businesses. Darryl currently heads a Brisbane based business.

Membership of any political party has never been of interest to Darryl, although he was involved in the LNP campaign for the federal seat of Griffith in 2013. Darryl is married to Sharon; together they have three adult children, Kate, Tom & Lib, living in Brisbane.

© Darryl Barber 2016

All rights reserved. No part of this publication may be reproduced, stored in a retrieval system, or transmitted, in any form or by any means, electronic, mechanical, photocopying, recording and/or otherwise without the prior written permission of the author. This script may not be lent, resold, hired out or otherwise disposed of by way of trade in any form, binding or cover other than that in which it is published, without the prior consent of the author.

## Contents

Preface

1.     'Great Southern Land'

## A. Current State & Issues – The 'Why'

2. Australian Politics - Current State
3. Political Parties – Democracy in Action?
4. Global Political Lessons
5. The Concept of Nations Competing
6. The Beds May in Fact be Burning
7. The Political Process Is Counter-intuitive
8. Is Avoiding Our Reality an Option?

## B. Getting Australia 'Off the Doom Loop' – The 'What'

9. Effective Governance
10. Values & Culture
11. Strategy
12. The Planning Conundrum
13. Managing Political Leadership Talent
14. Our Institutional Structure
15. A Sustained Focus on Productivity is Vital

## C. Regaining Momentum on the 'Flywheel' – The 'How'

16. Confronting the Brutal Facts
17. A True National Debate
18. Grass Roots Reform of our Core Institutions

19. Regaining Momentum on the 'Flywheel' – Discipline and the Dashboard

## D. Where to from Here – A Call to Disciplined Thought and Action

20. Where to from Here
21. Summary of Suggested Ideas and Actions

## Appendices

## References and Endnotes

# Preface

In 2012, a unique confluence of events found me doing something I didn't think I'd ever do. After the company in which I was a senior executive was acquired by an international company, I found myself temporarily not working. As it happened, my brother-in-law was at the same time being pre-selected by the Liberal Party as their candidate for the Federal seat of Griffith to run against, as it turned out, the incumbent Prime Minister.

Never one to shy away from a battle, my brother-in-law enlisted all the resources at his disposal, including his politically naïve, at the time underutilised brother-in-law. While I had no background in politics, I was 'drafted' to assist with the management of people and logistics, although I soon found myself substantially committed as part of an energetic team in everything from strategy to fundraising to day-to-day campaign operations, and even dealing with some of the off-the-street 'barrow pushers' that any campaign finds itself dealing with.

It was an extraordinary campaign, which almost saw a sitting Prime Minister unseated. Bill won the primary vote by almost 2%, losing only on preferences, and achieved the largest swing (5.5%) away from a Labor incumbent in Queensland. On election night, Mr Rudd in his concession speech on national television, was un-prime ministerially moved to remark, "it would be un-prime ministerial of me to say Bill Glasson, eat your heart out, so I won't". Bill's campaign team could not have received any greater affirmation that Bill had mortally wounded his opponent, or the Australian community any more poignant insight into Mr Rudd's emotional intelligence famine.

But that's not really why the experience was extraordinary. My brother-in-law was an outstanding candidate, who would have made an exceptional envoy for his electorate. He had moulded a wonderful, committed, passionate team around him, and the local 'burghers' of Griffith were empathetic, because they had a straight-talking, enthusiastic local advocate, who actually cared, and who they related to. The campaign team swelled to over 800 volunteers (and one horse - a story for another time) during the course of the campaign. I'll always be inspired by the passion of Bud, Virginia, Martin, Sue, Doug, Jennifer and the team of volunteers known as

'Glasson's Gladiators'. The sight of Malcolm Turnbull and Bill alighting from the ferry at Oxford Street Bulimba during the campaign for the Oxford Street Festival, surrounded by 700 high spirited people in Glasson shirts carrying balloons and spiritedly chanting Bill's name will stay with me for a long time!

Such are the highs of politics. However, even these circumstances were not the extraordinary personal insight.

What was truly extraordinary about the campaign was the understanding I developed of the inner workings of both major parties, their lack of professionalism and consistency, the trepidation volunteers held for the 'party machine', and the glaring focus on influence and funding. I became aware of the 'ugly machinery' of both major parties, and I didn't like what I saw. The raison d'etre of both parties it seemed, rather than providing a conduit for representative democracy, was instead an unadulterated drive for power. The constant pressure to fundraise, in preference to swaying voters was immense, despite and perhaps because Bill's campaign was one of the LNP's top electoral contributors during that campaign.

I believe, to this day, that Bill lost the election (on preferences; he was first past the post) because the LNP would not let us run the campaign we wanted to run, and in fact unwittingly hindered the campaign in various ways. Instead of allowing us to showcase Bill's credentials and his character, we ran the party's stock standard slogan campaign. Had we run the campaign we wanted to run, Bill would, I believe, likely be in Federal Parliament today. Bill was 'schooled' in the party methodology more than once by the party executive in Queensland, and, to be honest, another volunteer and I disregarded the party's instruction in one instance without Bill knowing, releasing a brilliant campaign video produced by some of his more dynamic supporters, which drew over 40,000 hits in the 48 hours leading up to the election. I watched as a number of faithful, tireless party stalwarts involved in the campaign began to question their party loyalty through the tension of the campaign. There were many other aspects of the culture and practices of Liberal, Labor and the Greens that were distasteful, and quite distinct to the professional, 'slick' culture one would expect at the apex of Australian leadership.

As Mark Latham candidly summarises, "you'd have to be a mug to stay in the system".[i]

Three years on, I've had time to reflect. Like most Australians, we continue to have heated discussions with family and friends about what is wrong, and what needs to be done to renew politics in Australia. Those discussions haven't uncovered all the answers, and neither will this book. All democratic systems have their issues. I'm writing because most Australians can see something wrong with our institutional system, however feel powerless to influence it for the better. But improve it must, and it will only do so if we collectively engage to 'encourage' it to happen. We have to urgently develop a platform for meaningful reform, because the party system is almost beyond repair in its current form. The Australian Institute of Company Directors pointedly refer to "the lack of progress on substantial national reform"[ii], which they cite as of 'serious concern'.

There is a mood of disquiet, an edginess in the electorate which cannot be ignored. Tony Jones notes 'Hugh Mackay had sensed a stirring, a restlessness in the national mood'[iii] in 2008. In 2016, that restlessness remains unrequited, perhaps heightened.

As a citizen and voter, who is represented - or rather more often, misrepresented - by our politicians, we retain the right to seek a mandate for strategic, long term style government. We can't simply leave it to politicians, lobbyists and journalists, and expect reform will occur in a popular way. It just won't happen. In fact, we have to play a stronger role, as 'activist shareholders', pressuring our institutions to break the shackles (from over-government and poor political process, for example) inhibiting our national progress. As Tony Featherstone writes, "Australia desperately needs a deeper conversation on the urgent need for reform."

Like the outcome of a recent governance summit agreed, governing for the long term is the key to sustainable value creation. This is as true for national government as it is for business.

I am, unequivocally, a proud Australian. I have no vested interest, other than abhorrence for short termism and waste, and a desire to see change for the better. Personally, I wouldn't dream of running any enterprise I was involved with the way we allow our major political parties and government institutions to function. The spectrum of core political activity, from lack of visible strategy, through the dark art of donations (which to this day remains open to corruption and gaming), and the 'you scratch my back' political favour remain the abhorrent principle source of internal political currency. Much of the process is counter-intuitive to sound organisational practice.

The risk for business, social and cultural leaders of publically speaking their mind, challenging government, assuming their comments support the public interest, should never outweigh the reward of frank debate. But they often do, constricting debate. My background is in business rather than government, and, while business is not government, it doesn't make sense to run any organisation the way we currently operate government.

Having decided, as an ordinary Australian, that I wanted to voice my opinion about the state of the Australian governance framework, deciding how to participate became the challenge. Both major parties are fraught with factions and infighting – joining a major party didn't make sense. Starting a new party or becoming involved with a minor party did not seem the best way to direct my energy, especially when I was questioning whether parties will look the same in the digital age, where a social revolution can start in less time than a bushfire. And so, the idea of writing as a means to start meaningful and productive conversations (and perhaps even some positive action) seemed like the most appropriate course of action to embark upon.

I've spent some time as a consultant to business, which leads me to be naturally wary of reports. Reports typically end in bottom drawers, seldom to be dusted off again. Government is renowned for producing reports, many if not most of which are, after time, shuffled carelessly aside, as the business of government moves inexorably onward.

This book found its genesis in countless aligned conversations rather than deep research or public opinion; it is a summary of personal insights based on a career in strategy and a curiosity for political processes and institutions. Some of the views expressed here will undoubtedly draw dissenting views and opinions. It is intended to kick-start a national debate as it has kick-started numerous 'micro-debates'. I've been heartened by the genuine passion and interest people have held for the topic of systemic political and partisan reform, particularly as I've told them about my writing.

The trigger for the title was a movie - 'Lions for Lambs'. Tom Cruise starred as the passionate, articulate but politically correct and morally tainted Senator; Meryl Streep as the liberal, seasoned, wary journalist. While the politician argued in support of an intended military action in the Middle East, the journalist became concerned she was being used as a potential vehicle to disseminate government messaging - 'propaganda'. Meanwhile, a sub-plot unfolded, with two determined university students arguing passionately in a political science class, ultimately deciding, at the cost of their lives, to put their pride on the line by fighting for their country, lambs to the slaughter at the behest of a bold new political strategy.

One of the students, at the height of an argument, shouted, "Every country should want to be better." The student's plea was to me, almost a personal call to arms. All the discussion, the mistakes and missteps, the rhetoric, ultimately is intended to achieve the outcome of a better nation; our national pride dictates that we all want Australia to be better, more decisive, agile and flexible. Effective, positive leadership is better for us, our families and our community, whether better means safer, more communal, equal and inclusive, wealthier or happier. We are utterly sick of the jargon, pointless and unnecessary parliamentary feuding and point scoring, and conversations without outcomes which are not assisting but impeding national progress. It will, however, require lions to facilitate change.

We realise that the problems faced by our government are typical of those faced by most if not all forms of government. It would be unfair to isolate our government as being different, or worse than other democracies. We are in fact better than many, if not most. However it is equally important that we do what we can to improve, not timidly ignoring issues in the context of what is normal, as lambs would do.

We have placed the blame on poor leadership, particularly in more recent times, however it is my thesis that if we investigate more thoroughly, we will find it is our system of government which is letting us down. It is time we relegate our focus on people, and direct our energy towards improving our governance framework. While we may have had some less than wonderful leaders in recent times, we should be asking whether we have a system which develops and selects leaders who are best skilled to lead, or a system which enables them to lead as we'd expect them to lead.

The intent of this book is not to outline a panacea, but to recognise the significant scale of change required to position us for future prosperity. The opinions expressed here will no doubt ruffle a few feathers and test some sensitivities and sacred cows – at least it is hoped that they do, for the sake of frank and earnest public debate, and advancement of robust outcomes in the national interest. Disciplined debate and action will provide the foundation for change. Let's have some conversations around the hard, tough changes Australia needs to make in our own collective interest.

This book is not intended to emphasise the ills of our major parties – they are creatures of their past and situational influences. The malaise we are in seems to have been a feature of Australian politics over the last decade or more; in fact, it likely has its genesis in the formation of federalism over a century ago. One could ruefully speculate whether we wouldn't be better off with benevolent authoritarian leadership, which has worked for countries such as Singapore. But of course, authoritarianism depends on the continued will, temperament, and benevolence of the leader, and typically fails to ensure adequate governance checks and balances. Democracy is the best of all conceivable government systems, however it is time to ensure our democratic system is as lean, efficient, communicative and effective as it can be, to ensure it provides the best outcome for our country and people.

My hope is that this book generates discussion about our nation's future, but more poignantly that we agree action which starts to address the real roadblocks hindering our progress, including the need for constitutional change. Put simply, we there is a united public plea that we continue to develop a happier, healthier, more engaged considered, cohesive and inclusive national community which is the envy of other nations around the world.

To do so, we need to communally wake up to ourselves in a few key areas. We cannot go on spending more than we earn as a nation, and hope to maintain our current standard of living – a return to sustained budget balance or surplus is imperative. We have to start playing the long game, rather than continue to myopically focus on our short game. We must provide a foundation for those with smart ideas and 'get-up-and-go' to prosper, which provides traction for more Australians to be successful, that we encourage empathetic, talented, skilled people to be motivated towards government leadership. We have to value and respect our political and institutional processes for what they provide – a stable, free democracy - but at the same interrogate them seeking continuous improvement.

There are many people to thank for their contribution to this book, whether that input was in the form of insight, edit, counsel, proofreading, or just providing me the spur to get on with it. The people who should be acknowledged are many, and know who they are. To attempt to name them all here would do them a disservice; I would undoubtedly overlook people who deserve credit.

To my wife Sharon, and our three children, who pondered what was going on in the study at various stages, thank you for your patience and forbearance. I'd be lying if I said this was a popular family project, although it has grown on them with time. They are more used to a father who is away from home than one tied to a desk. I am grateful for their unconditional love and support.

I am blessed with a wonderful wider family as well, and enjoyed significant input from various family members to this project, including Bill and Claire, to whom I am grateful for the opportunity to live and breathe the experience of the campaign trail, and to my parents, who encouraged me to explore broad horizons. I have also drawn on a wide circle of fantastic friends from diverse walks of life who have provided, whether they know it or not, significant input to this work.

Although I've never met them, I should thank Jim Collins and Michael Porter, whose concepts for outperformance and strategy apply just as adeptly to nations as they do business. Mr Collins conducted extensive empirical research on businesses which provided foundations for my views on leadership and transformation throughout my career. I have had the opportunity to read his books over the years, and apply his lessons in commercial environment to enhance culture and results. Mr Porter is a leading global authority on strategy and competitive advantage, with an insightful helicopter view and a laser-like lasso to lure complexity into understandable concepts. There is significant opportunity for our government to apply many of their principles in the ongoing tussle for global competitive advantage.

This book is also dedicated to the many good men and women who've entered politics and public service. Public service is, not that we give it its due, a selfless livelihood. I'm sure that life is not always what they expected it to be. To effect change, we will rely on the lions (and lionesses!) among these men and women to have the strength of their personal convictions to help us deliver a more effective governance framework for the future.

I have made every attempt to ensure the authenticity of source material for this book. Inevitably, some quotes, phrases and sources are second or third hand – hopefully their reincarnation here does justice to their originators.

It is the undeniable energy, resourcefulness and vigour of our people, their desire to 'be better' which will dictate our future, and which is often dampened in the fires of partisan conflict. Government needs to reposition itself to lead the generation of this revised framework to take shape effectively. Transforming our institutional processes will provide the impetus to hasten and strengthen our economy, vigour and social cohesiveness. I experienced that strength and vigour again and again in my brief time on the campaign trail; we all see it on street corners whenever an election rolls around.

The warning though is clear – politicians and the citizens represented by them need to converge, to address the 'hollowing gap' between politics and the community they represent. We, as voters, have the right to expect more from our politicians. Equally, our politicians have the right to expect more from us. We have a tendency to be hard on our leaders, in large part because they are so hard on each other. While support should never be unequivocal, it is important we are more respectful of the difficult task of civil representation. There is middle ground for us all to find, which is why addressing systemic issues is so important. It is systemic failure which often undermines that trust.

We don't have a problem we can't handle ... at least, not yet, although we could have if we don't address the situation in front of us. Jack Sparrow's philosophy (refer quote Chapter 6) rings true – it's our attitude to the problem (or problems) which will decide our fate. We cannot afford to be apathetic, or to permit ourselves the luxury of contemplating these issues will go away.

I do hope this book provides some food for thought, starts some conversations, and provides a foundation for real change for the better. The alternative, perhaps a Donald Trump type demagoguery vying for power, does not bear thinking about.

*Politicus (Latin) – 'of citizens'*

# 1. 'Great Southern Land'

*(from the song title by Icehouse)*

*"National prosperity is created, not inherited. It does not grow out of a country's natural endowments, its labour pool, its interest rates, or its currency's value, as classical economics insists." (Michael Porter)*

Aristotle once said, 'Man is by nature a political animal.'[iv] This is as true today of human nature and the desire for power and authority as it was in 350BC. Unlike the inheritance of great philosophy though, Porter's warning is clear – Australians can no longer afford to rely on our inherited prosperity, for if we do, we will undoubtedly become victims of our past success. Nor should we rely on economic 'triggers' as saviours – it is our character, as Nick Cater asserts[v], that is "the nation's greatest renewable resource".

The one thing most Australians have in common, regardless of our background, is an opinion of what is right, but more often what is wrong with our political landscape and leadership. Politics, and our political framework, are central to so many discussions, be it in book clubs or Blacktown, business lunches or Longreach, Newcastle or the National Press Club. Whether involving local councils, state government, through to the machinations of federal politics, we have strong opinions and vested interests guiding conversations about how our leaders are performing. These conversations are fuelled by the certainty that there is no absolute right or wrong view to most issues and decisions.

Despite the opinions we express, and the media content politics consume, there is a scarcity of effective debate centring on addressing these formidable institutional issues and challenges.

**The Good**

Tony Abbott, whether you are a fan or not, is quite correct in declaring that "Australians are entitled to take at least a measure of pride in our country's achievements."[vi] However, in an increasingly competitive and homogenous world, we can take only take the luxury of a defined period to bask in the glow of past achievement; instead we need to be looking forward to the next generation of change and improvement to determine how we can take the bedrock of our democratic system to the next level of performance, rather than accept the status quo. Porter reminds us in the opening quote that luck is not a strategy which can be relied upon, just as prosperity cannot be endlessly inherited.

Nick Cater commented that "Australia's pioneers mined their reserves of enterprise, energy, and ingenuity to build the greatest civilisation of the south", based on an overriding principle of fairness. This is the base of our modern egalitarian society, although Cater warns that this egalitarianism is threatened by an urbane 'Johnny-come-lately' breed – the "presumptive ruling class". It was this character which enabled us to build momentum, an energy which saw Australia outperform other advanced nations over several generations.

Without question, we are truly the lucky country, with a social freedom, a country of abundant beauty and resources, and one of the better institutional systems in the world today, at or near the top of many of global 'league tables'. Australia has enjoyed an extended period of sustained prosperity, although in recent years, some of the advantage we developed has deteriorated, as we wasted what inheritance was left previously, and failed to assiduously create new shoots of future wealth.

George Megalogenis' observes in 'The Australian Moment' that the good decisions of our political leaders to open up and deregulate our economy afforded us the best position of any country coming out of the recession of the last decade. However, 'The Australian Moment' appears to have come and (if we are not careful) gone. Our short sightedness, together with a slight whiff of collective indestructibility now threatens that position. To remain on top demands constant review and change; we've not been let down, but rather let ourselves down over the last ten or more years. The system issues though go way further back than the last decade. They are the symptoms of a framework under duress.

## The Bad

Donald Horne's downbeat assessment was well ahead of its time when analysing the social 'soul' of our nation penning 'The Lucky Country'. The irony of his title was deep and largely misunderstood. We have on occasion ridden our luck; however it has become increasingly harder to do so as other developing nations play 'catch-up'. As Hugh Mackay summarises in his preface to a recent edition of Horne's book, 'lucky' means 'lucky to get away with it' rather than lucky to be who and where we are. Horne's view is that prosperity has dulled our reflexes. The difference is that where Horne focused on a social apathy and lack of intellect in 1960's Australia, we are now more confident in ourselves; the corollary is that we now have to apply our substantial expertise, confidence and intellect to change our processes to meet changing times. A failure to do so would reflect the apathy and deficit of intellect Horne observed in his 'lucky country' of fifty years ago.

Horne saw the challenges for Australia as our geographic position (now addressed largely by more efficient supply chains, increased mobility and modern technology), "the need for a revolution in economic priorities" (the lack of stability in science, innovation, research and culture policies, and a focus on lifetime learning to cope with change, highlights a failure), and "the need for a bold redefinition of what the whole place adds up to now". The second and third challenges remain largely the same today. That 'revolution in economic priorities' and 'bold redefinition' of what we stand for has never been more important than it has now become.

It may be possible that both politicians and political commentators have become too close to the manner in which we 'play' politics, and too absorbed on the personalities to step back and see our institutional framework through a reform lens. In addition, changes such as the ideas that will be mentioned in this book and have been mentioned in countless summits and dinner conversations are tough to make. However, that is the very reason it is time to make such changes – because such change is tough, and will only become tougher with time.

Cosgrove notes Australians to be simultaneously "politically lazy and acutely politically sensitive"[vii]. The 2015 Lowy Institute poll found that 51% of Australians aged 18-29 don't view democracy as preferable to any other kind of government (although this is down from 61% in 2012); the worrying trend is that 26% don't believe it matters what kind of government they have, up from 23% in 2012.[viii]   Politics is progressively disengaging the freshest generation of voters.

The young are, by and large, less engaged with politics than ever before, leaving the youth partisan groups, political staffers, and ambitious lawyers and unionists as the most likely nursery for our future leaders.  While this is in fact not much different to our recent past, it will increasingly polarise and further disengage the youth vote going forward.

People, and especially younger people are turning off because there is a sense of 'political inertia' arising from a process of political consensus driving strategy and policy which was developed in ages past, and which is now well past its use-by date.  The pendulum has now swung.  As a nation, we've imperturbably lost momentum in recent times.  Regaining momentum on a national scale is a considerable challenge.

**The Positively Ugly**

At the time of writing, Australia has been through a period of significant leadership instability, with five changes in the position of Prime Minister in eight years, and an election which may increase this statistic.  Only two of those changes have been wrought by popular vote.  For the decade prior to and including the ascension of Malcolm Turnbull to Prime Minister, we have likely never seen Australians so disillusioned with and disengaged from what happens in government.  If a culture survey had been taken across the nation at almost any time over that decade, it would have likely shown record low levels of interest and engagement in politics.  The quality of debate in parliament has descended to the point where both major parties seem 'Monty Pythonesque', with their key objective ostensibly to be to inflict mortal flesh wounds on their opponents. Partisan conflict has become bitter and personal.  While the national interest is of most concern to much of the community, it feels like politicians are fumbling towards the comical definition of insanity – doing the same thing, over and over, expecting a different result.

When we were children, facing a long trip in the car, Mum would do whatever she could to keep us busy. The most common activity was 'I Spy', which kept us busy; I'd try to spot something I thought my brothers had no hope of spotting. If we 'spied' the object at the same time, outrageous argument would ensue as to who guessed first. With four boys arguing vociferously, Mum would typically need to arbitrate. It is this game which for me best reflects the current state of parliament. It has become a competition for ideas and who came up with that idea first. Surely our politicians are sufficiently emotionally mature to understand by now that politics should be a game where everyone plays together, with the reward the sustained implementation of good ideas, not the 'we thought of it first' whinge which appears in the ascendancy.

Like it or not, Australia has become the easiest democracy in the world in which to successfully stage a bloodless coup.

The easy answer is that we have lacked good leadership in recent times; however this conclusion seems somehow unfair to the high calibre human beings who have taken on the mantle of leadership. The underlying issues which caused Australia's malaise are far deeper and more profound than leadership. It is our reliance on outdated structures and processes, such as historical partisanship, and the lack of a values framework, a clear national strategy, and enunciation of long term plans to address current and future challenges, which is feeding the disillusionment of the voting public. The partisan structure, aligned to vested interests, is equally bad in both parties, and all the worse given those vested interests represent the few rather than the many. It is the institutional structure which is crying out for reform.

Ross Garnaut[ix], recognising the debilitating impact of vested interests on the political process wrote, 'vested interests have become more effective at shaping policy. The policies that emerge from the democratic process today are more likely to benefit special interests over the broader community than they did in the past. These changes have caused standards of living of large numbers of people across the democratic developed world to stagnate or fall ...'

Whenever I reach out for a pencil (when will we be able to vote online by the way?) at the ballot box, I am typical of many voters. My chief consideration in selecting a representative is to determine which candidate best reflects my values, and offers the integrity, strength and character of leadership I am seeking. Counter to this, the main focus of political parties appears to be slogans and policy, while belittling the opposing approach and cross accusations of mimicry. In truth it is typically challenging to separate the slogans and policy of the two main parties. The voting decision has become more problematic as candidates show less of what they stand for, as they've gradually morphed into a party sandwich board, often times sprouting policy they neither had a hand in developing, don't fully agree with, nor truly believe in.

Despite a nadir of engagement, politics has seldom been a more emotive topic of conversation at gatherings than it currently is. Many arguers hold little 'hope' for the future, and selfless Australians who embark on a career in politics are roundly assessed by silent assassins who don't know them as 'inept' and 'useless'. This is both unfair and untrue; anyone reaching the top echelon of political leadership is likely to be of considerable talent and fortitude.

The issue for many Australians is that we don't believe we have the capability in government to swing the pendulum towards forward momentum, while others remain apathetically disconnected or indifferent to what happens in government.

At the time of writing, the Liberal Party had recently replaced Tony Abbott with Malcolm Turnbull, (hopefully, but not definitely) completing that volatile decade of leadership thrills and spills. Turnbull's appointment appears, at first blush, to have settled Australians, who regard him as talented and progressive. However, the regressive nature of our current politics and party factionalism has ensured his honeymoon is a short one. If Prime Minister Turnbull fails to build momentum on the 'flywheel' before his term is up (more about the 'flywheel' later), our nation will be at a tumultuous tipping point, where the realisation will dawn that no one may in fact be good enough to lead us.

**Hope on the Horizon? ...**

In 2015, the Liberal Party ousting of sitting Prime Minister Tony Abbott, (effectively replicating the Labor Party antics of some years prior) and replacing him with Malcolm Turnbull was born of Mr Abbott's poor popularity and Mr Turnbull's ambition. The polling impact for the Liberal Party was instantaneous, with Mr Turnbull recording high results. Unfortunately, this is no new phenomenon – at one point Mr Rudd's polling was also at the stratospheric highs recorded by the new Prime Minister. Mr Turnbull's ratings have subsequently taken a 'Rudd-like' turn for the worse; and yet, blind Freddy should have realised that was on the cards.

In itself, the appointment of someone seen as capable and progressive as Prime Minister who is, at the time of writing, popular and largely respected, is not enough to resolve the systemic and framework issues which have contributed to our recent turmoil, and which will ultimately result in his demise. We are seeing this already. Mr Turnbull, despite his best efforts, may yet fail for reasons largely beyond his control, unless we make the effort to renew our political process to enable the Prime Minister, and the typically capable people around him to reform and cultivate the governmental and institutional processes of the future. Such reform would enable decent people to make effective, timely decisions which ensure Australia remains 'ahead of the game', the game being the global competition between nations.

**... Or Yet Another False Dawn?**

Meanwhile, the deep, thorough debate we hanker after as a nation is not mirrored in the quality of debate in Parliament. Key issues of importance such as institutional effectiveness and process reform are largely ignored – the modern day equivalent of Nero fiddling as Rome burns. People have had enough of pathetic, pointless argument and counterpunch. Is it too much to ask that we seek to hold substantive, disciplined conversations, resulting in a clear set of thoughtful actions, and a documented implementation roadmap?

Our national failure has been to establish a clear strategic framework, supported by long term planning to drive action to support that strategy.

The election cycle, the flip-flopping of policy between parties can be variously blamed, however the bottom line is that, however we aspire to achieve it, we require a consistent long term strategy to meet economic and growth targets. Strategy sets the stage for the redefining of a modern, vibrant Australian culture, and a unifying roadmap which provides a clear direction for Australians, a governance framework which ensures the public good is placed ahead of partisan interests. The lack of a clear long term plan for infrastructure[1], health, education, and the like creates inefficiency, and is extremely costly in terms of wasted resources. A lack of strategy results in ceaseless policy change, which makes it difficult to create legislative sustainability.

In August 2015, the latest in a series of National Reform Summits was held, with leaders from various industry, union, and other influential social bodies involved. The Summit highlighted many significant issues and challenges with which our nation is confronted, which require fierce conversations and, in some instances, transformational change. Most Australians, if polled, would not be clear on the outcomes and plan of action coming from the Summit. There have been many such Summits over the years, not least of which the Rudd 2020 Summit, which despite its significant promise and an insightful list of almost one thousand 'ideas' ultimately fell short of its objective to provide "an alternative form of democratic participation".[x] Professor Davis' comment is apt, however democracy only achieves participation if such summits are formalised as a routine, established component of a framework to advance strategy and manage democratic change.

The objective of this book is to initiate conversations which drive a culture seeking improvement for a better Australia. Citizens have the right to agitate, to outline an alternative, a way forward for change in this country, and in particular its institutions, recognising that they are considered among the world's best, but acknowledging that we do not obtain the outputs we

---

[1] Note that Infrastructure Australia, an independent statutory body, has recently released an Australian Infrastructure Plan (February 2016), although this plan can only provide recommendations across all levels of government, and is effectively developed in isolation of any other national planning mechanisms. There is at this point no accountability for the adoption or execution of the Infrastructure Plan. For more information see http://infrastructureaustralia.gov.au/policy-publications/publications/files/Australian_Infrastructure_Plan.pdf

should expect from effective government. The inescapable truth is that while it may not be politically straightforward, there are undeniable and profound opportunities for improvement in service, cost, productivity, and governance within the framework of Australian government.

We need to think hard, to discuss fully and honestly, considering changes wrought by time and what is needed in future on this question – how can we ensure our democracy works best? This is the base upon which we solve perplexing issues such as climate change, social equality, and economic underperformance.

**Government and Business**

For most of my career, I've worked across the scale of business, from my own business to global ASX listed companies. Government is not business, and business is not government, however there are parallels between the two. Both are there to satisfy stakeholders, both are dynamic, operating in increasingly complex environments. Both are subject to disruptive technology and innovation. Business has toiled to remain competitive, reducing cost, de-layering, simplifying processes, and improving service and quality in an effort to survive. Without the same survival imperative, government has not fought this same fight at the requisite pace, and remains, with some exceptions, fundamentally bloated and distant from its stakeholders. It would be unfair to say costs haven't been reduced over the years, however the allocation of budget, management of cost and allocation of projects is not driven with the same rigour as the commercial sector. Figure 3 highlights public service employment as one of Australia's key growth industries, despite considerable rhetoric to the alternative. The subsequent, intensified post-float refocus on cost reduction and improved customer service of government entities, including Telstra and Aurizon, provide clear corroborating evidence of this commercial gap.

Many political leaders have transitioned from political careers to business – Nick Greiner, Robert Webster, Warwick Smith, John Brogden, and Mark Vaile, to name a few. Less successful businessmen have transitioned to politics (Malcolm Turnbull being one, however the jury is well and truly out on Clive Palmer at this point!). The skill sets are not mutually exclusive.

There are philosophies of business which have, and will continue to be useful to government, to improve the way government is conducted.

While Government should not ever take the view that it is a business, it can learn from business.

Don Argus reminds us that the 'basics' of good business are also the 'basics' of good government. "... one learns very quickly that the only way to succeed (in business) is to nurture independent, motivated people who will assist in building healthy high performance organisations. Easy to articulate, but difficult to deliver unless one establishes an adult relationship with one's working colleagues. This relationship is crucial because it is the glue that holds enterprises together, connecting its strategy, structure, systems, and technology." In many ways however, politics and government seem to behave counter-intuitively to principles of healthy relationships and trust; that adult relationship, while so rudimentary, seems anathema in the modern political arena.

Government can utilise, and has utilised, more commercial approaches to certain facets of government. In business, markets are extremely dynamic, change is continual, and companies fight a cut throat battle to stay ahead or keep up with their competitors. Government is becoming more like business in terms of finding itself competing in dynamic markets. However to change government to become more strategically and commercially focused, where appropriate, is a change of significant substance, and is problematic for leaders of public institutions in a 'choppy' political leadership environment.

To facilitate change, redefining our national identity, values and culture (or as Peter Cosgrove[xi] refers to it, 'our ethos') is integral. In summarising 'The Lucky Country', Horne raises the concern about whether our luck will last. He comments, "Australia seems to have lost both its sense of a past and its sense of a future. In making appeals, in attempting to make policies 'rational' there is nothing to appeal to, no sense of purpose; yet people need some sense of definition to which they can relate their actions as an individual needs a sense of identity: a sense of having had a history, of having reached a particular point in it and of facing a certain kind of future." Without that unifying sense of identity (our national 'ethos') and long term strategy, we appear to be firmly anchored on the here and now.

The cost of government in the modern era is excessive. This will be covered in more detail later, however the proposal to reduce a layer of government is not one which should simply be dismissed as banal, ridiculous or too hard. The very foundation of government in Australia is based on the states maintaining their power, whether in the national interest or not. The employment figures in Figure 3, and the section 'Politics by Numbers' reinforce this point.

While the current framework is generally fit for purpose, it is not 'fighting fit'. In the modern era, we must seek to have that expectation. There is no question we do not have the best institutional framework available to us at the time of writing. We have laboured under a colonial system for over 200 years, which spawned local councils as the scope of government and the population increased. Finally, after more than ten years of debate at the end of the nineteenth century, the nation opted for federalism, albeit with some colonies dragged along for the ride, to deliver the system of government we have today, with some modest adaptations over time. We are victims of that flawed genesis; we should not simply accept our institutional fate.

Although the term 'reform' is often used loosely, the time has come for grassroots transformation and reformation of our institutional systems – to develop a system of government which can take us forward into a new era of prosperity. Reform is about ensuring 'match fitness' and should be engrained in our 'ethos'; transformation is about step change, and is typically needed when the culture of maintaining match fitness has not been in place.

It is the quality of our political leaders, the stakeholder relationships they develop, & the decisions they take which guides our futures & those of our children. However it is the frameworks behind them which influence their decision making and the effectiveness of leadership, which allows them to govern to the best of their ability.

These are questions and observations that are pertinent in considering whether our political structure remains appropriate, and how the framework should change to meet our future needs.

In the world today, across democracies, we are seeing a trend in liberal politics from conservative to progressive leadership in countries such as New Zealand (John Key), Canada (Justin Trudeau) and the United Kingdom (David

Cameron), as well as in Australia. In Australia, 'social progressive' factions are increasingly influencing global democratic power, reflecting the electorate's mood for change. While such changes potentially will create significant internal party conflict, indications are that this change is supported by the electorate, who are expressing their desire to see progression in our democratic process and way of life, providing a short term buffer from factional conflict.

At the time of Prime Minister Malcolm Turnbull's ascension, Don Argus[xii] penned a newspaper article, effectively offering gratuitous advice to our newly minted Prime Minister. Argus provided great insight into the depth of change he regards as necessary to Australia's core institutions to achieve the objective of restored economic competitive advantage. Argus argues that 'people, politics, culture and business are inseparable' in his quest to 'reinvent government'. However, this is broader than an 'economic reset'; rather a cultural reset.

**Australia the Republic?**

The Queen met with then Prime Minister Paul Keating at Balmoral in 1993, where he deftly advised Her Majesty that the monarchy had 'gently drifted into obsolescence', to which the Queen responded by asking Mr Keating if he'd like a drink[xiii]. Although the British are long over the see-sawing republican discussion, seemingly more accepting of it than we are, the Australian obsession remains today. Meanwhile, the Australian 'ethos' continues to gently drift, not because we haven't become a republic, but because, in part, we continue to fascinate over the symbolism of republicanism.

Given Mr Turnbull's profile in the republic debate, that discussion has gained momentum since he became Prime Minister. However, he has fittingly realised that there are far more pressing and profound governance and economic issues which need to be dealt with ahead of the issue of Australia becoming a republic. 'Cultural reset' is, as Argus attests necessary; the republic is relatively low on the list of cultural and economic reset priorities.

Our ties with Britain, which the Republicans sought to sever (at least procedurally) without success some years ago, are largely ceremonial. There is little if any economic benefit in separating. If an argument can be mounted that these ties are impacting us attitudinally, there may indeed be a case for Australia to become a republic. However, among the many reforms needed in our country, separating from Britain appears, on face value, to be towards the bottom of the priority list. Commentators such as Bob Ellis foresee deeper social change emanating from a republic; it is the benefit for culture on which a republic should be assessed.

Nick Bowen's assertion[xiv] that Australia "continues to live in the shadow of 19th century England" highlights his English heritage and a significant lack of insight into our country and its people, although the British themselves remain bemused that we've not been able to make this happen. Perhaps the inability to convert to a republic is endemic of our action paralysis when it comes to big changes or decisions. This is not an argument against republicanism; simply an acknowledgement that it is a less meaningful reform than other initiatives we need to embark upon, subject to the positive insights for our ethos which may be derived from this change.

### Balancing the Books

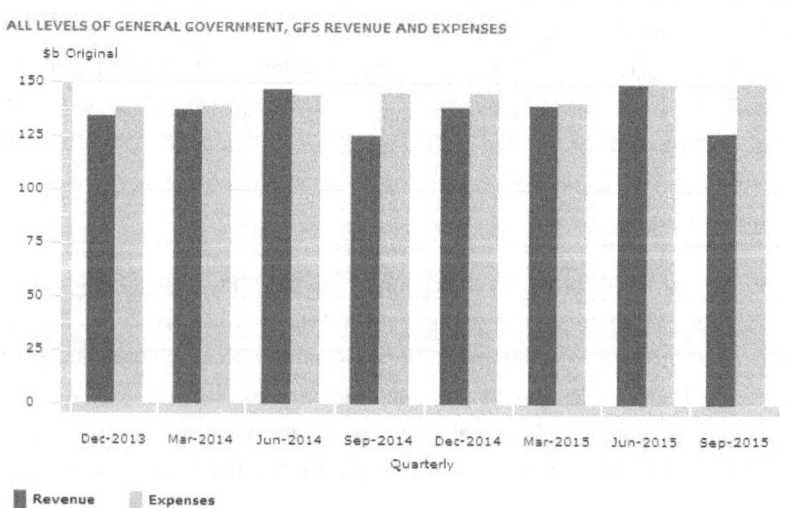

*Figure 1 – Trend of all government revenue and expense management by quarter since December 2013 quarter. In only one quarter from eight did revenue exceed expenses, and across the period expenses significantly exceeds revenue. Source: Australian Bureau of Statistics © Commonwealth of Australia.*

Of greater and more immediate importance to enhanced Australian democracy are a balanced budget and a growing economy. The futile anecdotal monthly payment of $2 billion in interest, money which could be diverted to so many more fulfilling functions, is a preventable dead weight on

our country which should infuriate us to our national core. Horne's warning not to ride our luck demands reiterating, lest any inheritance we have developed evaporates if we take it for granted.

As figure 1 disturbingly shows, we continue to live, day by day, week by week, month by month, beyond our means, wallowing in an ever increasing pool of self-inflicted debt, while self-defeating narcissism reigns in the halls of parliament.

**The System is Broken**

We have been accused of a 'leadership deficit' in Australia over the last decade or so. While this may be true, it is not the root cause of our political issues.

The alternative contention is that while we can attribute the volatile and abnormal number of leadership changes to poor leadership skills at the pinnacle of federal government, a key contributor to this instability has been a political process which is failing to set a long term agenda, or bolster the development of our national leadership capabilities. The electorate is unsettled by internal partisan factions, not behaving in a united, cohesive manner, and providing little difference in policy choice. These factions are tearing both major parties apart, offering no viable alternative; for Australians this results in an inconsistent, incoherent and vulnerable government narrative.

How can we admire leadership which engages in political spectacles such as the Senate debacle which was unfolding at the time of writing; the government attempting to implement minor party reforms to Senate, the opposition 'throwing their toys out of the cot', holding the Senate pointlessly to ransom, simply stalling the inevitable outcome. Such antics are a clear sign the system is failing us – we have to take note.

We should be admiring anyone who reaches the stature of high office, lauding their skills and dedication, rather than critically analysing every sound byte with the intent of cutting them down. Why wouldn't we though when our learning is that this is the normal behaviour of politicians towards each other, thinking such behaviour engenders approval in the church of public opinion. The media maintains its myopic, acerbic short term focus, which ensures this behaviour is reinforced. The 'attack dogs' of government, employing emotional vitriol laced with baseless 'drivel' fail to appreciate; sound, rational debate is acceptable, inane caustic contempt is not. The bitter vitriol of the political 'attack dog' class is no longer having the intended effect on a fatigued and wary electorate, and clearly illustrates the dysfunction of a fatigued system. We're ready to shout out the windows, Peter Finch style, screeching (or perhaps 'e-screeching') "we're mad as hell, and we're not going to take it anymore". The community wants to see government focus beyond themselves, on what's imperative and significant, rather than the urgent and trivial, and start to transform the fundamental internal processes of selection, partisanship, the framework of institutional government, and of decision making to ensure these processes are serving us appropriately.

If both major parties were in fact true to themselves, and able to cast the zero sum, 'winner takes all' approach to partisan politics aside in favour of the public good, there are many areas of policy where both parties could find agreement. Unfortunately, the ability to behave in a non-partisan manner appears to be confined to situations of security and ceremony in the current age.

Politicians past & present have commented on the failures of our system. John Brogden[xv], quoting a comment made he made himself some ten years earlier notes, "Our federal system is broke. It is a confused, duplicated and irresponsible mess of failed public administration. Council of Australian

Governments (COAG) risks becoming a club of Australian governors rather than a reform vehicle." COAG, although perhaps conceived as a reform vehicle is clearly now an entrenched negotiation vehicle, the dynamics of which vary based on the party composition of state & federal politics. The relationship between levels of government is, I'd suggest irretrievable if we are seeking unified, effective government.

Laura Tingle observed in her insightful Quarterly Essay[xvi] "it is wrong to see the anger of the last few years as a 'one-off', which might go away ... Voters are confused about what politicians can do for them in such a world."

Many of the views expressed in this book may be dismissed as one-dimensional and binary. That does not mean they should be ignored, but thought through further, along with other opportunities for reform by those with the expertise and attitude to enact change. Australians are competitive and embrace a challenge; the immediate challenge is to address the way we are governed, to break down barriers to progress, identify the waste, to develop a framework which enables good people to be selected and get on with the job we elect them to do. Australia's competitiveness in the global economy is at stake.

We are a lucky country, probably luckier than Horne made us out to be, and we should never lose sight of that fact. We have been handed a great legacy by our forefathers, and must ensure we pass that legacy on, with interest, to the generations that follow. We cannot expect to ride that luck. As we are regularly being reminded, these are dynamic and optimistic times. We have the opportunity to be so much more, but to do so, we have to break the shackles of our inheritance, and make the necessary, difficult changes to lay the foundation for future prosperity. It cannot however be left to government alone to paint a picture for all to follow. We all have a role we must play in ensuring government is structured to take the long term view.

The craft of politics is not new. Tom Butler-Bowdon, summarising the theory of power proposed by Niccolo Machiavelli[xvii] in 1531 articulates that "only states that are meritocratic, allow immigration, and have a desire to grow large will be able to command lasting influence." He adds to this "an emphasis on open government, a trustworthy judiciary, and an array of checks and balances that prevent any one person or party dominating". We are fortunate, in that Australia has got much of this right. Yet there is so much more to do, and it won't be achieved by fiddling around the edges while the slow burn lingers.

As Butler-Bowdon[xviii] summarises, "It is a strong nation indeed that can not only let people speak their mind, but remain open to ideas that bring political renewal." So this is a plea, a call to speak our minds, agree our reality, allow ideas to come to the fore, and take disciplined action to make Australia a still better country going forward.

The question is, are we decisively prepared to instigate action to fundamentally improve our core democratic framework?

Are we Lions or Lambs?

# Part A

# Current State & Issues – The 'Why'

## 2. Australian Politics - Current State

*"To understand where you are going, you must understand from where you came" (Welsh proverb)*

*"You may say to yourself, well ...how did I get here?" from the song 'Once in a Lifetime', Talking Heads*

Australia today, in terms of culture, governance, and outlook, is very much a reflection of our past. Founded as a British convict colony, expanded quickly on the back of the gold rush, a nation of explorers and adventurers discovering our vast land, a group of disparate colonies who eventually united in the view that federation was the best way to protect and manage our nation - Australia has developed its institutions based largely on these historical foundations.

While federation has delivered the system of government and prosperity we enjoy today, there can be no guarantees it will, in its current state, continue to optimise equality and prosperity for Australians. Tiernan[xix] writes of a 'narrative of failure' which 'permeates debates about Australia's federal system'. While the Commonwealth has shown an inclination towards reform, it also suppresses it with 'the result that it is difficult to transcend the tensions that are borne of the centralisation of money and power that reform needs to address'.

**Historical Drivers**

"Unlike the United States of America, whose constitution was born out of conflict and revolution, and which consequently has an iconic status in the minds of most Americans, the Australian Constitution and federal system was the fruit of discussion, agreement and peaceful evolution."[xx] The White Paper goes on to note that "perhaps because of this we tend to take our federal system for granted, as something in the background of our national life, and not as something that requires periodic re-assessment as to how it is affecting our economic and social wellbeing."

Politics in Australia today is enigmatic and even bewildering in many respects. Excessive levels of government, despite our relatively small population, have become designed overkill. Government is one of the key growth areas for employment in Australia. The cost of maintaining separate, misaligned government infrastructure (technology platforms, systems, processes and procedures, duplicated structure, no shared services) across multiple levels borders on the obscene.

The bureaucratic, multi-tiered nature of government has its genesis in the reformation of six colonies, reporting separately to Britain, who came together to facilitate the birth of our nation. The key driver for federation was born from the threat that the colonies separately may be insecure from invasion from neighbouring colonies held by world powers France (Tahiti and Polynesia) and Germany (New Guinea) in the late 1800's. The precursor to Federation was a Federal Council, formed in 1883, of which perversely the mother colony New South Wales was not a member. Henry Parkes, known as the 'Father of Federation', while arguing passionately for federation from an early age, voted against the Federal Council, leading to the New South Wales Parliament voting down their involvement during the long debate founding federation.

Federation was no easy task. In a time of primitive communication, the unification of independent, geographically diverse colonies despite considerable disapproval was a feat of perseverance. Australia was ruled as a set of colonies of Britain under a Governor and a small Legislative Council, until the early 1840's when discontent with the lack of representation of government provided impetus from William Charles Wentworth and others to influence the British Parliament to pass the New South Wales Constitution Act (effectively covering all colonies known loosely as Australia). Australia's first formal election, held in 1843, resulted in riots and scandal. Earl Grey in London, noting the tensions within the newly formed government, drafted the Australian Colonies Government Bill, which was given assent in 1850, enabling Victoria to be separated and establishing its own Legislative Council. Seeking an end to the colonies paying tax to Britain, Wentworth continued to agitate for further reform, whereupon the colonies were invited by Britain to establish their own government. Henry Parkes, the 'Father of Federation' took up the fight for independence from 1867 when he first brought the colonies together until his death in 1896, just 5 years prior to federation.

Federation in 1901 established the institutional platform for a growing sense of national identity, built on the creative nineteenth century writing of Banjo Paterson, Henry Lawson and Dorothea Mackellar which beautifully captured our harsh unforgiving land and its audacious people. Australia developed a national psyche as an up and coming nation of adventurers, larrikins and rebels, fuelled across a twentieth century of global conflict and industrialisation, and stimulated by a continuous wave of migration - a relatively new nation bent on developing its future prosperity, providing abundant opportunity for newcomers. The World Wars profoundly altered Australia's sense of identity; World War I created the legend of ANZAC, reinforced by acts of Australian bravery across many fronts during World War II. After the Second World War, 6.5 million migrants from 200 nations brought with them immense new diversity to their adopted home. Many were enticed to work on nation building projects such as the Snowy Hydro Scheme and the building of the nation's capital in Canberra. Our country was diversifying and developing quickly, as a national image of energetic drive and entrepreneurship evolved laterally.

Reform of the economy, clever regulation of economic and legislative levers, and the progressive vision of our leaders and governments of both persuasions, particularly between the 1970's and the 1990's provided a strong foundation for our current prosperity. However that prosperity has eroded, relative to other countries, since that time.

While it is important to acknowledge the decades of effective government reform during the forty years to 2008 which have bequeathed a solid regulatory and governance framework, we have turned over Prime Ministers like used dishrags in the period since, typically leaving a similar tainted smell. All capable and talented people, with, like all of us the usual human flaws, they have nonetheless played their part in dragging Australia's international reputation down a notch in terms of our stability and governance capability.

In one of the quintessential management texts 'Great by Choice', Collins & Hansen open with the approach, "we cannot predict the future. But we can create it." This line seems in some ways to have been written with Australia in mind; we seem to have spent considerable periods in our past creating our future, but have over the last decade allowed our future to overtake us. We have allowed the car to assume control, taking us wherever it wants, rather than retain control as the driver.

Australian politics founders on key structural weaknesses which are impacting the nation's performance and our ability to create our future.

We are likely the most over-governed country in the world per head of population, with even the most moderate of commentators (and widely revered as one of our best leaders), Peter Cosgrove, referring to the need for "an evolution in the relationship between the tiers of Australian governments"[xxi]. We remain saddled with unnecessary over-government across a relatively small population of 25 million, featuring a remarkable lack of integration across those three tiers of government. This multi-tiered government platform not only creates waste in its own right, but creates further inefficiency by adding an unnecessary layer to the continual negotiation and justification at all levels of government about income (tax) and cost distribution. As a nation, we should be considering what value this complexity adds, as opposed to identifying the most effective whole of government approach to income and cost.

**Decisive U-Turns – Short Termism in Action**

A lack of long term planning seems to result in changes being based on a change of government, and with a number of changes in government in recent years, all contributes to Australians being preserved in a fog of uncertainty. We'll refer later to the flywheel; rather than having continuous forward momentum, our momentum constantly gathers and loses pace as government recycles, driven by the election cycle and opinion polling. We move forwards a step, then backwards a step, never able to build the momentum needed to impel ourselves continuously forward. Rather than developing and implementing sustained long term transformational change, the interruption of the electoral cycle initiates 'stump' and 'reinventing the wheel' change. In simplistic terms, we seem to spend the first 12 months of a change of government undoing the work of the previous government, the next 12 months implementing the agenda of the government of the day, then the final 12 months developing new and improved policy and planning for the next election. If a change of government occurs at that election, the now new, improved previous government perpetuates this cycle.

At a state level, the East West Link in Melbourne is a classic example of a lack of poor business case planning. In short, the Victorian Liberal Government went ahead with the project, committing the state to a liability when the project was axed of approximately $1 billion. The Labor Government campaigned on the scrapping of this infrastructure project and abandoned the project when it came to power, triggering the liability provisions of the contract. The question here is not whose approach was right and who was wrong, but rather how the project managed to proceed on the basis it did, only to be terminated at a later date. There have been many such circumstances where successive governments have undone previous government policy, which have resulted in massive unnecessary cost to taxpayers, not to mention the impact on government credibility. If such projects were subjected to an appropriate governance framework which incorporates appropriate community feedback, then such expensive, wasteful about turns would be less likely to occur. It is likely in the case of the East West Link that this was a political failure rather than an assessment failure, supporting the view that strategy should be separated from politics. The concept that non-partisan, long term decisions be separated from government, with government taking the role of facilitator has merit.

The form of change which takes place through a switch of government can extend to repackaging old policy and swapping out senior bureaucrats to shore up partisan support. The impact on government departments after election change is often significant, and undoubtedly adversely affects their operations for a period even though the day-to-day business of government goes on. Some projects are curtailed, others brought to the table, all of which is unsettling as capabilities are rematched to the new 'normal'. While difficult to avoid, this is not a recipe for good government, even with talented, capable people at the helm. We have to seek remedies to this short termism, lest Paul Keating's 'banana republic' jibe rear its head again. If we cannot find basic long term agreement on core policy in areas such as health, education and infrastructure, whether within the parties or beyond them in an alternative democratic model, we are condemned to continue in this fog of uncertainty and significant unnecessary and wasted cost.

The demise of John Howard, for example, was considered to be less about a swing towards the up and comer, Kevin Rudd, than it was a desire by Australians to seek change, because the Liberal Party wouldn't provide regeneration itself. Kevin Rudd became the most available public conduit to achieve this outcome given Howard was not willing to stand aside. Despite considerable up front promise, it is likely that what Australia thought it was getting in 2007, and what it did get in the form of new leadership, were likely quite different. That Rudd and the Prime Ministers which followed him lacked the core capabilities for effective leadership is undoubtedly a contributing factor for Australia finding itself in its current malaise, a situation hopefully addressed by Prime Minister Turnbull. Only if Turnbull is given, or takes the opportunity to be courageous and bold, in the tradition of Hawke and Menzies, will we have the prospect of making tough decisions and addressing systemic failure. If his political legacy is less than this, we are destined to make do with what we have. Even a succession of strong, capable Prime Ministers cannot, on their own, address the system baggage unless that baggage is specifically 'outed' and pursued for reform.

**Governing Beyond the Election Cycle**

It is perhaps an indictment on our democratic system that change requires the leader initiating that change to have built a 'store chest' of political capital or public goodwill, rather than because it is the right change for the country. At time of writing, Malcolm Turnbull is, anecdotally hamstrung by the conservative factions within his party, despite an overwhelming public popularity. Unless we find ourselves at a crisis point, it is difficult to imagine he will indefinitely maintain the support to propose the pervasive change that would best serve Australia, particularly among a conservative faction acting the injured party. The more likely scenario is that his high popularity will gradually dip, the end of the 'honeymoon' period will be called, and the opportunity will be lost.

Four year election cycles would help, but are not in isolation the remedy. The strategy and planning cycle has to be somehow structurally divorced from the electoral cycle, or we stand little chance of enhancing the effectiveness of our ability to set strategy and long term plans in place.

Election results are shaped by the movement of a 'nomadic' group of voters, wedded to neither major party, who flock towards the party who is least inoffensive, or to a minor party if they are sufficiently disenchanted with the politics of both major parties.

Paul Kelly summarised succinctly the legacy the Rudd/Gillard/Rudd years have left us[xxii]. "The process of debate, competition and elections leading to national progress has broken down. The business of politics is too de-coupled from the interests of Australia and its citizens. This de-coupling constitutes the Australian crisis." In truth, we were probably headed down this path, but may have arrived sooner as a result of the turmoil of this recent chaotic period. Bowen[xxiii] also points to the poor state of public debate in Australia. Most of us could not help but agree that crisis seems not far away.

In the main, Australians tend to take a passive view towards politics, which somehow, unfortunately, inures us from crisis until it is too late. At the same time, this allows vested & special interests (such as unions and lobby groups) to dominate political influence. Over time, special interest groups, working to protect their members, create inefficiency by lobbying the interests of those members ahead of the total constituent group in return for the political support of that interest group. Such a situation creates a moral dilemma for major parties and government.

Governments can never afford to lose sight that they require the tacit consent of the people to govern, however the heartland interest groups are significant contributors to political outcomes. The needs of society at large however, should never be subjugated to those of special interest groups, and yet they are more often than many of us realise. Special interest groups can redistribute income through their negotiations, but rarely will they contribute to the overall growth of the pie, which society as a whole has the capability to do. Special interest groups also inhibit the change process, making change difficult to undertake. Our ability to implement change going forward will be a strong symbol of our ability to be successful.

As Olson[xxiv] remarks, special interests "will develop ever more complex regulation that reflects a non-level playing field", creating conflict and larger government, which is needed to manage this complexity. The special interest agenda is further muddied by political donations, which like it or not offers the spectre of something in return.

In Australia, Parliament is the legislative branch of government; the executive branch is responsible for the administration of those laws, while the judicial branch provides for the interpretation of legislation and laws, including the Australian constitution.

**Federal Government**

Federation proved a turning point for Australia, its conception and architecture conceived by the colonies. Until federation, Australia existed as a collection of six British colonies which were partly self-governing but under the law-making power of the British Parliament.

At several stages of its genesis, federation appeared bound not to take place, as states opted in and out of the discussions and negotiation. The outcome, the Federation of Australia, required in excess of ten years of intensive debate. That federation succeeded despite the vested interests of some colonies (notably Western Australia, New South Wales & Queensland) is testamentary to the power of the people, who kick started a process which appeared moribund and doomed to failure on several occasions. David Hill offers a detailed insight into the process of federation in his book, 'The Making of Australia'.

The Commonwealth of Australia Constitution Act provides the legal framework for how Australia is governed. It was drafted at a series of constitutional conventions held in the 1890s, and passed by the British Parliament in 1900, taking effect on 1 January 1901. Since federation, Australia has progressively removed its constitutional ties with Britain, culminating in the passing of the Australia Act (1986) which removed all remaining legal links between the Australian and British governments.

The Australian political system is in some ways like the British system (eg. the Prime Minister and cabinet are responsible to parliament, and elections can be called at any time), and in other ways like the American system (eg. separation of powers, an independent judiciary and a written constitution).

An area of significant constitutional discussion has revolved around the Australian Constitution not including a Bill of Rights, which offers a single document protecting human rights. Australian human rights are protected by a combination of the constitution, legislation and case law.

Unlike the New Zealand Constitution, which is not entrenched or formal and can be changed simply (although seldom) by a majority vote of its Parliament, the Australian Constitution can only be changed by referendum. For a referendum to occur, a supporting Bill must be first passed by Parliament, then sent to the Governor General to issue a writ, enabling a referendum. The referendum must be passed by a majority of people in a majority of states and a majority of people across the nation (known as a double majority). Since 1906, we've held nineteen referendums, with forty four questions put to the people – only eight have been passed, underlining that change through referendum is problematic and complex.

As the key stakeholders of federation were the colonial governments, it is perhaps inevitable that state government survived and thrived beyond federation. The idea that we don't need state governments ad infinitum is not a new concept. As early as 1920, the Labor Party strategised the redistribution of states into 150 regional boundaries reporting into the Federal Parliament. Even today, the executive powers of the federal government in the modern era are not as strong as they could and probably should be, because the architects of those powers were motivated not only to unite but to retain their own influence beyond Federation. The idea that we can do without state governments has been allowed to fester by various former Prime Ministers.

The Federal Parliament is a bicameral (two chamber) legislature – providing single member representation for each electorate for the House of Representatives (the lower house), and multi-member representation, fixed for each state for the Senate (the upper house). Legislation has to be approved by both houses before it can become law. Most legislation is initiated by the House of Representatives, which currently has 150 members, elected for a maximum term of three years in proportional single-member constituencies with a system of alternative vote known as preferential voting. The political party (or majority which can be cobbled together) with the most seats in the House of Representatives forms Government following an election.

The Senate is effectively the 'rubber stamp' or review point for legislation accepted in the Lower House. The party composition in Senate can be different to the House of Representatives, which can contribute to delays in legislation being passed. One of the Senate's original roles was to ensure that laws were fair to all states, which is why state representation is equal. Voters elect twelve Senators from each State and two Senators from each of Australia's two Territories, a total of 76 Senators.

Phil Ruthven[xxv] identifies the make-up of the Senate as a key contributing factor to ineffective government. That the people of Tasmania should have the same voting influence as the people of New South Wales or Victoria is, as he suggests, nonsensical. Some hard questions need to be asked about the role of Senate, terms for Senators, and the appropriate structure to ensure proper governance and decisive outcomes to best serve the Australian people in the modern era. Lobbying & trade-offs are now the standard order of business in the Senate. Substantive transformation of Senate process is vital to enable the Senate to establish a more effective and decisive governance function.

Most recently, minor parties have been increasingly 'gaming' the preferential system through strategies including preference swapping and harvesting, which enable minor parties to optimise representation. This 'gaming' though is a clear expression from the electorate that it wants alternatives or change. The gaming loophole is being carefully considered for reform currently, however if the major parties have their way, the loophole will be closed whilst simultaneously cementing the power of the major parties. It is important that the distractions of minor parties are managed so that minor parties are not an undue distraction to the electoral process. It is equally important that reform is based on the will of the people, not the will of the parties. At the time of writing, the Turnbull government was in the process of having Senate voting reforms signed off by Parliament to reduce the opportunity of 'gaming'.

The proportion of special interest groups, even within the major parties, now influencing the Senate vote and therefore our key federal decisions has now reached almost ludicrous proportions, as evidenced by the Palmer United

Party candidates which joined the Senate at the last election on a wave of dissatisfaction with the major parties, then subsequently imploded. As Ruthven notes, "Paul Keating once referred to it as a house of 'unrepresentative swill'. It is now a house of ideological and narrow interest members. And it doesn't follow the Westminster system, since the upper house can reject bills of any kind forever, rather than just stall them", a fact many Australians would not be cognisant of, and which contributes to a conservative and highly negotiated and compromised approach to the passing of legislation.

**State and Territory Government**

As mentioned previously, state and territory governments are the foundation of Australian government. It was the coming together of the colonies that generated the framework for federalism in the 1890's.

State and territory governments are broadly responsible for those powers not administered by the Commonwealth Government. Every State and Territory has its own Parliament and its own Constitution Act (which can be amended by its Parliament), but they are also bound by the national constitution, which takes precedence. All State Parliaments other than Queensland are bicameral. The Parliament of each Territory has only one House. State and Territory governments are responsible for matters including public health, education, roads, public land use, police, fire and ambulance services, and local government within their territory.

In situations where state and federal legislation conflict, the Constitution ensures that federal legislation is upheld.

Although it remains a powerful component of our government framework today, state government is effectively a relic of our colonial roots, which predated our federal government by more than a century. It is this genesis which now contributes to Australia's high level of government intervention. While state and territory governments are the building blocks of our nation, the open question is 'do we need them anymore?'

When the State parliaments appeared to be 'dragging their heels' in moving towards federalism, one of the many Federation Leagues which had formed in support held a historic meeting at Corowa in July 1893 to expedite the process, at which the 'Corowa Plan' became the basis for a bill and proposal that each colony commit to elect national delegates to draft a national constitution. Today, it can be argued that state governments continue to be an anchor to our national ship.

| State/Territory | GFS Net Operating Balance ($m) | Operating Statement | Cash Flow Statement |
| --- | --- | --- | --- |
| | | GFS Net Lending (+)/Borrowing (-) ($m) | Surplus(+)/ Deficit(−) ($m) |
| New South Wales | −278 | −3,707 | −3,012 |
| Victoria | 1,344 | −1,154 | −1,145 |
| Queensland | 186 | −2,321 | −2,356 |
| South Australia | −479 | −380 | −300 |
| Western Australia | 177 | −1,638 | −1,838 |
| Tasmania | −386 | −459 | −79 |
| Northern Territory | 79 | −667 | −642 |
| Australian Capital Territory | −446 | −862 | −555 |
| **Total State Government Balances** | **197** | **-11,188** | **-9,927** |

*Figure 2 - State Government balances 2014-'15. Combined State Government budget balances have fallen from a surplus of almost 1% of nominal GDP to a deficit in excess of 1% of nominal GDP over the last 7 years. Source: Australian Bureau of Statistics*
http://www.abs.gov.au/ausstats/abs@.nsf/mf/5501.0.55.001

The Federation when formed ensured that all trade between states would be tariff-free, with the national government retaining exclusive power to collect duty on imported goods, in turn reimbursing the states from this income. Today, this principle continues to form the basis for budgeting at a state & federal level. Budgeting is a process, like many government mechanisms, that is confounded by the relationships between levels of government.

While state debt and operating balances receive little exposure in comparison to the federal balance, in the current era, (as shown in figure 2) the states are consistently operating in deficit, with high borrowings. ABS trend graphs show that combined state budget balances have fallen from a surplus of 1% of nominal GDP to a deficit exceeding 1% of GDP over the last 7 years.

The states will typically lay the blame for this parlous position on reduced federal government funding, but that is the point. It is difficult, nigh impossible, to accord accountability for fiscal responsibility in such a situation.

The states are confronting a flagging revenue base, and increasing federal intervention in areas of traditional state functionality, which Tiernan and others conclude is contributing to increased centralisation in the federation. It is also creating inefficiency and overlap. The Business Council of Australia[xxvi] estimated in 2006 "that eliminating duplication and overlap and 'ending the blame game' among the tiers of government could save in the order of $20 billion a year, or 3% of GDP", improving productivity, simplifying government interactions for people, clarifying roles and responsibilities, and supporting Australia's drive for international competitiveness.

Popular thought is that the 'holding entity', the federal government should have ultimate authority for the management of our finances. The continual punch and counter-punch between federal and state governments has ultimately destroyed 'shareholder value'. It is time we got serious reviewing the national governance framework, and put a stop to this internal bickering, which is unproductive and expensive for taxpayers.

Over management and mis-management is not manifested simply in the finances. In areas such as land management, where local councils best understand local land management issues, state government interferes unnecessarily and inappropriately, achieving sub-optimal land management outcomes. It is not intentional interference, but simply a poor relational framework for managing such localised concerns, where local council marches to the regulatory beat of state government rather than form the true 'service provider' role it should in land management.

The Council of Australian Governments (COAG) provides one of the key mechanisms for the working relationship between state and federal government. However, given the continual turnover of parties and leaders at both levels, the irony is that a stable group seldom has the opportunity to work together without partisan conflict for an extended period. The COAG process is itself problematic in the modern era, particularly as the working stability of such a group is impacted as Premiers and Prime Ministers are being rotated like laughing clowns, and parties vie for public attention.

**Local Government**

Although local government does not rate mention in the Australian Constitution, local government is the foundational form of people's government in this country. It is where the interests and strategy of government are most closely aligned with its constituents. Local council is effectively the service provider of core local services.

We undoubtedly have too many local councils, and need to find the balance between financial sustainability and local oversight. In addition, the roles and services of council can vary extraordinarily from council to council and between states. A common service platform, differentiated for local variances would provide a more useful basis for benchmarking.

Various sources (including Wikipedia) indicate that local councils number a 'hotch-potch' collection of 561 local government areas (LGA's) in Australia (including some islands and ski resorts which are counted as 'unincorporated bodies'), each varying in powers depending on the state government to which they report. Local council is, in many ways, the 'poor relation' of government, sourcing funding from state & federal governments, and often undertaking work passed on by those governments. That being said, local government is uniquely placed to understand and meet the needs of its local constituency. We simply have too many unsustainable councils, a factor that all state governments recognise and have attempted to change without significant success, although at time of writing, the NSW government were seeking to amalgamate 43 Sydney councils into 25 under their 'Fit for the Future' proposal.

On recent data, about 260 of these councils represent less than 10,000 constituents, which would appear inefficient & counter-productive, as it would be difficult for these smaller councils to be heard. In fact, the smallest 100 local councils represent on average just 858 constituents, which while providing a local focus, appears to illustrate the issue of over-management.[xxvii]

The objectives, processes and frameworks of these councils also vary significantly, increasing the total burden of local council on the economy.

As mentioned, various state governments have or are attempting reform, with varying success, however there remains insufficient accountability to manage the effectiveness or cost of local government. And as the lowest rung of government in a bureaucratic, multi-tiered governance framework, local councils are largely poorly financed, independent and splintered. In addition, with so many councils in place, they have not been immune from governance issues, examples including Wollongong and Auburn councils.

As local council is the responsibility of state governments, the authority, scope and powers of local government vary from state to state. They also vary according to local constitutions. For example, some local government bodies operate transport and energy enterprises while others are far and away the largest employer in their territory. Most levy rates as well as receiving funding from the higher tiers of government. Local government responsibilities typically include town planning, supervision of building codes, local roads, water, sewerage and drainage, waste and sanitary services, and community recreational facilities. Over time, some of these councils have been aggregated, however attempts to implement such efficiencies have typically been thwarted by local interest groups.

It is only recently that standards and codes of practice have started to trickle through local governments to provide a 'how to' and offer some uniformity of process. Inevitably, the Banana Shire Council, despite some similarities, will typically operate quite differently to the Adelaide City Council, simply due to the nature of the spread of community, the nature of constituents, and the types of services offered.

Our great need is to unshackle local government from state control to reduce cost shifting between tiers of government, provide national efficiencies in service delivery and infrastructure, improve the level of resource, information and technology sharing (best practice), improve access to direct federal funding, aggregate to provide the best opportunity to balance their budgets, thus enabling all councils to operate efficiently and service their local constituencies, while providing better feedback on strategic issues to federal parliament, so that the higher levels of government are better attuned to local council needs.

**Politics by Numbers**

The number 9 is an important number, as it best displays the duplication and paralysis in Australian politics. Across our federation, we have 9 Education Ministers, 9 Health Ministers, 9 Ministers for Transport – you get my point. Okay, so some ministers cover multiple portfolios; however this does not mitigate the impact such duplication has on operational effectiveness, ability to change, and the effort to standardise and simplify. Yes Minister, there is only room for 1.

The number 3 is also important; the current term of federal government and the number of tiers of government. While there is argument increasing the term of federal government to four years or more would improve our myopia, the fact that not one of our last five Prime Ministers has been able to see out a 3 year term of government.

In total, across all levels of government, we have (in the order of) 226 federal politicians, 598 state politicians across the houses of the states and territories, and something in the order of 4,500 - 5,000 local politicians in Australia across 561 council authorities, a total approaching 6,000 politicians

|  | 2007- '08 | 2014 – '15 | Change |
|---|---|---|---|
| Federal | 237,000 | 235,000 | -0.8% |
| State (All) | 1,340,000 | 1,470,000 | 9.7% |
| Local (All) | 172,000 | 187,000 | 8.7% |
| **Total Public Service Headcount** | **1,749,000** | **1,892,000** | **8.2%** |

*Figure 3 – Public sector headcount 2007-2014 (Source: Adam Creighton, The Australian, 19 March 2016, per Australian Bureau of Statistics)*

across the country. This accounts for politicians only and excludes the political staffs and bureaucracies supporting our elected representatives. The numbers are breathtaking, and emphasise the need to substantively streamline our bloated political framework. Political support and public service headcount reinforces that public service is one of the key sectors of employment growth across the nation (per Figure 3 above). The most recent budget carefully hid a recent decision to provide $5m to lift the number of political staff independent senators can employ from two to three. Australia already has the most and highest-paid political staffers in the world - such measures completely undermine the cost focus of government affecting the voting public.

Bowen points out[xxviii] that "volatility has become the new normal in Australian politics. Over the past thirteen years there have been 64 leadership changes at the federal and state level …"

Whereas our focus is typically on national debt, the Australian Bureau of Statistics provides a summary of debt by jurisdiction. These numbers are meaningful in total, but meaningless at a specific level given the level of cross subsidisation (refer figure 4 below).

Debt levels and operating cashflow statements across all levels of government make harsh reading if you were treating government as a going concern. While there are cycles to economic performance, the trend is not our friend, and demands an enterprise type approach to both revenue capture and expenditure across all levels of government, in order to reduce total debt.

Instead of flip-flopping between whether we have a revenue problem or a spending problem, it is important we recognise it is in fact both, then quickly move on, because that itself is not the heart of the Australian financial burden, but rather the development of a sustainable system which enables consensus as to how intergovernmental financial relations are structured, to stop the cycle of blame (termed the 'vertical fiscal imbalance') and deliver accountability for the management of public funds. As Eccleston and Smith[xxix] intimate, 'we need to either ensure all tiers of government have adequate and sustainable funding, or find a way of operating reformed government which achieves this outcome'. Figure 4 confirms this is not the status quo.

| Surplus(+)/ Deficit(−) | Common wealth | Multi-jurisdictional (a)(b) | State | Local (b) | All levels of government (c) |
|---|---|---|---|---|---|
|  | −26,819 | −1,381 | −9,790 | −1,137 | −47,608 |

(a) The multi-jurisdictional sector contains units where jurisdiction is shared between two or more governments, or classification of a unit to a jurisdiction is otherwise unclear. The main type of units in this category is the public universities.
(b) Data for local government and multi-jurisdictional are estimated.
(c) The sum of individual levels of government may not agree with the All levels of government figures due to transfers between levels of government.

*Figure 4 - Cash Flow Statement for all Levels of Government 2014-'15. Source: Australian Bureau of Statistics*
http://www.abs.gov.au/ausstats/abs@.nsf/mf/5501.0.55.001

The numbers seldom lie. There are too many politicians, there have been too many leadership changes, and there is too much debt to enable good government. There is undoubtedly significant scope to enhance our performance across these key areas of governance.

**Legal Institutions**

John Locke[xxx] wrote "Where there is no law, there is no freedom." Australia enjoys significant democratic freedom, because that freedom and equality is safeguarded by the independent application of the law under strong legal institutions, with Australians accepting that the rule of law will be put into effect as legislated.

The principal function of the High Court of Australia is to interpret the Constitution and to settle disputes about its meaning. The High Court, established in 1903, has the power to consider Commonwealth or state legislation and determine whether such legislation is within the powers granted in the Constitution to the relevant tier of government. The High

Court has the power to invalidate any legislation or parts of legislation that it finds to be unconstitutional.

Under Australia's common law system, the High Court of Australia and the Federal Court of Australia have the authority to interpret constitutional provisions. Their decisions determine the interpretation and application of the constitution, most famously in cases such as Mabo v Queensland (1992) and the Gordon River dam case (Commonwealth v Tasmania, 1983).

Our legal system is similar to the American system in that our constitutions are entrenched ie. cannot be changed through the law making process, although Australian law may be changed through referendum, while an Act of Parliament is sufficient for constitutional change in the United Kingdom. It is noteworthy that ultimate power for the Constitution resides with judges (who are not elected to office, but appointed by federal government, on advice to the Governor General) rather than democratically accountable politicians, providing definitive separation of constitutional power from a governance perspective.

One of the key issues for our legal system is that it continues to interpret the Constitution, a document which has not changed since federation, despite huge changes in the way we now live. There have been calls for changes to the Constitution, or the development of a US style Bill of Rights, however the call for change is lethargic. The Australian Constitution has become something of a natural 'wet blanket' in terms of enabling reform. Examples include more recent social and environmental issues which may cause significant change in the way we lead our lives, such as global warming and terrorism. The failure of the constitution, or some other mechanism (such as a Bill of Rights) to deal with specific relevant social issues may make it difficult to provide and direct the requisite community support to develop and enact appropriate social outcomes.

While we have Law Reform Commissions, the inherent weakness of these commissions is that they cannot instigate change without parliamentary assent, which extends the leadtime and typically requires negotiation for change to take effect, as has occurred in the ALRC's review into national security legislation.

The failure of our legislators to appropriately and sufficiently confer personal responsibility to the individual has created a minefield of bureaucracy and unnecessary legal case load. Special interest groups such as the unions have intensified this issue. The inadequate focus on personal duty of care has an additional impact on productivity, and has been applied poorly in some industries to unacceptably transfer responsibility to employers and contribute to a lack of competitiveness.

At some point, individuals must take responsibility for their actions without government departments, companies and statutory bodies being concerned by the need to address every conceivable potential legal liability which may arise. For example, employers and office holders should be making the workplace as safe as possible, but can only make the workplace as safe as employees act in a given situation. In the work environment, the greatest prospect for zero harm is to ensure that employees who do not maintain an appropriate duty of care for themselves and their fellow workers are held personally responsible, particularly in the event of an accident caused by such failure, so that safety becomes truly institutionalised.

If it is possible to do so, we need to develop a standard for individual duty of care which can be applied to place appropriate responsibility to all individuals across all work and social situations which clarifies what a reasonable person would do to plan for, and protect their safety, and those of others.

In general terms, we appear to be over legislated, to the point where only legislators and lawyers can keep up with legislation. This is not assisted by the varying standards which apply from state to state. The removal of unnecessary and unproductive legislation, and to continue to unify towards national legislation, would benefit the nation by streamlining and simplifying our legal system. This of course is difficult when it comes to negotiation, and every state believes it has the highest legislative standard in the nation.

The clarion critique of our legal institutions is that justice takes too long and is too expensive. The law is generally perceived to lack the stakeholder management and service ethic of commercial entities who rely on a positive customer experience to ensure return custom. Mediation, the typically less expensive and expedited outcome, is not yet used to the extent it can be, despite ongoing improvement in the way mediation is applied. So many conflicts which go to court could be resolved just as effectively in mediation.

The modern era, with terrorism just one threat to our society casting a global pall, perhaps illustrates that the time has again come for a more integrated federal methodology to be bolstered, to deliver us the security we seek as a nation. An integrated national approach to terrorism is, for example, proving more problematic with seven State and Territory government policing systems, each with differing designs, operating systems, and cultures, interfacing, often manually with a federal policing system. It is important that we face this threat on a national front, with an integrated national policing system, yet we are not geared to do so to the extent that we should, constrained by the complexities we've allowed to develop over time, despite the best efforts of skilled, and committed people.

From a criminal standpoint, police remain somewhat hampered by archaic state jurisdictions. The ludicrous situation persists today whereby crossing state lines buys time for criminals, as jurisdictional bureaucracy crosses from one state to the next, often delaying and impeding apprehension and prosecution. If only the criminals faced the issues with state boundaries that our police do. Or better still, those boundaries did not exist.

The other great challenge for legislation and legal institutions is that globalisation is creating both new jurisdiction and case law at a brisk rate. Managing global business, social media, cross border issues, all relying on cross border negotiation, sometimes with institutions aligned differently from ours, provide new challenges for legislative and legal institutions.

These points aside, our legal system is regarded as one of the best, most stable systems in the world. Society however is changing at a rapid pace (globalisation, technology, and changing social values to name but a few) and all legal systems are struggling to keep up. While the key focus is on technical reform of law, deliberation is needed to determine how we can make the legal system, seen as staid and conservative, able to support a global environment which is rapidly changing.

**Financial Institutions**

As the information age facilitates more available taxonomy and comparison of global data (albeit that it remains even in the modern era difficult to compare oranges and apples!), various social and media bodies are attempting to compile global rankings across a range of indices.

According to the 2014 – '15 OECD rating of global competitiveness (refer Figure 9 and Appendix 1), Australia is rated 6th in terms of financial market development, our highest ranking across any of the OECD competitiveness pillars. We have a capable Treasury, a strong and independent Reserve Bank, and active regulatory bodies including Australian Securities and Investments Commission (ASIC) and Australian Prudential Regulatory Authority (APRA) to name a few.

During the global financial crisis, our banks were ranked among the safest in the world, due principally to the safeguards which had been built in by prior governments.

We have significant institutions underpinning what is a solid, if perhaps at times bureaucratic financial regulatory environment. While a royal commission into financial institutions scores easy political points, the supervising bodies already in place have greater regulatory and reform clout than a royal commission would have.

Of all the roles in government, arguably including the role of Prime Minister, the role which requires the most conscientious contemplation of personal attributes and fiscal capabilities is the role of Treasurer. Despite the political clout of our key financial institutions, the government of recent times has experienced a series of Treasurers who failed to take heed of advice from, and align themselves with, the experience and financial nous of our core financial institutions, or understood the nuances of our political dynamics. As Ruthven observes, "history demonstrates that nothing ever really goes right unless finances are well managed; balancing the budget over a term of government." Despite this significant support structure, Australia finds itself facing significant budget deficit, a failure to store funds for such times, and an unclear way towards light in the fiscal tunnel.

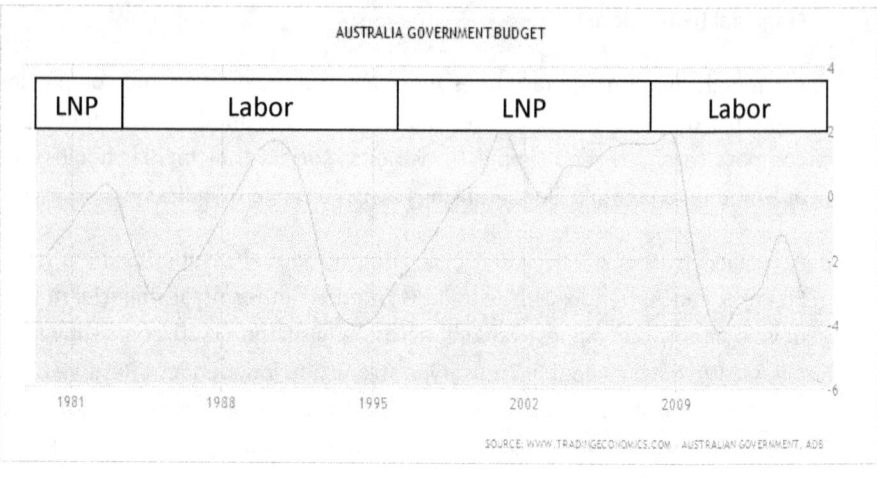

*Figure 5 - Trend of Australian Government Budget surpluses & deficits 1979 – 2015. Source: http://www.tradingeconomics.com/australia/government-budget. Overlaying the budget, we have placed a timeline of government.*

The government of the day cannot be solely accountable for budget balances; there are global influences beyond their ability to manage, however government does have some control in terms of their ability to manage incoming revenue and spending. The legacy of the Costello era, highlighting the peak of the long running resources boom, (shown in figure 5 above) has been abused by fluctuating trading terms & successive poor decision making since – in Horne's parlance, it could be said that our luck appears to have run out.

**Disruption**

The truism of politics, business and life is that expansion is not readily accessible to any entity with excessive debt, as so much revenue is devoted to debt repayment. It becomes difficult to spend on initiatives, such as Prime Minister Turnbull's eminently sensible emphasis on innovation, which support growth, when current spending is already exceeding income and we are borrowing to sustain our current standard of living.

With respect to innovation, we have a lot to learn from other nations, who are supporting and financing innovative technologies for the national benefit. Israel is a prime example. While it is not our intention to become another Silicon Valley, much of our best innovation is appropriated overseas early in the development cycle because we have failed to provide domestic support. Of course, it is inevitable that for every Atlassian, we have one hundred or more innovation projects which won't make the cut, which reinforces the need for a sound governance framework to support the innovation 'revolution'.

The key business terminology of the moment – disruption – is another phenomenon which needs to be incorporated into the reform debate. If we are not seriously identifying initiatives to utilise new technologies to enable our institutions to be more responsive, effective, and customer friendly, we are establishing a productivity liability for future generations. It is vital that we have a window on the world of technology and on best institutional practice around the world to ensure we continue to remorselessly streamline institutional processes and reduce the cost of administration.

Disruption is as much an issue for government is it is for business in the modern age. Disruption will impose the impetus for grander scale reform, which is why we should be striving to 'transform' (change in form, appearance, or structure, to metamorphose) government process and structure as well as 'reform' (improve or amend what is wrong). Reform remains important, but it is no longer in itself enough in an age of rapid change. There are many cases in which the 'wunderkind' innovations of five years ago are already the mature, waning 'dogs' from a life cycle perspective.

**Crises or Opportunities?**

Our politicians appear to bear more than reasonable scorn by the general population despite most working extremely hard for modest pay relative to what they may earn in the private sector. However, while salaries are modest, it is the structure of politician's pay, including spurious allowances and uncommonly generous superannuation arrangements which cause most concern. Allowances, and their potential misuse, remain a historical anachronism which requires reform. The fact is that few politicians misuse allowances, however they are seen as profligate by voters, with any indiscretion reflecting badly on the process. And then of course there is the age-old argument that if we are all tightening our belts, any perceived misuse of allowances is seen as profligate.

Abbott and the Prime Ministers preceding him expressed their concern about a 'febrile media culture'. No recent Prime Minister has managed to harness the media in a meaningful way, or establish a sense of urgency in their narrative to distil this febrility. No politician in a democracy can afford to overlook that free press is a building block of democracy, in spite of the polarised local media ownership which has developed. A process which sanitises this short term focus by lengthening the span of our forward view would go some way to removing the day-to-day media culture we perceive to be in place now.

A summary of Peter Hartcher's Lowy Institute paper[xxxi] surmises that "the great crises that threaten Australia's national prosperity come from abroad. So do the grandest opportunities. But in Australian politics the big matters are commonly crowded out by the small." This is to say, it is vital our leadership is focused on the big issues and opportunities, rather than the minutae which seem to have occupied headlines in recent times. Our 'big ticket' agenda (not simply slogans) needs to be clarified and enacted to allow us to better address crises and take advantage of opportunities from abroad. All Australians should understand the direction in which the government of the day intend to take us. In fact, remarkably few do.

Whether we can assume control of 'the car' again and drive it in the direction we want to go (that is, create the conditions to develop our future prosperity) remains to be seen. The resources boom, based on China's growth has foundered, central banks globally have already pulled the levers at their disposal (some seventeen nations already have negative interest rates in place) to bring to life a spluttering global economy. We will need to become more resolute, more diversified, geographically and industrially, and proactive to regain control of our economy, the growth agenda, and our global competitiveness. The challenge for us as a nation is, as Collins & Hansen suggest for companies, how to master our own fate despite the upheaval, uncertainty and disruption going on around us.

We have many challenges ahead for Australia and its government - tax reform, infrastructure planning for the future, innovation, productivity improvement, to name a few. Given the depth and breadth of these challenges, how attuned is the average Australian to the elements of our national strategy, despite media attention to policy? How many Australians understand the big picture? The likely answer is that many of us are blissfully unaware, content to 'row our own boat', and prepared to apathetically rely on our representing officials to 'do the hard yards' for us.

Then Prime Minister Rudd's (2008) ambitious 2020 Summit brought together hundreds of the best minds in the country, "throwing open the windows of our democracy, to let a little fresh air in"[xxxii] and discuss the nation's future, putting aside political considerations or constitutional barriers. Our expectations and appetite for the summit at the time were enormous. Many big ticket, 'cut-through' ideas were proposed, and committed to a report which is worth reading if you have the opportunity, although the public perception, correct or not, was that the inspiration and good intentions arguably came too little in the form of concrete outcomes.

With key exceptions, we have largely failed to advance good ideas into outcomes. Attendees such as David Marr noted the role of facilitators as gatekeepers, preventing ideas raised such as the abolition of crown copyright from even reaching the final summit report.

Unfortunately, it seems the many ideas proposed at the summit have been wasted, despite the fact that the convergence of these committed, talented people with the common interest of the national good, because we could not fulfil the promise of ideas with the process of implementation, identifying what ideas work, clarifying the priorities, establishing a work plan, and a forum for updating and communicating progress – none of these core issues of process were in place. Now that's waste.

Such summits have become the symptom for what is wrong – we have no problem understanding what our issues are, or what needs to be done. We simply don't seem to have the fortitude to bring unpopular (or at least not universally accepted) but necessary notions to fruition. Too often, small minded vested interests slow or terminate important debate.

The government is well aware of governance issues; reform of the federation is in the spotlight of cabinet on an ongoing basis. A taskforce within the Office of Prime Minister and Cabinet developed five 'Issues Papers' and a White Paper within the last few years. In Issues Paper 1: A Federation for our Future[xxxiii] presented the concept of subsidiarity, 'whereby responsibility lies with the lowest level of government possible, allowing flexible approaches to improving outcomes'. However, the Paper also points to some key issues – the difficulty in 'operationalising' subsidiarity, and the most exasperating challenge of providing appropriately for each tier of government with sufficient income to meet their expenditure obligations.

The republic is the best known of notions which are currently supported by a majority of the population which cannot reach fruition. Tax reform is another recent matter which appears to have tripped up on itself. This is an issue of process, a 'missing link' in the reform agenda, the need to implement our best concepts and move on. Instead, we seem to be caught in the political equivalent of 'Groundhog Day'.

The final report of the 2020 Summit, despite its perceived failure to convert ideas to measurable outcomes, did summarise the issues ahead of our country, as have many documents before and since.[xxxiv] Across the areas of productivity (incorporating education, skills, training, science and innovation), the future of the Australian economy, population, sustainability, climate change, water and the future of our cities, future directions for rural industries and rural communities, a long-term national health strategy, strengthening communities, supporting families and social inclusion, options for the future of Indigenous Australia, creative Australia—the future of the arts, film and design, the future of Australian governance—renewed democracy, a more open government (including the role of the media), the structure of the federation, and the rights and responsibilities of citizens, and Australia's future security and prosperity in a rapidly changing region and world.

Summits provide an excellent platform for strategy. They offer 'outside the box' thinking, an opportunity to fearlessly debate options, and a means to engage with the wider community. The importance and value of summits is understood by most, however to become part of the fabric of Australia's strategic fabric, they necessitate being taken beyond a one-off event and infused within our ritual governance framework for strategy development.

While we have to take lessons from the past, it is vital we are not bound to it for the future. Australia's forward prosperity depends on us, like any dynamic enterprise, understanding the reality of our situation, agreeing what is working and what could work better, establishing through disciplined discussion and debate the democratic framework we need for the future, then playing the 'long game', to transform those mechanisms of the framework of government requiring change to meet our requirements now and for the future.

David Marr remarks[xxxv] that "at the heart of democracy is a contest of conversations". That contest of conversations in Australia has indeed become messy and, at times, aimless. On similar lines, George Brandis has said[xxxvi] "the art of legislation is compromise". This is not only undoubtedly true, circumstances have caused it to become the political currency of choice. The problem is that while the parties have developed their approach to compromise with each other, the standard fare of politics, the community they represent has become disengaged from the process of policy development. Citizens have to be brought back into the conversation, and governance mechanisms developed which support decisive strategy rather than political compromise to reflect the fast paced world of today. We need instead to review the processes of government, so that legislation supports strategy and public narrative rather than rely almost purely on political compromise. This 'science' incorporates clear national objectives and priorities, long term plans, resulting in accountable, auditable action.

We have to acknowledge this disengagement, and understand the cost impact of disengaged Australians on our national productivity. That cost may largely be opportunistic, and may come in the form of good people electing not to go into public service, a lack of debate leading to economic debilitation, and the continuing influence of vested interests undermining productivity, filling the void left by capable people opting out.

Tiernan concludes[xxxvii] that 'a reset in habit and cultures of intergovernmental relations' is required, and unless we see 'something more collaborative and invested in shared problem solving, and supporting architecture embedded through reform of federal financial relations and the governance of COAG and IGR, we are unlikely to achieve desired reforms'. While federation showed reform was possible, it must do so again.

The platform of stable democracy provides the best opportunity for economic development and therefore national prosperity. It falls to us to ensure stability, and to push for more effective planning, not only to ensure that stability is maintained as a foundational brick in the wall, but to provide the platform for growth based on stability. Stability alone is not sufficient to ensure prosperity, as we have learned to our chagrin over the last decade. The organism has to grow to survive.

Just as Australia has been at the forefront of global reforms of the past, we now have to determine how we can be at the forefront of the global reforms of the future. The environment for such change has to be 'forward-looking, dynamic and challenging'[xxxviii].

# 3. Political Parties – Democracy in Action?

*"There is no act of treachery or meanness of which a political party is not capable; for in politics there is no honour."* (Benjamin Disraeli)

As a young boy, collecting stamps was an interest. We'd collect, saving multiples as potential trades, and trading took place with impassioned negotiation. We were always on the lookout for something rare and unusual, something others may want, for which we could trade for our sought after stamps, with the intent of achieving a worthwhile collection. Trading power and influence in Australian politics has, over time, become similar to the art of collecting and trading stamps. Key influencers store information and favours, constantly on the lookout for a market for its use, constantly searching for a way of maximising or 'trading on' their collection of power.

A survey conducted by the Australian National University Social Research Centre[xxxix] found that for the majority of Australians surveyed, it no longer matters which party is in power. While the major parties fight a battle of attrition for power, more and more Australians are becoming disengaged with them, particularly younger (18 – 24 year old) voters who not only divorce themselves from the major parties, but from the enrolment process itself. Perversely, the major parties appear to be at this time, our only electoral choice.

At some stage, idealistic followers joined the major parties yearning for input to policy. Now, membership of these same parties has become a search for political currency, the currency of donations – their views are not of interest to the party unless they offer tangible support in the form of money or time, at which point their views, often vested, may get lip service. Most midstream party members, realising this, have run for the hills, resulting in a deteriorating membership base.

A yawning chasm has swelled between the rule of the parties and the will of the Australian people they represent. The only way an increasing number of voters can now express their dissatisfaction is to nomadically switch from one party to another in some misty, obscure political twilight zone. The major parties (not the representatives themselves, but the parties they also represent) have become so divorced from the people they supposedly represent, as they wage a pointless competitive race to the middle ground, that the Australian people should simply cite irreconcilable differences, and walk away from both of them. But where do we walk to? Unfortunately, at this time, we have no alternative for the inhabitants of the twilight zone, although there is a groundswell of support building to figure out an alternative.

We are 'blessed' to live in what Francis Fukuyama labels a liberal democracy, which is broadly supported by two key parties with core fundamental views of how this liberal democracy is best maintained. Unfortunately, both parties are stricken by factions and vested interests, and it often seems that the greatest rifts are within parties rather than between them. This pattern correlates with less people identifying with specific parties.

Cater hypothesises that "Labor and Liberal have paid a high price for following outdated maps of the cultural landscape drawn on a more familiar grid of working class and middle class, country and city. They have blundered back and forth across the trenches, uncertain of where the battle lines are drawn and unable to tell their allies from their enemies; the casualty rate has been high."

**Partisan Antics**

The party system has displayed laudable resilience despite an ongoing propensity for fraying at the edges. Mark Latham's chilling critique of the Labor Party can be applied in measure to the Liberal Party as well. Such criticism is not new. Vere Gordon Childe, private secretary to NSW Labor leader John Storey commented in 1923 that his party of choice had '... degenerated into a vast machine for capturing power ...'.[xl]

Latham writes, "The Party's defining purpose now revolves around power and patronage, the fuel that sustains its factions, but that ultimately drains the True Believers of conviction and belief. It has become a conservative institution run by conservative people, the worst elements of machine politics. The problem of social democratic reform in Australia has become insoluble."[xli] This is not intended as a shot across the bows of the Labor Party; my 'outsider's' brush with the Liberal Party revealed not dissimilar traits, albeit my view of the future is more optimistic.

Shorten's targeted attack on the LNP at the 2016 Federal election, referred to as 'Mediscare' is widely seen as an attack without merit or basis in fact. Despite this, it has proven successful in scaring wavering voters back to Labor at the 2016 election, which of course was the intention of this tactic. The long term consequence however is that it will now be difficult for either party to enact reform or improvement of Medicare without significant political fallout. While a successful campaigning tactic, however offset by its long term damage to government on both sides to implement systemic change in one of the key areas which will affect Australia's budget position in years and generations to come.

Both Labor and the Liberal Party, it could be argued, effectively communicate 'liberal democratic' policy, and there is little to be discerned by comparing and contrasting the philosophy underpinning the policies of both parties. Both parties appear to be in a race to placate middle Australia, the outstanding difference being that Labor has the support of unions, while the Liberal Party has a classical conservative backbone. Both parties trumpet fairness, equality, justice and inclusion as core values. And yet, their interface in government does little to reflect the social harmony we seek as a society.

One of the key issues we face in Australia (and in fact most democracies) is that while we can vote for whoever we like, our choice is narrow. The major political parties act almost as filtering agents, based on their own interpretation of the public agenda, what might be popular, and what will enable them to retain power – this lust for power "as primordial as a salmon going upstream to spawn".[xlii] The voting decision will likely be determined for many based on who they perceive will make the better leader, with party policy a shadow. As a result, the trend has become that the key policy platform of the major parties don't appear too different, and are nuanced to 'meet the market'. The focus falls further towards the character and qualities of our leaders as the constituency attempts to discern difference. Edward Bernays[xliii] may have described it as democratic propaganda, "a consistent, enduring effort to shape events to influence the relations of public to an enterprise, idea or group" or engineering a viewpoint.

This viewpoint is further coloured by the political numbers game. Resources and investment are more likely to be devoted to 'swinging' seats than 'safe' seats, in order to curry favour with voters in those swinging seats, whereas votes in safe seats may be taken more for granted. Safe seats held by opposition representatives are renowned for being tough to attract investment – after all, what is the point for an incumbent government who doesn't believe such investment will change its political fortunes.

The very common public perception is that the leadership of our country has spent excessive energy working against each other, rather than working in unison to enable better outcomes for the nation – across parties, and levels of government. There is no sense that we are pulling in a common direction, towards a common goal. This is despite the supposed similarity of the party policy platforms. Effectively, parliament now operates on the basis of argument for the sake of argument. Politics has become based on personality rather than substance, and the aim of the key parties is power rather than the public good. These are generalisations & perceptions, but they highlight how we have allowed our politics in this country to go 'off the rails', and the impact this has had on our international competitiveness.

While both major Australian parties were more closely aligned with distinct social groups in their genesis, these lines are now blurred in the race for the middle ground. Disturbingly for parties, current and future generations are less likely to simply follow the allegiances of their parents as they did in prior generations.

Our parties are, whether we like it or not, driven by factions which don't typically reflect the views of the wider electorate. However, they are able to influence, and even distort the public agenda with a powerful voice.

The widening gap between parties and people is being expressed around the world with the rise of demagogue politicians; we need look no further than the US elections, and the rise of Donald Trump, who will tell the American electorate whatever he thinks they want to hear. Until Trump's agenda, of leadership at any cost, is clear, they'll continue to lap up the rhetoric, because, to many, the choice of a non-politician is intended to give traditional politics a 'black eye', rather than a choice based on its own merits. Clive Palmer's hapless political rise was based on a similar approach.

The Australian Labor Party (ALP, or Labor) formally began in 1892, and is the country's oldest political party. Labor was the first party in Australia to win a majority in either house of the Australian Parliament at the 1910 federal election. The party formed from labour parties founded in the various Australian colonies by the emerging labour movement in Australia, and according to Labor folklore has its origins under the Tree of Knowledge at Barcaldine. The ALP pre-dates both the British and New Zealand Labour Parties.

The Liberal Party was founded in 1945 to replace the United Australia Party, and has spent more time in government than any other federal party. The Party's ideological heritage stretches back to the anti-labour movement, including a fusion of earlier groups including the Free Trade and Protectionist Parties, which were brought together by Menzies in response to the growing popularity of the Labor Party, on a more conservative fiscal policy of balanced budgets and debt reduction.

Fast forward to today, and both parties are now ideologically positioned in the middle ground. However the direct middle class influence of both parties is waning (only typically building as the lesser of two evils); membership of a political party no longer holds the value to the broader population it once did.

Recent analysis highlights that Australia has the lowest level of party membership in the western world. Arguments will diverge as to whether this is a sign of comfort and confidence in our system of government (generally a proposition of the parties despite continuing efforts to increase membership), or of disengagement and apathy. I'm tending towards the latter.

As the major parties continue to 'tighten the screws' to their grip on power, the membership base of both parties is dwindling dramatically. While it is difficult to get transparent information on party membership, it appears that both major parties have suffered a significant loss of membership over the last decade. In fact, membership appears to have declined to the point where the combined affiliates of both parties anecdotally represent less than

2% of the population, with approximately 70% of members over 60 years old. Contrarily, as former Prime Minister John Howard notes[xliv], this reduction in membership has made parties more susceptible to vested interests and vested control of the candidate selection process. Howard's proposed solution, a branch plebiscite process enabling local branch members a greater say in who represents them, is currently being trialled by the Liberal Party.

Despite the ongoing partisan conflict which symbolises Australian politics, Christopher Pearson[xlv] some years back referred to a substantial, yet 'tacit freemasonry across the political class' drawing on the Monty Python spoof election coverage between the 'Sensible' Party & the 'Silly' Party. Pearson wrote that despite their differences, 'what they have in common is a set of broad assumptions about the national interest and the value of stable institutions and a belief that duty and friendship should normally trump partisan advantage and sectional allegiances.' That freemasonry is rarely on show in the modern era, at least to the public. It is conversely available to be drawn upon when necessary, a mutual survival strategy.

In the past, politicians could more readily put aside their partisan differences, and maintain strong friendships across the political divide. This enables mutual interest to be progressed. In the current era, such relationships are not only difficult, but frowned upon by the parties.

Contrived power, the almost legendary power of the 'faceless men', is to this day a significant force behind Australian partisan politics. Horne points out in the original (1964) version of The Lucky Country[xlvi] 'indeed a great deal more of the affairs of Australia are carried out in an underground of conspiracy than most people realise.' Contrived power, although an impediment to good government, is a means of short circuiting decision processes which may otherwise be more cumbersome. It enables vested and special interests to pursue specific agendas and outcomes which are not necessarily in the national interest. Of course, contrived power is a feature of all democratic governments.

Partisan junkies talk in another language, referring for example to partisan styles such as wedge politics (a political or social issue, often divisive in nature, which dissects a demographic or population group) and triangulation (presentation of an ideology as above or between the left and right sides of the partisan political spectrum). Less common is talk of consensus or visionary politicians (Hewson, Beazley and Kennett might be considered in such terms); typically such politicians finish in politics before their time, either frustrated or derailed by partisan style.

**Core Voter Factions**

Partisan debate is impacting our effectiveness as a nation, and the influence of the major parties needs to be somehow wound back, or finished. As Australian media executive Kim Williams has been quoted (per Stephens)[xlvii] we have to stop "the often tiresome parades of intellectual conceit between 'left' and 'right'" and their "descent into simplistic binary views on politics and society". The standard of parliamentary debate and media comment is too often appalling, pointless and personal, effectively failing the people that debate represents.

I've formed the view that the majority of Australians 'shop' their political support between six core 'class' or 'interest' factions, the nomadic migration of support between which political polling and election outcomes is guided. This breakdown of groups does not reflect the party factions (which is far more complex), but rather the way the parties are viewed by the electorate.

1. Labor Progressives (Centre) – this is the group most responsible for developing Labor beyond its union and socialist roots to develop a more progressive political agenda. This faction grows and dwindles in its support in alignment with the Liberal Progressive faction & special interest groups such as the Greens;
2. Liberal Progressives (Centre) – this group appears to be most closely associated with middle class families and capitalist business groups, who are seeking advancement in science, technology, social and economic systems to improve society. The faction fluctuates in support in alignment with the Labor Progressive faction, and special interest groups such as the Greens, when voters are not satisfied with the platform of either party and seeking an alternative;
3. Liberal Conservatives (Far Right) – this is the largely 'rusted on' liberal cluster, unlikely to consider changing their vote, historically influenced by family, social and class background, and bolstered by a solid

denominational support group.  Their challenge as a group is that their party has, and will continue to change to reflect middle class Australia; some of these values may become inconsistent with the core conservative group;

4. Socialists/Unionists (Far Left) – these are the 'rusted on' Labor voters, also unlikely to consider changing their vote, historically influenced by family, social and class background.  Their challenge as a group is that their party has, and will also continue to change to reflect middle class Australia;

5. The Greens (Centre/Special Interest) – the Greens, and other key minor parties are at their most popular when support for both major parties is on the wane.  Various other parties, including Palmer United Party and the Australian Democrats have tried to attract support in the centre, however all have failed to sustain that support;

6. The National or Country Party – principally reflecting the interests of country and regional Australia, this party was once described by Horne as "the most powerful pressure group within the Government".  This statement was made prior to the amalgamation with the Liberal Party, which has probably resulted in some loss of this power over time.  It is vital this group retains influence and avoids splintering, as it remains the key means of maintaining pressure on government to support our rural and regional communities.

It is from the dynamics of these six core voter 'factions' that voter intentions are typically driven.  On inspection, the differences will, to many, appear clearer between these 'core factions' than they do between Labor & Liberal/LNP.  It is likely that, were we to go to an election on the basis of these voter 'factions', we might well see an entirely different leadership outcome, and the downstream consequences for factions which currently influence our political agenda (ie. the far right and left), but which failed to attract support in such a vote may well be severe.  On the other hand, we would likely witness the rise of what Ian MacFarlane and Gary Gray referred to in their 'farewell' interview[xlviii] as the 'extreme centre'.

If we can't find a reasonable marriage between parties representing the 'extreme centre' and the people of Australia, this 'hollowing out' will continue unabated.

**The Hollowing Gap**

The Australian Democrats, the Greens, and the Palmer United Party have at various times tried to fill the gap in the centre, however starting a new political party is fraught with problems (no need to convey this news to Clive Palmer), and there is a failure within the governance framework to ensure party start-ups meet appropriate minimal guidelines.  Not only do new parties of any consequence become a point of focus for the major parties, who are concerned with any potential vote leakage, Stephen Mayne noted his learning from the formation of People Power in a Victorian election some years back, where his party became a lightning rod (what he referred to as a 'grievance factory') for all the disaffected, disenfranchised people with a barrow to push who couldn't gain credence elsewhere.  These will be the types of issues the Nick Xenophon Team (NXT) will face as it tries to develop as a viable alternative to the major parties.

While it often occurs beyond the public gaze, there is considerable fighting, 'trade-off' and negotiation going on between these core factions in the generation of policy.  However, it is becoming increasingly difficult to understand the difference in values and policies between the factions and vested interests of the major parties. Horne's observation, now 50 years old, seems not only true today but applicable to both parties, "Power within the Labor machine can become a satisfaction in itself; activists are more concerned with keeping their position in the machine than with winning elections. In this way they can enjoy a feeling of importance and exercise power and at the same time preserve their emotional security (their 'integrity') by never testing their 'policies'."[xlix] The 'faceless men' are just as faceless, yet just as powerful on the Liberal side of politics.

It is the influence of these factions which often drives electoral outcomes at the ballot box.  The point is probably moot, as the parties would not be willing to 'open themselves up' in this way, however it would be interesting indeed to see the outcome of a grand factional spill, which would allow these six core voter factions to stand on their own, instead of within the party apparatus.  A likely outcome would be the elevation of a more aligned, centrist government to power, (possibly a coalition of the two centrist voter groups) with the more extreme factions of the major parties taking a back seat. The 'country' party could well lose power in the short term, but gain significant influence in the longer term, allowing them to renew their position as a pressure group for regional Australia. Over time, we could possibly see the influence of left and right factions, which retain a tight interest on political outcomes at the moment, wane in the face of changing social and political attitudes towards government.

**Muddy Waters**

Donations have become the currency of 'soft corruption' in politics - a term bandied around ever increasingly in recent times. The argument against political donations is fuelled by (yet again) differences in legislation between states and state and federal legislation, and a deliberate lack of transparency in reporting, particularly at the federal level, where reporting on donations during an election campaign (where the major transacting is done) is delayed until months after government is elected.

The rules around donations to political parties reveal another 'dark underbelly' to norms of transparency and accountability. According to the current governance regime for donations, only donations over $12,800 have to be declared. However, this declaration limit applies only for donations to a single branch, which allows an organisation to donate $12,799 to the federal Liberal Party or Labor Party) and the same amount to each state branch without any obligation to declare it. It should be noted that the Labor and Greens parties now declare donations over $1,000. Crikey recently reported[1] that almost 40% of major parties' income is not disclosed, with almost 60% of Queensland LNP income not disclosed. Payments for goods or services, however spurious the service (for example, fundraising dinners) or significant the cost, don't need to be disclosed. Donors can also mask their contributions under the guise of associated entities, and donate under multiple entities. A review of the 2014-15 federal Labor Party return, for example, shows the single largest income description line as "Other receipt". The disclosure regime, and party culture is murky indeed in this respect.

Following the New South Wales ban on developer donations in 2010, Liberal Party members channelled suspect donations through a federal body ('the Free Enterprise Foundation'), which then 'laundered' donated money to the

NSW Liberal campaign, a technique exposed during the Independent Commission Against Corruption (ICAC) investigation. Various groups within the parties maintain the unhealthy culture of 'finding a way around the rules, rather than offering true transparency.

The oversight failure relating to income also extends to party expenditure - there is generally very little apparent information available on how funding and donations are spent by the parties. The entire system of reporting revenue and costs is open to gaming, which leads to ordinary voters questioning the integrity of those who represent them.

The lack of process and transparency highlights a fundamental failing of governance, and sets the stage for poor culture which has been highlighted by the Queensland LNP and Palmer United Party in particular. The development of an independent process, perhaps by the Australian Taxation Office, which regularly reports all sources of political party income is the necessary antidote to what has effectively become a high class charade. While a Senate Committee has reviewed and reported on the shadowy world of partisan financial accountability, outlining a number of recommendations to overhaul electoral funding and increase transparency, no real progress has been made in converting these recommendations into legislation. Both Canada and the UK have reformed partisan income and expenditure in different ways to improve accountability and transparency.

Based on recent results at state and federal level, Australians appear to prefer 'divided' or small majority government, as this electoral outcome forces the parties to collaborate towards the centre, which is the where the majority of voters vacillate. It also offers the electorate some pretence of accountability. This electoral outcome is also a function of both left and right attempting to maintain its political influence. The unfortunate consequences of divided or small majority government include the febrile Federal Senate we've endured over the last three years, and the flipping of parties at elections to install the other party, resulting in constant policy change, which are both counter-intuitive to the development of long term strategy and effective decision making.

Peter Mair writes, "the age of party democracy has passed. Although the parties themselves remain, they have become so disconnected from the wider society, and pursue a form of competition that is so lacking in meaning, that they no longer seem capable of sustaining democracy in its present form." This quote from Mair[li] was written to describe European democracy, however few would disagree that the quote could have been written for Australia.

Doing nothing about partisan politics, which is a fundamental building block of our Australian democracy, is not an attractive option. The title of Mair's book ('Ruling the Void: The Hollowing of Western Democracy') colourfully expresses the issues of partisanship. If we do nothing, the void will continue to hollow out, the sense of disengagement and dissatisfaction will increase, and the political and electoral climate will become increasingly volatile. Whether we increase the governance framework around all parties, find a substitute for partisan politics or develop a sustainable 'third force', or significantly reform the structure and organisation of the major parties, or a combination of all these actions, something must be done. Changing the philosophy of the party system to reflect the modern values of the electorate is the foundational stone on which other fundamental democratic change will be enabled.

While Mark Latham Prime Minister would have been an interesting turn of events indeed, one can but admire his brutal honesty and perspicacity. In describing the party he led, but realistically applicable to large political parties generally, Latham writes, [lii] "this is what the Australian Labor Party factional machine does to people. It is an endless series of deals and compromises, which bit by bit, drains away the idealism of mind and soul."

# 4. Global Political Lessons

*"Differences in national values, culture, economic structures, institutions, and histories all contribute to competitive success. There are striking differences in the patterns of competitiveness in every country; no nation can or will be competitive in every, or even most industries. Ultimately, nations succeed in particular industries because their home environment is the most forward-looking, dynamic, and challenging."* (Michael Porter)

**Applying Porter to Nations**

Michael Porter is the doyen of business strategy. Extending his research beyond businesses to the national factors which influence competitiveness, Porter analysed country competitiveness and the role of government in encouraging national competitiveness. "In the continuing debate over the competitiveness of nations, no topic engenders more argument or creates less understanding than the role of the government. Many see government as an essential helper or supporter of industry, employing a host of policies to contribute directly to the competitive performance of strategic or target industries. Others accept the 'free market' view that the operation of the economy should be left to the workings of the invisible hand."

Of course, national competitiveness is more complex and variable than business competitiveness. The strongest governments are typically those who can balance the books while ensuring their social obligations are maintained. However, those that can best support their national trade and commerce, without getting in the way, are best able to lay the foundation for prosperity. Porter asserts that neither the 'hands on' or 'hands off' view is on its own correct, concluding that either on its own would lead to the permanent erosion of a country's competitive capabilities. Excessive government assistance for industry frequently propose policies that would actually hurt companies in the long run and only create the demand for more help, in effect as welfare does. "On the other hand, advocates of a diminished government presence ignore the legitimate role that government plays in shaping the context and institutional structure surrounding companies and in creating an environment that stimulates companies to gain competitive advantage." This is particularly true for Australia, which relies on small and medium sized business as its engine room for growth.

The underlying point is that, like it or not, just as business competes for a finite global market, our country is competing with the other nations of the world, for finite capital, lifestyle, productivity and growth.

**Democratic Comparisons**

Gross Domestic Product (GDP) is the most common comparative measure of global performance. Professor Ian Lowe[liii] starkly illustrates the issues associated with this measure; it realistically represents the best comparison we have. Lowe highlights a speech by Robert Kennedy months before his demise, highlighting the pitfalls, but also the enormous 'wealth' GDP fails to capture:

"Yet the Gross National Product does not allow for the health of our children, the quality of their education or the joy of their play. It does not include the beauty of our poetry or the strength of our marriages, the intelligence of our public debate or the integrity of our public officials. It measures neither our wit nor our courage, neither our wisdom nor our learning, neither our compassion nor our devotion to our country. It measures everything in short, except that which makes life worthwhile."

Of course, all governments and types of government systems have their issues. Micklethwait and Wooldridge[liv] argue that some established democracies such as South Africa face increasing corruption, while countries such as Russia, Turkey and Hungary 'have become increasingly illiberal.' Micklethwait and Wooldridge are of the view that the biggest challenge facing the world in upcoming decades is fixing government, citing the unsustainability of a welfare state, and the desire to 'combine social provision, economic growth and personal freedoms'. There is of course, a significant prize for the nations which can conquer such issues and inefficiencies – a sustainable platform for increased prosperity and growth.

John Kilcullen has reviewed various political systems and identifies issues with various advanced democracies, noting that the political systems of Australia, Britain, Canada and the United States all have shortcomings. "In the not-too-distant future these societies will need to deal with issues that may require extensive changes to life-style and social organisation, issues such as global warming, terrorism, religious conflict, energy shortages, and war. None of these 'democratic' systems does well in focussing the attention of a large enough proportion of the population on a problem and giving people suggesting possible solutions an opportunity to mobilise enough public support to carry any solution out."

Kilcullen goes on to note that the US system is, in his view, particularly unsatisfactory, which is of grave concern given their dominant position of power, and strong influence in negotiation across issues including trade, armament, and international intervention.

At the time of writing, the US system appeared to be in gridlock, facing an 18 month election cycle with a 'children's birthday party' line-up of candidates, at a consequential cost to the nation. There will also be consequences for active management of the nation's resources, not to mention business impetus. Even prior to the campaign commencing, independent analysts indicated that the majority of legislation passed by the House of Representatives is not even considered by Congress, and government has been unable to finalise a cogent budget now for nigh on five years. Much of the resource in the US appears to be dedicated to maintaining the lethargy of the political system.

Kilcullen notes the chief defect of the US political system is the fixed terms of office of Congress and President, resulting in a lack of accountability for executive government (beyond impeachment). US candidature for government also appears to be a case of the candidate with the most money having the firepower to see off potentially more worthy but less wealthy leaders in a campaign process both drawn out and arduous. The length of campaigning can also draw attention away from strategic initiatives, and leave incoming leaders 'owing favours' to valued supporters. Finally, Kilcullen points to the lack of flexibility for constitutional change, making it difficult to address defects in political process.

Writers noting some of the legacies faced by America, such as Fareed Zakaria[iv] point to their apparently mediocre school system, low savings, increased regulation and red tape, high corporate tax rate, government gridlock, costs of healthcare, and loss of manufacturing jobs offshore. The problem, he says, "is that 'a can-do country is saddled with a 'do-nothing political process', taken over by money, special interests, a sensationalist media, and ideological attack groups." His warning resonates with an eerily familiar echo.

America's auxiliary great political and cultural weakness is the social burden entrenched within the Bill of Rights the nation seems unable to face up to or overcome; the right to bear arms which, although enshrined in legislation, is contributing to the deterioration of the American social fabric from the inside out.

Kilcullen also expresses views about the voting systems in Britain, Canada and the US, although he acknowledges based on feedback to recent polls that certainly Australia, and likely no other country has found the right mix to maximise attendance and voting preferences. Kilcullen expresses the view that "it should be compulsory to attend the polling place, but not compulsory to actually vote, and not compulsory to express any more than one's top preference (though possible to express lower preferences if one chooses)," noting that "a voter should be able to cast a vote that straightforwardly expresses their view." The benefit of preferential voting is that it "gives a better chance for smaller parties to compete with the traditional 'major' parties, thereby making possible the political realignments that may be needed to deal with emerging problems." Our experience would be that preferential voting, while working, does not yet enable voters to express their view in a straightforward way. Electoral reform, as stated previously, also needs to enforce greater governance around party formation and management.

Kilcullen also draws reference to the common make-up of the lower house in Australia, Britain, Canada and the US, suggesting that these "single member constituencies give a distorted reflection of public opinion, since it is possible for a party to win a majority of seats with less than 50% of the vote". This also establishes a heightened "distinction between 'safe' and 'marginal' seats, which leads parties to concentrate their campaigns on the undecided voters in marginal seats". He suggests an ancillary impact might be that sitting members in safe seats become unresponsive to public opinion and factionalism becomes intensified, although this is less true in Australia than other countries, where a politician considers his seat safe at his own peril.

He identifies potential remedies including the adoption of multi-member constituencies, which existed in the United Kingdom until the 1950's, and proportional representation, although these suggestions would likely cause as many issues as solutions.

The current reality for Australians is that while we have a sound, relatively stable political system in this country, it has its shortcomings, & we should be looking to improve it, albeit incrementally, with a view to the long term. We can harness the best of processes and initiatives other countries have implemented. Automating basic processes for example, and reducing the costs associated with non-value adding activities such as voting, transactional activities and tasks, duplicated control of electoral boundaries and other similar reforms would be useful places to start. There are a myriad of other initiatives to be considered.

The stability of the government is a key factor considered by business when seeking to establish long term relationships. The leadership instability of the decade to 2016 has undoubtedly impacted business confidence and the desire to invest, both domestically and by international investors in an environment where growth options are already minimal. Nations such as China and other Asian nations have watched the intriguing machinations of Australian politics in recent years with some bemusement.

**The Scorecards**

The articulate lesson proposed by recent philosophers such as Acemoglu & Robinson[lvi] is that politics guides economics. It is not a matter of chance, but rather the symmetry between political systems, and those constituents the system is established to serve. Australia has a solid base to work from. We take for granted in Australia that, while bureaucratic, we have a core system which supports entrepreneurialism, while other countries have institutional systems which inhibit similar industries in other countries competing. Socialist economies for example have in the past operated less efficiently, which in turn reduces their ability to compete internationally. Often the macro decisions

|  | 2006 | | | | 2013 | | |
| --- | --- | --- | --- | --- | --- | --- | --- |
|  | Billions U.S.$ | % of Nation GDP | % of World GDP |  | Billions U.S.$ | % of Nation GDP | % of World GDP |
| **1. Largest Deficit Economies** ||||||||
| United States | −807 | −5.8 | −1.60 | United States | −400 | −2.4 | −0.54 |
| Spain | −111 | −9.0 | −0.22 | United Kingdom | −114 | −4.5 | −0.15 |
| United Kingdom | −71 | −2.8 | −0.14 | Brazil | −81 | −3.6 | −0.11 |
| **Australia** | **−45** | **−5.8** | **−0.09** | Turkey | −65 | −7.9 | −0.09 |
| Turkey | −32 | −6.0 | −0.06 | Canada | −59 | −3.2 | −0.08 |
| Greece | −30 | −11.3 | −0.06 | **Australia** | **−49** | **−3.2** | **−0.07** |
| Italy | −28 | −1.5 | −0.06 | France | −37 | −1.3 | −0.05 |
| Portugal | −22 | −10.7 | −0.04 | India | −32 | −1.7 | −0.04 |
| South Africa | −14 | −5.3 | −0.03 | Indonesia | −28 | −3.3 | −0.04 |
| Poland | −13 | −3.8 | −0.03 | Mexico | −26 | −2.1 | −0.03 |
| **Total** | **−1,172** |  | **−2.3** | **Total** | **−891** |  | **−1.2** |
| **2. Largest Surplus Economies** ||||||||
| China | 232 | 8.3 | 0.46 | Germany | 274 | 7.5 | 0.37 |
| Germany | 182 | 6.3 | 0.36 | China | 183 | 1.9 | 0.25 |
| Japan | 175 | 4.0 | 0.35 | Saudi Arabia | 133 | 17.7 | 0.18 |
| Saudi Arabia | 99 | 26.3 | 0.20 | Switzerland | 104 | 16.0 | 0.14 |
| Russia | 92 | 9.3 | 0.18 | Netherlands | 83 | 10.4 | 0.11 |
| Netherlands | 63 | 9.3 | 0.13 | Korea | 80 | 6.1 | 0.11 |
| Switzerland | 58 | 14.2 | 0.11 | Kuwait | 72 | 38.9 | 0.10 |
| Norway | 56 | 16.4 | 0.11 | United Arab Emirates | 65 | 16.1 | 0.09 |
| Kuwait | 45 | 44.6 | 0.09 | Qatar | 63 | 30.9 | 0.08 |
| Singapore | 37 | 25.0 | 0.07 | Taiwan (Prov of China) | 58 | 11.8 | 0.08 |
| **Total** | **1,039** |  | **2.1** | **Total** | **1,113** |  | **1.5** |

*Figure 6 - Largest Deficit and Surplus Economies, 2006 and 2013. Source: IMF, World Economic Outlook database, www.imf.org/external/pubs/ft/weo/2014/02/pdf*

taken by governments are only understood well after those decisions have been implemented. The Hawke/Keating initiative to reduce local tariffs, although difficult on many iconic local industries, and unpopular at the time, set Australia up on a sustained path to prosperity in the late 1980's. The

Rudd stimulus during the global financial crisis, while giving the economy a 'sugar hit' in 2008, still reduces our ability to withstand subsequent economic shocks eight years on, leaving Australia as one of the highest deficit nations per GDP as per figure 6.

Our performance relative to the world's leading economies is discomfiting, having come through a prolonged resources based boom, and highlights our challenges, as the International Monetary Fund comparison (per figure 6 above) shows. The IMF analysis puts into perspective Australia's economic performance on the global league table. We are consistently in the worst performing countries in terms of largest deficit (per GDP) economies, and while we have performed better than countries such as Canada, who have a similar economic base (focus on mining, relatively spread population, etc.) as Australia, the US have, to their credit, halved their deficit over the same period. We gaze on in envy at the largest surplus economies, some of whom like us are blessed with significant natural resources, while others such as Germany appear to simply outperform economically.

While Australia's deficit as a % of GDP has reduced from -5.8% to -3.2% over the period, the inference drawn from the data is that we are running hard to stand still, with our actual deficit increasing. What is clear, from an economic perspective, is that our current capital structure is not sustainable. The impact of a continuing deficit is on the wallets and accounts of all Australians, who have to bear responsibility for that debt. It is no mistake that the some of the most influential nations of the world also operate with the highest economic surpluses.

We cannot afford alternative rhetoric to the simplest explanation of Australia's deficit. Make no mistake, country debt is no different to company debt and household debt. As long as it is not excessive, supporting growth, and supported by sustainable income it is manageable, however in the long run, Australia's great challenge is to spend less than we earn on a sustainable basis, so that funds that are now allocated towards debt repayment can be channelled towards our future. An interest payment of $2 billion adds no value in economic terms, but leaves an unwanted legacy.

As mentioned above, there has been action taken on the US deficit, although it must be noted they have been at a different stage of the economic cycle to Australia. The figures confirm the need for decisive action in Australia, even if such action is not electorally popular. We have to demand superior long term resilience from our financial system, and strive to achieve the sustainability and flexibility of nations operating in surplus such as Germany.

On the income side, Phil Ruthven[lvii] points out that "Australia's taxes at 28% of GDP make it the second-lowest taxing nation of all advanced economies in the OECD", with some nations, such as Denmark and France closer to 50%, and the average 37%. We may not like it, but the argument to increase GST or other taxes in light of these figures appears quite rational, particularly as our GST rate is among the lowest in the western world (according to Ruthven, the average GST rate across the OECD group is 17.5%).[lviii] The bottom line is that we need to instigate action on both the revenue and spending lines, and a disciplinary framework which ensures the work is strategic and sustainable, not undone by successive governments.

Of course economic prosperity is not the only measure of competitiveness, although it is fundamental. The tiny kingdom of Bhutan has come under scrutiny for its alternative approach to measuring national 'success', and has been more recently frequently labelled among the happiest countries in the world. In 2008, Bhutan transitioned from an absolute monarchy to a constitutional monarchy, and held its first general elections. The leadership reviewed the constitutions of 80 countries around the world, as the basis for the development of its own constitution. The kingdom developed a measurement[lix] in the 1970's which reflects its Buddhist spiritual values - the 'Gross National Happiness' (GNH) index, in contrast to other countries which focus on Gross Domestic Product (GDP).

Bhutan has a focus on long term goals, which are reflected in the index, and based on the four pillars of preservation and promotion of cultural values, sustainable development, conservation of the natural environment, and establishment of good governance. To quote the third Dragon King of Bhutan, Jigme Dorji Wangchuk, "today, GNH has come to mean so many things to so many people but to me it signifies simply - Development with Values. Thus for my nation today GNH is the bridge between the fundamental values of kindness, equality and humanity and the necessary pursuit of economic growth."

Success, the basis for influence, is at the core of these various 'league tables'; the ability to develop and influence global relationships, recognised by the term 'soft power'. Monocle, a magazine launched in London in 2007 focusing on global affairs and culture releases a 'soft power' ranking by country each year[ix]. In 2015 – '16, Germany, the US, Great Britain, Japan and France were nominated as the top 5 'soft power' nations in the world, while Australia is optimistically ranked at no.6. New Zealand is the survey's 'bolter' moving up significantly in the rankings in recent years to no.13. While Australia should never harbour ambitions as a super power, our ability to delicately wield 'soft power' is significant to our global influence going forward. China's soft power ranking is perhaps understated by Monocle, at no.21, down two places since last year, understating their significant regional and global influence.

**China – A Snapshot**

I have had the good fortune to visit China on several occasions. The Chinese culture is more nationalistic than outsiders might expect, and the economy appears to be successfully combining a market system and socialist principles to develop an economic trajectory which will prove sustainable in a society of momentous change. This adjustment is massive, and will have its hiccups along the way. Despite the country's size and the enormity of the transformation taking place, there appears to be a strong, coherent set of values, a clear long term plan, and an enduring sense of national pride. The immediate challenges for China are to stamp out corruption, manage the transition of their middle class, and improve productivity, which has been based in the past on an abundant supply of cheap labour.

China has a distinct and deliberate approach to planning. It has various planning horizons phased out fifteen years or more, and recently released its latest rolling five year plan. China anecdotally have a five year plan locked & loaded, a further five years out a plan being formulated, and a further five year plan (ie. fifteen years out) under early formulation, providing a clear long term planning horizon. These plans, while complex, are communicated succinctly in a style enabling its people to understand the key priorities for their government. Planning is vital to the world's largest economy, as it transitions through a change in style, and addresses significant historical issues, while mindful that such evolution typically impacts growth rates.

UBS[lxi] succinctly summarises the objectives of China's latest plan, which is communicated as a national narrative, as:

1. **Growth is still a top priority** - Doubling per capita income by 2020 from 2010 levels requires an annual average growth rate of 6.5% over the next five years, which will likely be the growth target of the new five year plan. The government wants to promote innovation and accelerate reforms to help unlock new sources of growth.
2. **Go green** - The new Five Year Plan (FYP) places more emphasis on environmental protection and cleaning up. Expect more investment in non-fossil fuel energy, new energy products, an environment tax, and more spending on cleaning up air, water and soil pollutions.
3. **Poverty reduction and social welfare** - The new FYP aims to lift 70 million people out of poverty by 2020, with the help of an improved minimum wage system, free secondary education for poor children and a better social safety net. The government plans to expand pension and serious illness insurance coverage to the whole population, assisted by the transfer of some state assets to social security funds.
4. **Go global** - China wants to further integrate with the global economy by further opening up the domestic market as well as pursuing "going out" strategies such as the "One Belt One Road" initiative. China plans to expand free trade zones, regional free trade agreements, and playing a more active role in global economic governance.
5. **End of the "one-child" policy** - After more than 30 years, China finally announced the full relaxation of the "one child" policy nationwide, against a backdrop of a shrinking working age population and rising social issues. The relaxation will likely lead to a higher birth rate in China, but how much higher than the current 1.2% is uncertain as birth rates in its East Asian neighbours are also very low. Short-term benefits of the policy relaxation will be limited, as demographic shifts tend to be very long term.

By comparison with Australia, where the average Australian would have difficulty nominating the country's top five priorities, such a narrative substantially simplifies the complexity of government into the issues of priority for government, and communicates a clear plan to the Chinese people.

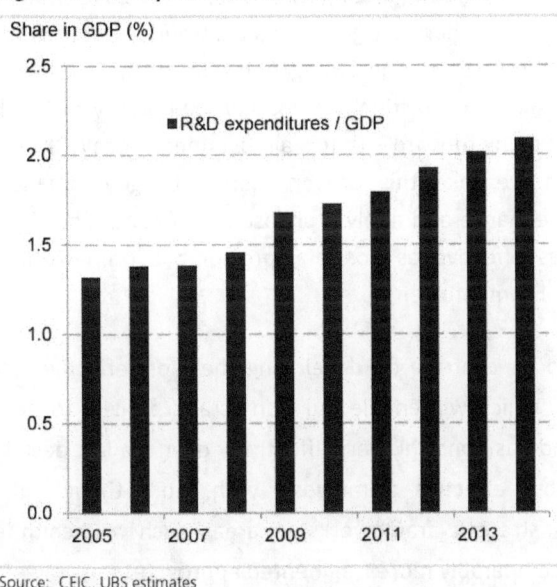

*Figure 7 - Chinese planned commitment to increase research and development expenditure as a % of GDP. Source: UBS – Takeaways for China's New Five Year Plan*

The Chinese government has also committed to increasing R&D expenditure as a % of GDP as manufacturing costs increase and an immature supply chain is addressed, supporting the expanding infrastructure of their manufacturing industry (per figure 7). Unsaid but implicit is the point made earlier, that addressing endemic corruption will continue to be a high priority.

While there is a prevailing view that China's economy is faltering now that its advantage of low cost manufacturing is eroding as its middle class develops, there is also anecdotal evidence that it is moving from an export economy to a consumer economy as domestic household wealth increases. It is in fact a visible strategy in progress.

**'Best in Class' Governance Framework**

Democracy remains the most efficient and effective system to support economic growth. There is a general global trend towards hybrid democratic government, in countries including China and some of the former soviet states. It is not a question of whether democracy is the best form of government going forward – that is almost unequivocally true. The question is how can we take this proven system of government in Australia, modernise, enhance and apply a philosophy of continuous improvement so that it is as effective as possible, providing a framework for improved international competitiveness.

We need to concentrate on developing the most effective framework and the outputs which will enable our democratic process to be best in class. New Zealand has done this very effectively over the last decade, developing a flexible but effective framework, with more thoughtful effort being devoted to strategic frameworks in areas such as health compared to Australia's comparably more fragmented approach.

China, while undergoing dynamic social and economic changes, is more stable than stock markets attest, and it at least has a long term plan as the country transitions through one of the most dynamic historical transformations for any modern nation. Of course, planning is the easy part; the greater difficulty comes in effectively executing the plan. The certainty of a plan which outlines clear goals and is readily available to all provides an essential building block for effective execution to take place. Such planning does not increase the level of bureaucracy or control (the big government fear), but provides greater certainty and stability for entrepreneurs to develop, knowing the environmental factors under which they are operating, providing greater freedom to flourish.

The development of strategic relationships with Asian nations generally requires time, patience and stability, as a means of earning trust. Despite the advancements we have made with many nations across Asia, they still observe Australia with some bemusement and unease, observing for example the continual leadership unrest. Planning for the long term is vital to build true, mutually beneficial cultural, social and economic relationships. The sovereign risk currently placed by some Asian nations on Australia does, on occasion, impede our efforts to build such relationships and attract capital.

Our international image is important, and is not necessarily viewed by other nations as we view ourselves. A dent in national image can occur quickly, but heals interminably slowly, requiring significant toil, just as for business and other organisations. The development of strategic relationships with Asian nations requires significant time, patience and persistence. Saying we are part of Asia does little if anything to help. Showing that we are a stable, capable nation who is easy to work with does help that effort. We can learn from the tenacity and patience of Asian nations who take the time needed to develop trust and respect as the basis for long standing relationships.

The lessons for Australia are that we should be in no doubt that we cannot afford to take a myopic, internally focused view of where we are in relation to other nations, all of whom, like us, have their issues, nor can we afford to be lethargic about addressing these issues. It is a fundamental failure to understand and accept these problems, the drivers behind them, and the distinct action needed which see us in our current economic predicament. Prolonging that failure will see us fall behind those countries seeking proactively to improve their global position. Ultimately, our national prosperity, our jobs and our livelihoods are at stake in the ultimate global race.

# 5. The Concept of Nations Competing

*"Man is a competitive creature, and the seeds of conflict are built deep into our genes." (Robert Winston)*

In Barack Obama's 2011 State of the Union address, he articulated to the nation that America had to "out-innovate, out-educate, and outbuild the rest of the world", with the objective of being "the best place on earth to do business." The concept of nations competing, while for many years universally tacit, is now very much in the open. Australia's greatest allies are also our keenest competitors.

Australia's relatively small population, the flexibility our size offers, attractive climate, well regarded education, proximity to Asia, established and cordial connections with global powers including America and the United Kingdom, our entrepreneurial and innovative spirit, relative equality and diversity and sense of community are significant strengths which bolster our position as a global competitor, so long as we continue to plan to our strengths for future growth.

This is particularly evident in some niche & produce markets. The export of orange juice for example[lxii] highlights the competitive dynamic between the US, Mexico, and Brazil, in comparison with Australia. The US, Mexico and Brazil collectively produced 1.7 million metric tonnes of orange juice in 2014, of which 1.3million metric tonnes was exported, constituting the bulk market. Australia is a niche player in the export market; production of orange juice has fallen from 145,000 metric tonnes in 1984 to 9,000 metric tonnes in 2014, with exports of 1,000 metric tonnes. Australia is able to leverage off the quality of our produce, proximity to Asia, and stability of supply in such markets, however a significant increase in Australian export of such products barely causes a ripple in global commodity markets, which represents our great opportunity. Interestingly, we exported 4,000 metric tonnes of orange juice in 1984, and so appear to have lost ground in this specific example. It is such niches, with growing markets, and where we can sustain and grow a competitive niche that we need to specifically identify to strategically encourage.

The concept that nations compete, while simultaneously allying with each other, is not new. While the United States values its relationship with Australia, our sugar & other primary industries compete head to head. This does not create an adversarial dynamic; the competition is tacitly acknowledged. It simply means that if we are to continue to develop the standards of living we now enjoy, we have to select growth industries in which we offer an advantage, and invest smartly, for the long term, in the global competitiveness of those industries.

Paul Kennedy[lxiii] notes that "a lag of only 1% of economic growth compared to other countries can turn a world power into a small one in less than a century, as happened with Britain." While there are inevitably other factors at play, we cannot afford to take our forward growth for granted. The end of the resources boom is a timely inflection point to remind ourselves of the importance of targeting new sources of strategic national growth.

**How Do We Rate?**

According to the Global Innovation Index[lxiv], Switzerland, the United Kingdom (UK), Sweden, the Netherlands, and the United States of America (USA) are the world's five most-innovative nations, while China, Malaysia, Vietnam, India, Jordan, Kenya, Uganda, are among the countries outpacing their economic peers in 2015. Australia ranks 17th in the global index, ranking below countries including New Zealand, Germany, Singapore, Ireland, and Hong Kong, providing a compelling narrative for PM Turnbull's emphasis on innovation. The report further confirms the close alignment between innovation and productivity.

In another global comparison, Forbes, through the World Justice Project, ranked the top 10 governments in the world in terms of openness and accountability in 2012[lxv] (refer figure 8 below). To make it into the top 10, national laws had to be assessed as efficient and fair, enforced and accessible. The Justice Project further assessed that justice is delivered by competent, ethical, and independent (non-partisan) representatives, and the adequacy of resources to judge a case, and reflect the makeup of the communities they serve. Australia figured well in the Forbes rankings at No. 5, ahead of the UK, USA, and Canada which all ranked outside the top 10.

| Rank | Nation | Score | Rank | Nation | Score |
|---|---|---|---|---|---|
| 1 | Denmark | 0.93 | 6 | New Zealand | 0.87 |
| 2 | Sweden | 0.92 | 7 | The Netherlands | 0.86 |
| 3 | Norway | 0.90 | 8 | Austria | 0.82 |
| 4 | Finland | 0.89 | 9 | Germany | 0.82 |
| 5 | Australia | 0.88 | 10 | Japan | 0.80 |

*Figure 8 - Top 10 World's Best Governments by World Justice Project ranking, 2012*

The World Economic Forum rates global competitiveness across 144 nations on a regular basis[lxvi] (refer figure 9 below). Australia ranks 22nd on the index in 2014-'15, equal with France & Saudi Arabia, and behind countries including the UAE, China, New Zealand, and Malaysia. Qatar, an autocracy with questionable human rights policies, and recently at the centre of a bribery scandal involving FIFA topped the WEF list for efficiency, although it would be churlish to consider money could have changed hands.

It is Australia's rankings across the individual pillars which make the most interesting reading, highlighting the OECD view of our strengths and weaknesses relative to other countries, albeit observing that much of the measurement is qualitative.

| Pillar | Category | Aust. Rank/144 | Aust. Score/7 |
|---|---|---|---|
| 1st | Institutions | 19 | 5.1 |
| 2nd | Infrastructure | 20 | 5.6 |
| 3rd | Macroeconomic Environment | 30 | 5.6 |
| 4th | Health & Primary Education | 17 | 6.5 |
| 5th | Higher Education & Training | 11 | 5.7 |
| 6th | Goods Market Efficiency | 29 | 4.8 |
| 7th | Labour Market Efficiency | 56 | 4.3 |
| 8th | Financial Market Development | 6 | 5.4 |
| 9th | Technological Readiness | 19 | 5.6 |
| 10th | Market Size | 18 | 5.1 |
| 11th | Business Sophistication | 28 | 4.7 |
| 12th | Innovation | 25 | 4.4 |

*Figure 9 - World Economic Forum, Global Competitiveness Index 2014-'15 – Australia's Rankings by Sub-Category (refer to Appendix 1 for detail scores in each sub-category)*

In the survey, Australia ranks relatively weakest in terms of global competitiveness in the areas of budget balance as % of GDP (86/144), co-operation in labour/employer relations (109/144), flexibility of wage determination (132/144), hiring & firing practices (136/144), effect of taxation on incentive to work (80/144), pay & productivity (125/144), and value chain breadth (95/144).

These rankings condemn our productivity and effectiveness in these key growth-stimulating factors.

We can also improve our competitiveness in the areas of gross savings (42/144), degree of customer orientation (46/144), redundancy costs (50/144), female workforce participation (54/144), and government procurement of advanced technology products (73/144). These rankings provide a reality check of comparative performance, and show we have substantive reformatory work to do if we intend to improve our competitiveness.

Finally, the World Bank published the Worldwide Governance Indicators report[lxvii] (refer figure 10), evaluates the efficiency of world governments on six indicators - voice & accountability, political stability & absence of violence, government effectiveness, regulatory quality, rule of law, and control of corruption.

The latest rankings (at time of writing) were:

| Rank | Nation | Rank | Nation |
|---|---|---|---|
| 1 | Finland | 11 | Luxembourg |
| 2 | Singapore | 12 | Australia |
| 3 | Denmark | 13 | Belgium |
| 4 | Sweden | 14 | Germany |
| 5 | Norway | 15 | Austria |
| 6 | Switzerland | 16 | Ireland |
| 7 | Netherlands | 17 | United Kingdom |
| 8 | New Zealand | 18 | Andorra |
| 9 | Liechtenstein | 19 | United States |
| 10 | Canada | 20 | Iceland |

*Figure 10 – Worldwide Governance Indicators Report – rankings of national efficiency. Source: World Bank http://www.countryranker.com/worlds-top-20-countries-with-best-government*

Again, this ranking highlights that Australia remains among the top tier in governance and performance, but not in a position which can be taken for granted. Most Australians would be wanting to see us higher up these rankings which reflect equality ... and definitely in front of our friends in the Shaky Isles!

Each of these rankings recognises meaningful opportunity for improvement in our system of government and governance institutions.

**How Do We Improve?**

Australia's ranking across the pillars must be directly and strategically addressed by government. Action may include, for example, redefining the budget system (more on this later) and approach to systematically return to surplus, while other initiatives require a change in mindset (for example, customer orientation & female workforce participation), and reduced influence of vested interests (for example, flexibility of wage determination).

The availability of such data globally provides valuable input into our strategy & decision making processes. The question is how we utilise such data to make sensible long term decisions and executable outcomes in the national interest.

Global trading is decidedly dynamic and fluid, dependant on macro factors including currency, commodity price and cost of living fluctuations. China established a vibrant manufacturing industry based on their ability to co-opt technology & the availability of cheap labour fifteen years ago. However, in recent times, the United States has regained their manufacturing competitiveness, thanks in part to a comparatively lower US$, cheap funding and energy costs, and a burgeoning Chinese middle class, which is impacting the supply of cheap labour in China.

Australia's manufacturing sector has not regained ground in the same way the United States has, however there is opportunity to regain a foothold in Australian manufacturing by eschewing mass production, paying greater attention to niche and technology driven manufacturing, improving workplace flexibility through employee/employer dialogue, and improved infrastructure, to name a few potential initiatives. Australia needs to retain a stable, skills leading manufacturing industry as the value adding link in the supply chain.

The world has undeniably and rapidly evolved in the last fifteen years, and Australia is struggling to keep up in the stakes of international competitiveness. We cannot hope to compete on a pure cost comparison basis, and so we literally do have to find smart ways to develop our commerce more productively and innovatively. Whether we've had it too good for too long, been too absorbed on digging dirt from the ground, demand has moved beyond what we supply, or social norms have changed, it appears possible that Australia could fall behind other comparative nations. Maybe it is, as Horne suggests that our luck has run out. We are a niche player, and must continue to maintain and improve our competitiveness in these niche areas which appeal to a mass market.

Michael Porter leaves us in no doubt that nations compete as companies do. He considers competition at a nation level at the macroeconomic level, driven by indicators including exchange rates, interest rates, and government debt, concluding that while these are influencers, nations prosper despite advantage or disadvantage across these indicators. He additionally considers labour and labour rates, however deduces that labour is highly variable over time, and increased prosperity can result in increased rates which can then reduce competitiveness, as is happening in China at this time. Porter also points to abundance of natural resources, however, as he concludes, this cannot explain the success of Germany, Japan, Switzerland & South Korea, which are highly competitive but not resource rich, for example.

Porter is less convinced that competitiveness is driven by government policy, indicating that while policy settings such as targeting, protection, import promotion, and subsidies have supported the penetration of Japanese and South Korean auto, steel, shipbuilding, and semiconductor industries across global markets, in Italy policy has proven ineffectual, while Germany intervenes rarely into the exporting dynamics of its companies.

Porter further declares that "a nation's competitiveness depends on the capacity of its industry to innovate and upgrade. Companies gain advantage against the world's best competitors because of pressure and challenge. They benefit from having strong domestic rivals, aggressive home-based suppliers, and demanding local customers." This assertion illustrates the notion of building in 'home grown' advantage.

In a world of increasing global competition, nations have become more, not less important to companies competing globally, both in the way they help and unintentionally hinder the company value proposition. As the basis of competition has shifted more towards the creation and assimilation of knowledge, the role of the nation has grown. Differences in national values, culture, economic structures, institutions, and histories all contribute to competitive success. Ultimately, Porter concludes, nations succeed in particular industries because their home environment is the most forward-looking, dynamic, and challenging.

Porter's final justification for national competitiveness is differences in management practices, including management-labour relations. This is of particular consequence in Australia given our comparatively humble OECD ranking in this area. However, Porter qualifies that different industries require different approaches to management. "The successful management practices governing small, private, and loosely organized Italian family companies in footwear, textiles, and jewellery, for example, would produce a management disaster if applied to German chemical or auto companies, Swiss pharmaceutical makers, or American aircraft producers." Porter also reports that unions are strong in Germany and Sweden, and both countries boast internationally preeminent companies despite the view that unionism inhibits competitiveness. This conclusion highlights the importance of tailoring the Australian approach to specify the industries and strategic support that will be offered.

Australia is failing to appropriately support some of the core capabilities Porter notes as pivotal to successful companies, which apply equally to nations:

- Companies which fail to improve and innovate will atrophy. "Sometimes early-mover advantages such as customer relationships, scale economies in existing technologies, or the loyalty of distribution channels are enough to permit a stagnant company to retain its entrenched position for years or even decades. But sooner or later, more dynamic rivals will find a way to innovate around these advantages or create a better or cheaper way of doing things." This is now a dilemma for China, as it is for Australia and indeed all nations competing in the global market. Is it any wonder innovation is a core plank of Prime Minister Turnbull's leadership methodology.

- "Successful companies tend to develop a bias for predictability and stability". Federally, we lack the predictability in our economy which comes from an unprecedented bias to industries such as mining. Forward budget estimates either failed to predict the macro movement of this industry, and the depth and length of the downturn. Improved forecasting would also enable us to take a more proactive approach to 'filling the gap' rather than the reactive hope that construction and other sectors will soften our fall after the event.
- Porter supports the posture of earnings diversity, as for companies. Australia now suffers from having too many eggs in the mining and China baskets, which has left us vulnerable. Our economy needs to shift focus, just as many companies in the market are diversifying their exposure to other markets, ready for an upturn in mining, but not relying upon it.

Zelleke and Zorn[lxviii] note that the US government does not appear in favour of developing a strategic framework; indeed strategy is almost regarded as counter-political. Barack Obama at one point told *The New Yorker's* David Remnick that he's 'not interested in a new grand strategy'. Zelleke and Zorn point out that "he could use better process for asking and answering core questions about the nation's direction. Americans can live with a published National Security Strategy that disappoints. But they will be hurt if the White House lets itself make new high-stakes decisions—or mindlessly perpetuates old ones—without the benefit of a clear and achievable guiding vision and the best possible strategic thinking."

Australia has to recognise that competition between nations is increasing; Peter Costello refers to a 'relentlessly competitive world'[lxix]. Costello's 'medicine' is to ensure we have taxes and spending as low as possible (ensuring that health, education, defence and security standards are maintained), but more is needed than tight cost control.

We cannot afford to sit on our historical laurels of rich resources, and proximity to Asia. Such arrogance will be our downfall. We must look forward to the next steps – identifying our capabilities for the future, resolving long term issues, and investing appropriately for growth. Our constant challenge is to continue improving at or above the rate of other nations.

# 6. The Beds May in Fact be Burning

*"The problem is not the problem. The problem is your attitude to the problem." (Captain Jack Sparrow)*

While the ABC series 'Hollowmen' offers a humorous parody of the back rooms of Australian administrative politics, one can't help thinking the comedy writers are uncomfortably close to the mark in cynically impersonating the decision processes of our politicians (refer Quote Chapter 9). The so-called 'Central Policy Unit' lurches from one crisis & impromptu policy initiative to another, dogged by the PMO who are determined only to manage the media cycle & boost Prime Ministerial popularity.

What should be becoming clear to Australians is that we simply cannot continue to structurally borrow against our future to fund today, particularly as a growing segment of our population ages. There has to be a repayment plan, or the debt will at some point become insurmountable. And yet, while Australians look for this narrative from our leaders, that narrative is not being communicated. Meanwhile, Australia continues to lose its 'antibodies' to fight global debt crises. It's what has been referred to me as the 'gradually, gradually, suddenly syndrome'. We see degeneration, almost imperceptibly over many years, the warning signs that things are not as they should be, until suddenly a crisis is brought on, seeded and compounded by the gradual degeneration over those many years. Meanwhile our ability to fight the crisis is worn down, which perhaps brings on the crisis in the first place.

Australia's recent ability to address key national issues is undoubtedly at question. Phil Ruthven provides a succinct (and perhaps generous in some respects) rating of Australia's key issues, and the extent to which they are being addressed[lxx] (refer figure 11, as at October 2015):

| | Australia's key issues: are they being addressed? | Yes | No |
|---|---|---|---|
| 1 | Balanced budgets, the first rule of good government | | X |
| 2 | Tax reform that includes GST and shifts taxes to spending | ✓ | X |
| 3 | IR reform that understands work and workers in the new age | | X |
| 4 | Innovation, IP and productivity; and how to get them | | X |
| 5 | Fully embracing the digital era for international competitiveness | | X |
| 6 | Long range vision, especially our role in the Asia Pacific region | ✓ | X |
| 7 | Reducing subsidies going to yesterday's industries that won't survive | ✓ | |
| 8 | Privatisation of low-productivity government activities | ✓ | X |
| 9 | Rational energy policy that includes carbon and nuclear power | | X |
| 10 | Developing the top part of our continent (especially top third) | ✓ | X |

*Figure 11 - Assessment of Success in addressing key issues in Australia. Source: Company Director Magazine.*

If we review Ruthven's conclusions of issue resolution in terms of Porter's assertion regarding national competitive advantage, it is clear the quantum of much effort required to improve our international competitiveness. Ruthven suggests that we have only fully addressed one of ten issues, the reduction of subsidies to sunset industries, with partial resolution across four other areas. Ruthven establishes that across five of the ten big issues, there has been no meaningful issue resolution, a poor scorecard at best. Former Prime Minister John Howard supports the view that institutional reform has stagnated.[lxxi]

Our immediate priority is to work towards a balanced budget, and embracing innovation and digitisation, which as noted Mr Turnbull has shown early interest in progressing. However, the work on IR, innovation and energy strategy are significant 'big ticket' outstanding items.

## Policy Without Context – 'Playing the Short Game'

The idea of developing northern Australia is notionally sound as a strategic imperative, with its reach into Asia, potential for population growth, and rich array of resources. The Japanese invasion during World War II prompted the desire to develop the north and improve our security. On becoming Prime Minister, Ben Chifley established the Northern Australia Development Committee (NADC). Development of northern Australia has been an ongoing policy, in particular for the Labor Party. It is though a clear example of the on again, off again planning philosophy which is driven by politics and election cycles rather than an emphasis on defined strategy.

What has become obvious in recent times is that many, if not most political decisions lack the context of strategic background. Former Prime Minister Tony Abbott's Paid Parental Leave (PPL) Scheme is an example, an initiative which had merit; a scheme which would support families and working women in particular. However, the electorate did not understand the context for this policy, given the cost of the scheme, particularly when Abbott himself had placed the mounting deficit front of mind for the electorate. If we had appreciated the PPL scheme in the light of a higher level strategy of increasing female workplace participation or reduced welfare for example, we might have recognised the strategic substance of the scheme. The rejection of the PPL scheme provided another nail in PM Abbott's leadership coffin, rather than being implemented as sound policy, based on clear contextual strategy.

The allocation of investment and capital is a perfect example of the inefficiency of the short game. As a nation, we were exemplified by the way we allocated capital to nation building schemes including the Snowy Hydro Scheme and the Sydney Opera House to name a few. More recently, our capital has been allocated poorly, characterised by stop/start and project variability, and influenced more by votes (particularly in marginal electorates), short term priorities and vested interests than what is in the best interests of the country-at-large in the long term.

Ensuring a rigorous, integrated process for capital and investment allocation is a cornerstone to the development of any nation. The Australian system for allocation of investment of capital gives every impression of being haphazard, fragmented and opportunistic.

Tiernan[lxxii] points to a trend which has occurred in recent times. "Officials have been supplanted as the primary source of advice and support. Their relationships with ministers are mediated through steadily proliferating numbers of partisan personal staff. Increasingly, officials are not in the room when policy decisions are contemplated." This additional layer of bureaucracy reduces engagement within the departments responsible for implementing policy and reduces the situational context of new policy.

Similarly, Tiernan notes the trend of recent Australian Prime Ministers to transfer their primary source of advice and support from the (permanent) Department of the Prime Minister and Cabinet to the (temporary) Prime Minister's Office (PMO). The PMO is in turn run with people from outside the public service who are selected in part for their loyalty. The impact, Tiernan concludes is reflected in a substantial loss of the 'institutional memory' of the bureaucracy.

It is difficult for companies to implement policy without sound, well communicated strategy; when it is so much more difficult at a nation level, why do we fail in such an elementary sphere as a nation? The lack of a strategic framework for government is a substantial systemic institutional failure which some notably better performing nations (eg. Singapore) don't make.

A common constituent argument is that many of our political decisions are perceived to be based on the necessity to either maintain or increase power, rather than decision making in the national interest. The fact is that radical change will rarely result in an improvement in political popularity, however the Australian voter is more astute now than ever, and understands the difference between policies designed to achieve long term good, and those intended to prop up an election result. Without a well-defined strategic framework, how can the government expect anything else but confusion and disdain from voters?

Our nation, despite enjoying more than three decades of relative economic sunshine, now find ourselves on the back foot, facing a massive deficit, with few economic levers left to pull, making decisions to manage fiscal crisis, in the face of a significant credibility gap. Change in this environment is a huge task, but more urgent than ever. With prices of our key commodities decimated in recent years, our manufacturing industry seeking urgent restructure to survive, and our arable land the subject of intensive offshore interest, it appears as though we have squandered our prosperous years and the inheritance it offered. Of course, it is not too late, and our best years do lie ahead of us, but not if we continue to engage in the figurative definition of insanity.

We are, as mentioned previously, a country which is over-managed & under led. Over-management has resulted in inefficient allocation of scarce resources. The signs of 'over-government' are testified to by the liaison between local, state & federal governments, often bickering for a slice of the same pie, and with whole departments established with the chief objective of 'dealing' with other branches of government.

Our governments are very good at analysis – white papers, submissions, green papers, summits, reviews, and commissions continually adorn the news. We are not short on information, but have developed a failure to execute, often because the safer political option is to do nothing. It would be a very interesting exercise to look at the reviews conducted across government over the last three years, identify the findings and recommendations, determine which of those findings has been agreed to be actionable, and then audit the extent to which those actions have been completed. Perhaps we need to have someone in government responsible for ensuring these outcomes (the Minister for Accountability?); it instead becomes a function of the media, typically by which time momentum has been lost. The key question from a governance perspective is what tools we are using to ensure government is held accountable to govern in the public interest, aside from elections? We need a more fact driven structure to ensure accountability, lest the 'Hollowmen' approach take root – 'ignore it; it'll blow over once the next crisis hits!'

There are other relatively recent policy U-turns which reinforce the quality of decision making in the context of long term conditional factors. The aborted introduction of the Resource Super Profit Tax (RSPT) was a notable policy backflip, a preliminary response to the Henry Tax Review proposed by the Rudd government in 2010, which was later repackaged and rebadged by the Gillard government as the Minerals Resource Rent Tax (MRRT). This proposed tax was an attempt by government to appropriate 'super profits' from the resource companies at the height of the mining boom, but failed to take into account mining cycles, was poorly communicated, and impacted our global competitiveness as a resources investment destination. The major resource companies ran a strong public campaign against the RSPT which resulted in the demise of the RSPT, saw mining capital diverted away from Australia, and contributed significantly to Mr Rudd's original downfall. The MRRT was subsequently implemented by the Gillard government, however the legislation was subsequently repealed by the Abbott government, having anecdotally earned less than it cost to administer. This series of policy changes did significant damage to Australia's sovereign credibility among major resource purchasing nations.

**National Productivity Matters**

Productivity is vital to growth, and yet we appear to be doing very little to address the rump of our productivity issues. Over 20% of our productivity measure relates to government owned activities; further shedding of these activities will contribute to productivity improvement as private enterprise establishes commercial drivers for productivity management. Our workforce flexibility ranking, a key measure of labour market efficiency is ranked 114 out of 144 nations; we are in fact ranked behind a number of third world countries on the OECD measure of workplace flexibility.

Any seasoned leader will attest to the fact that there is a time for narrative and building consensus, and a time for the courage to plunge right in and make prescriptive change. While Australia struggles for what seems forever with a Tax Review, and finding the answers to a significant budget dilemma, John Key, the New Zealand Prime Minister, as Ruthven points out "simply raised the country's GST without an inquiry and without disturbing the ongoing consumer confidence (consumer sentiment index) to any extent. That is courageous leadership."[lxxiii] This is not to suggest Turnbull should increase the GST in Australia, rather to acknowledge that there is a time for leaders to choose their moment, choose their issue, and to have the courage of their convictions, to implement without disproportionate debate. The Australian governance framework, it must be recognised, makes this difficult in practice.

Ruthven[lxxiv] additionally notes that although we have now reduced subsidies to sunset industries, it took almost $11 billion of the 2014 budget (0.8% of GDP) spent on protecting industries which are effectively lost causes before this lesson was learnt. This funding could be used so much more effectively to fund the growth of our industries of the future and reskilling labour towards these industries. Such decisions are courageous although not typically popular with special interest groups.

Ever since productivity was labelled as 'Work Choices', both parties have effectively 'walked away' from what is now one of our key national concerns. As Argus quotes Nobel Laureate Paul Krugman, "Productivity isn't everything, but in the long run it is almost everything. A country's ability to improve its standard of living over time depends almost entirely on its ability to raise its output per worker." This is a fact both major parties need to be cognisant of, particularly as relative productivity (v the United States) increased from 85 to 95% during the Hawke/Keating years, but has since returned to 84%. Productivity improvement, undertaken methodically, is unlikely to bring individuals back to the poverty line or increase unemployment, despite the howls of protests from union representatives. Productivity will increase our national competitiveness and provide more jobs, sometimes in new industries. It may require workforce retraining, but that is a preferable investment to propping up uncompetitive or dying industries.

Unions are one of the key self interest groups impeding advancement in areas including workplace flexibility and productivity in Australia. While we will always have a small number of outliers, those who seek to operate outside the strict guidelines of acceptable workplace practice, we maintain a strong regulatory framework which fortifies worker rights. The most effective method of enforcing worker rights in most cases is directly between employer and employees, and, while we all acknowledge there will always be a small element of unscrupulous employers, this is not the norm as the unions would have us believe.

Unions appear to have become almost anachronistic in the modern era, focused on their own enrichment & influence base in an attempt to remain current, but in so doing alienating themselves from their constituents and employers.

## And Then There's …

Mike Baird, Premier of New South Wales at time of writing, when asked what keeps him up at night[lxxv] did not point to terrorism or global warming. Instead, he alluded to the challenge of funding healthcare for an ageing population, which simultaneously erodes our per capita revenue base and increases per capita healthcare costs. He referred to studies by experts including PwC which forecast a conservative shortfall of $45 billion in 2030, of which health contributed $35 billion.

Saving remains an ongoing concern for households. The rate of savings in Australia has plummeted, principally because savings are being taxed. This makes little sense when superannuation is becoming a tax haven for the wealthy. Discussion has started around the idea of converting the superannuation taxation rate from 15% to the marginal tax rate less 15% with a floor of 15%. This contention, on face value, appears reasonable, however it has to be accompanied by changes to the tax rate applied to savings, which in the current low interest rate environment provides a disincentive to acknowledged savers, instead encouraging them to place their funds at risk.

Finally, the lack of respect politicians show for each other only magnifies the lack of respect voters in turn have for them. We have all made the basic mistake of focussing on personalities, 'playing the man', rather than addressing issues of governance process. We have allowed generally good people to become victims of poor process. If government were a racehorse, these limitations place extraordinary weight in our saddle bags; we have little chance of finishing, let alone winning, when we carry such heavy weight.

The words of Tom Northup ring clearly (refer quote Chapter 12) – 'All organisations are perfectly designed to get the results they are now getting.' Australia is getting the results we are designed to get, and if we want to change the result, we need to change the way government is designed. The process of government needs to be reviewed to ensure it is doing what it is intended to do.

# 7. The Political Process Is Counter-intuitive

*"Leadership is often about disappointing your people at a rate they can absorb it." (Ronald Heifetz & Marty Linsky)*


Nick Bowen aptly discerns partisan politics to be a zero sum game. For a vote to be passed in favour of one party, the other party is seen to lose. Unfortunately, it's the only game in town. The win/loss game undoubtedly causes antagonism and colours each parties' approach to negotiation, perception, and legislation. Surely, a win/win outcome is best for the nation. Paradoxically, win/win outcomes are a rare outcome in Australian politics.

In such ways, our current governmental processes are counter-intuitive. While we would expect decision making systems to be instinctive, when it comes to Australian politics, they generally prove not to be so. It is the dark secret of our governance system that is not talked about. While we have tinkered around the edges of parliamentary reform, so long as it is difficult to achieve win/win outcomes, our current governance processes are fundamentally flawed and counter-intuitive to sound practice.

Such are our core decision making practices, as we've already alluded to. We generally reach decisions through endless negotiation and side deals, to reach outcomes which are typically sub-optimal for the national interest. John Stuart Mill refers to such outcomes as 'fractional truths', an outcome which marries the interests of the people and the parties.

**Voting**

We've discussed preferential voting previously, however it is worth reinforcing the anachronistic reliance on voting methods such as preferential voting (particularly voting every square, rather than simply voting for your top (say) 3 candidates). This method of voting does not ensure the vote reflects the voter's intentions (for example, we are forced to vote for representatives we know nothing about), and increases the potential for a 'donkey' vote. Preferential voting requires amendment, to better reflect the voting intention of the electorate, and avoid the gaming which has created poor candidature in the Senate, for example. We would perhaps be surprised at the error and corruption rates which may occur in manual (paper) voting, besides which it is just plain inefficient. While this is not a priority, it is a signpost of inefficiency, and emphasises the innate absurdity of the process. As Tim Dunlop[lxxvi] notes, the current preferential voting system merely "reinforces mediocrity and rewards stasis".

Myriad papers and reviews have been written to explain and improve our voting system. Relative to other nations, our system is good. However, there are a number of reforms needed to make it more reflective of the voting intention of the public.

**Social Support Systems**

The complexity of our core social systems, many of which we transact with on a daily basis, is another key area of concern. Our health system, and the linkages between the supporting charging, rebating and insurance processes underpinning it are a source of increasing apprehension – the system is too difficult to be understood by many Australians, and provides opportunity for those who do to take advantage. Complexity is a protection mechanism for waste and inefficiency, just as it is a shroud for poor productivity. There are those who 'game' the health system while those without knowledge of the workings of the system become its victims.

Complexity is a natural outcome when you consider that the social systems we utilise are constantly changing and adaptive, have significant interaction and dependencies across departments and levels of government, and are based on historical antecedents. Often, incoming governments seek to solve symptomatic issues, which fail to consider or resolve the root cause of those issues, with the impact that additional layers of complexity are added over time.

## Leadership Selection and Development, and the Role of Media

The selection process for leaders is counter-intuitive, unlike any leadership assessment process utilised within an organisational environment, and effectively akin to survival of the fittest. Rather than assessing the skills of applicants, and matching them to the capabilities of the role, we have an arcane process of deal making and climbing over dead bodies to reach the top of the political leadership pile. It is likely that our last three Prime Ministers would not have made it to a shortlist for the role in a true leadership selection process, let alone be considered to have the necessary attributes to lead our country. Kevin Rudd became PM because we agreed that leadership transition was required; Julia Gillard because the prior decision had been impulsive. Rudd returned to 'save the furniture', giving Tony Abbott the virtual armchair ride he sought to become Prime Minister, until a series of gaffes convinced his party that he wasn't a Prime Minister in the same mould he was Opposition Leader.

Australia has had several periods since federation where we have revolved Prime Ministers as we have over the last eight years; in fact, we had five Prime Ministers in the five years following federation if we include Alfred Deakin's second stint. There is clearly something wrong with the way we select and develop talent for the role. Hopefully, we will be better served by Malcolm Turnbull, however the point is that the way we conduct the process guarantees a result akin to a lottery.

We have been vehemently regaled with the various reasons why we've faced the leadership issues of the last five years – the media cycle, an ineffective Senate, internal party factions, etc. To be continuously let down emphasis emphatically the role that poor process is playing in this drawn out drama. These factors may well have contributed to the problem, but for the answer of why it occurred, we have to glimpse deeper.

Margaret Simons[lxxvii] wrote at the time about why she declined an invitation to attend the 2020 summit, perhaps battle-hardened by a view of the symbolism of such events, citing "… the silly way in which politics is reported – as a highly managed spectator sport, rather than as though it actually mattered."

Kevin Rudd, Campbell Newman, and Tony Abbott each attributed their downfall in part to the role of media, for example. Mr Rudd harnessed the media to develop his profile and was unashamedly a 'media tart', although Newman, Gillard and Abbott never looked entirely comfortable in public, even when it was their media call. While there may be some truth that the media tended to forensically examine the minutae, these leadership failures would have likely occurred even if the media had taken a more 'stand-offish' approach, albeit that the media is attracted to a whisper of controversy as bees are attracted to flowers. Media, like politics, is focused on the short term, the headline of the day, whereas our leadership concentration has to be taken beyond day-to-day tactical issues to the long term view. We have to give the media a motive to focus on the longer term, and that is where the role of strategy comes into play.

Chris Kenny decries the role of the media[lxxviii], "the media cannot escape its share of the blame for preferring personalities over policy and posturing over substance", noting that if we have seen the end of 'solid and courageous' politicians of the ilk of Keating, Hawke, Howard and Costello, the media will have played its part.

There is no doubt the world is changing, and our political system has failed to keep up, however that's the point. These are symptoms of a greater issue. Issues of personality in leadership don't go far enough in explaining leadership failure of this scale. It is the way we develop and select our leaders which requires closer scrutiny. The way we allow leaders to lead, or not lead. Our democratic system has somehow become atrophied, unable to function as it should. This is not to diminish the necessity of the work done and the importance of the legal system, government departments and other mechanisms of the bureaucracy, but rather an assertion that we develop a process which provides a higher degree of certainty that our national leaders going forward have the requisite skills to lead, and are allowed the opportunity to lead.

Tiernan refers to the most striking conclusion of the Kemp Review[lxxix] as a question of philosophy. Kemp determined that it was unclear "what a Liberal Party government stands for, its public-interest framework and the values it brings to the task of governing", a function "perhaps of the tribal and careerist nature of the contemporary party and those coming through its ranks seeking pre-selection." Either party could draft a similar post mortem report, changing only the names and dates, so similar would the findings be for either side, and at various levels of government.

Our key interest as citizens is to ensure we select leaders who are capable to lead. We've not done this so well in recent times. The deeper issue though that we need to come to grips with is to ensure we are providing the infrastructure which empowers capable leaders to lead. It is this inability which has diminished the effectiveness of our governance.


**Special Interest Groups and Unions**

That special interest party factions have such resounding influence in policy is also counter-intuitive, particularly as they represent such a miniscule fragment of the fabric of the electorate. Both the conservative faction (Liberal) and union faction (Labor) have a disproportionate say in policy in comparison with their proportional representation of the Australian community. It is no coincidence that union membership has reduced dramatically, and that union membership is being 'propped up' by the delivery of large numbers of public servants to union membership. That unions are required in the public service is itself a nonsense, considering the checks and balances in place, such as whistle-blower policies and the nature of the employer.

The power of special interest groups is impeding growth and harming our international reputation. In relation to the China Free Trade Agreement Robert Gottliebsen[lxxx] notes, "Instead of embracing the China-Australia Free Trade Agreement we allow the building unions to hijack the debate. And it is the cartel between the large builders and the unions that escalates the price of developments in Australia and sees massive corporate payments to the unions to protect their big profits from the cartels. That money then goes onto the ALP, which must then oppose the free trade agreement. It's an awful look for any country that reckons it's a democracy, particularly if the market's fear of a looming recession changes the government." Unions generally have shown an inability to consider the big picture, however it is the way these groups peddle and impress their ideology and influence across the wider Australian community that is harming and threatening our Australian way of life.

Gary Gray observed the 'phenomenon' quite aptly in his 'farewell' interview on the 7:30 Report[lxxxi]. "We take too much notice of the amount of noise instead of the number of people making the noise; frequently, the smallest crowds of people are the noisiest, and too often it's the amount of noise that channels the public debate, the media attention and therefore the political attention. We need to get better at seeing through the harsh, loud cacophony, and seeing to the conclusion we want to get to for the benefit of the nation."

**Culture and Values**

Best practice for high performing business is based around the building blocks of clearly defined values, a well enunciated strategy, and carefully considered long term planning, and a management team continuously alert to service levels and the cost to serve. As stated previously, government is not business, and has important social obligations, however it should not be immune from the need to create these same building blocks with the expectation of performing at consistently high levels.

What are our values as a nation – what do we stand for? These questions are timidly but deficiently answered by policy; meanwhile policy is highly fluid. The important step before is missing – values provide the impetus for how we think and behave. They tell us what is good and bad, right and wrong. They tell us the 'should do's' and the 'shouldn't do's' of life. They help us determine which is more and less important. Unfortunately, leadership moments, their motivating capture of the values of the people they represent are most often remembered in times of crisis. Who can forget New York Mayor Rudolph Giuliani, hailed for his inspirational captaincy after the nightmare of September 11, or Queensland Premier Anna Bligh's rousing speech following the calamitous January 2011 floods – "I want us to remember who we are. We are Queenslanders; we're the people that they breed tough north of the border. We're the ones that they knock down and we get up again. I said earlier this week that this weather may break our hearts and it is doing that but it will not break our will …". We shouldn't have to wait for a disaster to remind ourselves of who we are.


**Strategy, Planning and Budgeting**

The concept of strategy seems almost anathema to Australia; if it's there, most of us are certainly not enlightened by our planning design. As a nation, what is our strategy, to improve as a nation and to compete on the national stage? Based on our cultural and values strengths, what are the plans driving progress? Any other business or organisation is floundering without these fundamental drivers. And yet, as a country, we are slaves to the electoral cycle. The major parties have generally vague plans, however we do not appear to have a coherent national strategy, beyond the next election, that we can 'hang our hat on'; it depends who wins office. How can we plan for the future in such an environment? Business, social organisations, trustees of financial funds all wait in hope, or attempt to second guess, the likely approach government will take. None of the building blocks for organisations can be effectively implemented while government has responsibility for strategy and execution within a three year election cycle, with the prospect for change beyond that. The long term lens is missing in infrastructure, health, education, welfare and the core areas of government planning responsibility.

Our system of budgeting and forecasting, despite utilising some of the best minds in the nation, is a noteworthy area for improvement. The cross subsidisation between government tiers and complexity of assessing the future without a clear roadmap must make budgeting and forecasting a nightmare. John Wanna offers budget repair advice to the government[lxxxii], in reference to what he describes as the parlous state of Australia's finances arising from a dysfunctional budgetary system, "Singapore offers a markedly different way of deploying and investing public spending in a developed society; and it is worth remembering that Singapore's achievements have occurred over the past 40 years or so. Before this it was once one of the destitute basket cases of south-east Asia with very low living standards, but now has a higher standard of living than most of the West and a per-capital income getting close to twice the Australian average". The practical benefits of addressing the stultifying, convoluted budget process to better reflect what we need rather than what we have to put up with would be enormous, as re-engineering the budget practice has abetted economies such as Singapore and Finland.

There are alternatives. Wanna suggests, for example, that Canada use an alternative "prudential system to limit federal spending within the current budget year by initially only allocating some 70 per cent of the budget outlays in the main estimates, and then trickling out additional supplementary allocations as and when its revenues are known and received." This, he concludes "prevents agencies' overspending against revenue that has not yet eventuated (or will never materialise), and allows governments to direct greater spending 'in-year' to any pressing priorities." Many Australians have been witness to government department urgency at the end of the financial year, as they spend their remaining budget with urgency but not necessarily prudence or discipline, lest they not have the same budget allocation available in the following year.

**Governing for the Long Term - Some Key Social Issues**

While our lack of a unified strategic approach across a range of social issues continually lets us down, there are three key cases where our lack of long term focus and strategy have been on occasion disastrous and expensive – climate change, indigenous Australians and industry support. In each case, the government of the day have responded to their short term situational bandwidth, resulting in sub-optimal legislative outcomes.

Climate change is a classic example of a counter-intuitive political approach. The potential consequences of climate change are clearly dire, and yet climate change has become a political sacred cow rather than a unified call to action, devoid of clear balanced argument, resulting in the electorate being continually misinformed. In truth, few everyday Australians (me included) actually understand the macro state of our planet in the millennial cycle of climate change. We do understand that we are living in a finite environment, for which we need to take responsibility and be sympathetic, and we have to be clear about the effect we are having on our environment. Although we understand we are likely having an impact and must manage our footprint better, climate change sceptics and alarmists punch and counter-punch; meanwhile we are little wiser.

My instinct tells me that direct action policies will have a greater positive impact, as they reinforce the evident action Australians must take to preserve our environment. By the same token, we are talking about the human impact on the environment (which has no doubt been substantial) over 200 years in an ecosystem which has been through cycles of millions of years. And yet, in this setting of unclear messages, we have been the subject of a highly emotional and political debate, incomplete, implemented and undone policies. The environment should not be a partisan debate. It requires bright, unfettered minds, clear measurement, and the long term national interest at the core. Having clear measurement in place is vital if we are to understand the truth of our situation, the impact we are having, and the action we must take to improve our relationship with our natural environment, and integrate with the global effort.

Recent policy on climate change has, it seems, generally been knee-jerk and ill-conceived, with a greater focus on a political outcome than the public good. Like most other areas, it should start with our values – our love of our natural environment and our desire to protect and maintain it. We should have higher order data in place to illustrate how we are interacting with our environment, and clear plans to affirm how we can manage our relationship with the environment more effectively. What is undeniable is that we need to take responsibility for our planet, we need to reduce pollution of all kinds and therefore emissions, and to protect the heritage of our natural environment. We need to establish education and measurement mechanisms that people understand, can relate to and act upon in their daily lives. We need to understand the issue in all its enormity, then draw on agreed accurate data to establish long term plans. We need to separate this debate from the politics.

The sense of fairness and 'fair go' we tout as distinctly Australian has not been extended to the Aborigines. For years, we have skirted around the problem of atoning for the disgraceful historical treatment of indigenous Australians, in so doing, skinning them of almost all hope of developing their sense of self-worth. We've afforded ourselves some cathartic moments of symbolism, but we've not been able to establish an appropriate structured framework supporting inclusiveness of indigenous Australians, aside from some entrepreneurial efforts, leading Aboriginal elder Pat Dodson to refer to his people as the 'playthings' of politics. Australia remains the only Commonwealth nation that does not have a treaty with its first peoples. Despite numerous discussions and policy 'flip-flops', we still cannot agree on formal recognition for indigenous Australians in the Constitution, we are yet to establish a mutual treaty to support the protection of aboriginal rights and culture, or consider appropriate indigenous representation in parliament.

Like climate change, how we resolve an issue of such consequence is not straightforward. As Noel Pearson points out, "what we have thus far failed to find is the appropriate middle ground between the competing philosophical extremes: the 'sweet spot' where rights meet responsibilities, where cultural prosperity meets economic achievement, where inclusion and equality meet appropriate recognition of enriching difference."[lxxxiii] While many aboriginals have taken their rightful place in society, we have much to do to empower the health, education, and effective independence of first Australians. To ensure this process justice would take considerable time, and, in the current governance environment, bi-partisanship, however both major parties are more interested in outdoing each other. While there is no magic answer to this long running issue, other nations have shown they can adopt a strategic approach to resolution, whereas we cannot. It is counter-intuitive that such issues continue to be administered as political footballs.

The third area, industry support, will be discussed in more detail later. Government has not taken the calculated, strategic approach to developing industry policy which promotes greater variety in innovation, a supportive environment to value add, and identifying and supporting industries of the future, rather than holding on, at great cost, to industries of the past. Government has to understand its strategic role in business – when to jump in, and when to stay clear. Whole markets have been destroyed by poor government policy and a misunderstanding of its role in improving growth and productivity.

**Foreign Ownership of Assets**

The foreign ownership of Australian assets appears to be another example of mediocre, counter-intuitive process which is impairing our international reputation. It doesn't make sense for us to be considering every significant investment, and arguing after an investment has been proposed whether it is in the country's best interests for that asset to be sold. Although prone to over-simplification, there are simple solutions. Why wouldn't we instead proactively 'A, B, C' classify our assets from the outset. 'A' class assets are core strategic assets, such as security, food and national interest resources. These assets are not available for international investment. 'B' class assets are non-core strategic, and may include Qantas and other Australian companies, non-strategic infrastructure, etc. 'B' class assets would be available for foreign investment on agreed models, such as maximum 49% international investment or other appropriate funding model. 'C' class assets are non-strategic, and available to be sold overseas. Rather than analyse every business case, the issue then becomes how we classify our assets over time to ensure the national interest is maintained. Such an approach is also helpful in negotiating free trade agreements, because the investment horizon is visible and understood.

**The Convolutions of Implementing National (Federal) Reform**

Consequential federal policy change seems to tie us up in knots, typically taking far too much time, and being difficult to 'operationalise' on a national front. The ongoing debate to develop a national curriculum, which has badgered successive governments is a case in point. As Tony Abbott describes, "The Commonwealth and states first agreed to support a national school curriculum in 1986 and established a national curriculum corporation in 1990. In 2007, a report found that only physics and chemistry had a high degree of national consistency. If the National Curriculum Board can meet its latest timeline, it will have taken 25 years to complete." Meanwhile numeracy and literacy benchmarking indicates our results are falling relative to other western nations.

Tony Abbott[lxxxiv], like those before him, recognised this before he became Prime Minister. "Meaningful reform is unlikely until one level of government can call the shots. As long as reform involves negotiations with the states, reform proposals will nearly always mean that the Commonwealth pays for changes that the states then have to deliver – a recipe for buck passing and blame shifting – or that an unwieldy state bureaucracy is replaced by an equally unwieldy and possibly even less accountable joint Commonwealth-state bureaucracy."

Even in the management of fundamentally federal assets, the regulatory and administrative regime is complex and counter-intuitive. Regulation of Australia's interstate and intrastate rail freight networks is a prime example underlining the complexities of reform, and the obstacles state government portend for integrated management of networked national assets. As at July 2015, all rail networks are regulated and administered under the Rail Safety National Law with the exception of Western Australia and Queensland, which are administered under state rail safety jurisdiction. The two national bodies responsible for rail safety, the Office of National Rail Safety Regulator (ONRSR) and the Rail Industry Safety and Standards Board (RISSB) have only advisory jurisdiction beyond South Australia, New South Wales, Tasmania, Northern Territory, Victoria, and more recently the Australian Capital Territory. Of the 196 accredited rail transport operators within Australia, 127 (65%) conducted railway operations accredited by ONRSR. It has taken five years of negotiation to garner national agreement to the collation of national rail safety data, with Queensland due to come on board in 2017. Despite the efforts of competent operators and regulators, the Australian rail industry is doomed to mediocrity without an integrated national approach to the management and development of the asset.

Inability to access an integrated federal rail network hinders our ability to educate and share knowledge, compliance audits and inspections, and an integrated approach to enforcement. Such jurisdictional nuances are problematic for the effective management of the safety and efficiency of such core assets, perhaps partially explaining our rail safety performance in comparison with the United Kingdom.

Across the board, change is very difficult to achieve and requires the explicit support of all levels of government.

**Governance Structure**

We have one layer of government too many, and that is a significant brake on reforms such as curriculum change.

In favour of maintaining three layers of government are the arguments that they ensure proper governance, provide a plurality of opinion and ideas, and provide more localised government. State identities remain relatively strong to this day – just ask a Queenslander when rugby league state of origin, or a Victorian when the AFL grand final is playing. Against the three layers of government are the arguments that they hinder government productivity and efficiency, add unnecessary cost and bureaucracy, and does not support the strength of local and regional councils. It represents on the basis of vested interests to federal government, which results in a lack of coherence, a culture of blame & finger pointing, and an inability to make sound, effective, timely, nation-building decisions.

The Senate has also become counter-intuitive in its function and form. Joff Lelliott[lxxxv] notes the historical context to the Senate. "Australia's constitution was written before the party system became properly entrenched, and in that context it seemed reasonable the Senate would allow state interests to be represented directly in Parliament. But the vast majority of Senate seats are now in the firm grip of Labor, Liberal, Nationals and Greens. Even micro-parties and independents generally push partisan positions over individual state interests." Proportional representation is not representative of the Australian population, and the minor parties have left an indelible stain on the function of the Senate. The Senate is no longer the house of review that it was intended to be, in the way it was intended to be; it is now closer to the 'unrepresentative swill' so poetically dubbed by Paul Keating.


**Government First Level Process**

The nation has failed to take a sufficient process view at a whole of government level – across federal, state and local council, understanding the needs of their stakeholders and customers, understanding the linkages between departments and processes, marketing products and services to meet those needs, and delivering products and services in an efficient and effective manner; what is known as first level process in process mapping parlance.

A proper process view cuts across government and functional delineation, ensuring that best applicable practice in one area is applied across similar processes in other areas, ignoring the siloed approach to process improvement which currently occurs. Where a common platform is developed, it also enables increased digitisation and greater data sharing across levels and functions of government. A natural monopoly is typically a nest for inefficiency, although it has the capability to be a model for superior efficiency. Taking a whole of government approach to process also provides better decision making for which functions are best maintained and which are best privatised or outsourced.

At time of writing, Mr Turnbull's appointment of Angus Taylor as the Assistant Minister for Cities and Digital Transformation is an overdue first signal that government leadership understands the need for process reform and more specifically the application of technology and innovation to process. Citing research from Deloitte Access Economics, Taylor acknowledged the enormous opportunity[lxxxvi] to reduce government transaction costs, across a base of 811 million transactions per annum of a calculated face-to-face cost of $17 per transaction to an estimated online transaction cost of 40 cents (also refer Leinwand and Mainardi's capabilities of extraordinary enterprises figure 13). It is further estimated by Deloitte that while 75% or more of commercial transactions are now carried out electronically, about 40% of these government transactions are still completed using traditional channels – telephone, post and face-to-face. 'Cutting costs to grow stronger' is ultimately our best defence to prepare for future growth.

The integrity of parliamentary checks and balances are a function of the composition of the houses of government at any point in time. The power of amendment and veto are, for example, circumstantially higher when the balance of power in the Senate is not held by the government, as in the current government; the composition of the Senate has caused it to become the home of vested interests, where negotiation to engineer support for legislation is the name of the game, reducing the balance of public versus vested interests. In the situation where the government of the day does hold the balance of power in the Senate, this counterbalancing authority can develop into little more than a rubber stamp, upsetting the balance of governance integrity in an entirely different way. We need to consider whether there are other institutional options which can provide the necessary review capability without the dynamic power of amendment and veto which now symbolises the Senate.

The areas we need to focus our attention as a nation, to achieve the gains in productivity, improvement in budget position and international competitiveness come down to attention to overhauling core processes and the governance framework:

- Deciding whether partisan politics is the way forward for democracy in the new age of social media options
- Developing values which reflect who we are and where we intend to go, which in turn develops appropriate culture to empower the Australian population
- The development of a clear, well communicated strategy which identifies the priority themes on which we will focus as a nation
- A systemic process for long term planning based well beyond and outside the election cycle
- A system for developing our political leadership capability, so that we are preparing those who may aspire to the toughest job in the country to be great leaders rather than great politicians
- A root and branch review of our institutional structure

**Is Australia Entering or In the 'Doom Loop'?**

Considering weighty issues brings with it the potential insidious label of pessimism. Hopefully, a contention that Australia could have entered or be entering what Collins refers to as the 'doom loop' (refer Figure 12) is not viewed as overly cynical. Taking the long term view, our country has been through a regressive and destabilising cycle of leadership change. However, a combination of continual leadership change, disappointing economic results, and a lack of alignment of our situation have all contributed to prior momentum being lost – the 'flywheel' (refer Chapter 19) effect Collins found in business has, it can be argued, arrived for government.

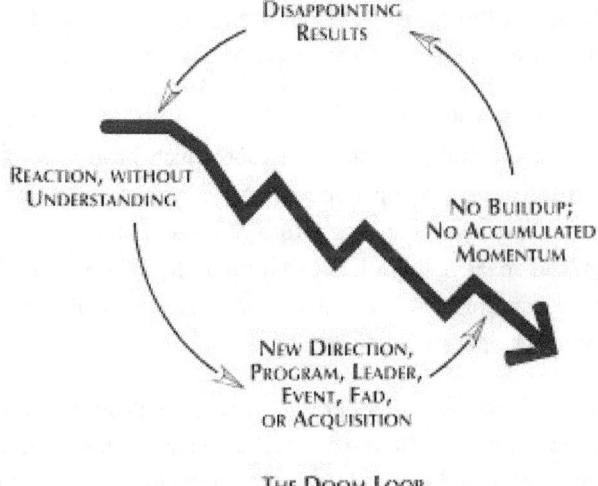

*Figure 12 – The Doom Loop. New leadership, following fads rather than strategy, not allowing momentum to build, all result in the flywheel not starting, slowing or stopping, or even going into reverse. Source: 'Good to Great', Jim Collins*


The symptoms Collins described as those of an enterprise in the 'doom loop' are:

- Implement big programs, rather than addressing the fundamental disciplines
- Chronic inconsistency, lurching back and forth
- A lack of disciplined thought (developing and sticking to a strategy)
- Not getting the right people 'on the bus' (a failure to select and develop the best people to lead)

Some of the symptoms Collins has described undoubtedly apply to Australia in enterprise terms. In fact, if we displaying the symptoms of the doom loop and recognise it, this may be just the 'jolt' we need to develop momentum, move forward and away from the loop.

Strategy should be about taking the action you want, when you want, rather than allowing an entity to be responding to its environment – creating our future. For example, we want to be selling assets because it is the right period to be selling those assets, rather than because we need the funds – forced asset sales are a typical signal we are in the 'doom loop'.

If we can agree as a nation that we are in fact in the 'doom loop', start to address the fundamental process and issues which have caused this, and think through and act in a disciplined manner, we can regain the momentum we need to set Australia up for the future of growth and prosperity we are seeking for the next generation. Fortunately, there are alternative democratic mechanisms being applied in various ways which can enhance the way democracy operates in Australia.

Thomas Jefferson once said, "I hold it that a little rebellion now and then is a good thing, and as necessary in the political world as storms in the physical."[lxxxvii] It may be time for some organised citizenry unrest, in the name of enhanced democracy.

# 8. Is Avoiding Our Reality an Option

*"There are three types of people in the world: those who make things happen, those who watch things happen, and those that say, 's---, what happened!'" (Adapted from an original quote by Niccolo Machiavelli)*

Post mortem is a typical post-election loss outcome; as Tiernan refers "a ritual of grieving".[lxxxviii] The Kemp review following the Victorian Liberal Party 2015 election loss highlights operational dysfunction at the heart of that government, not unlike similar post mortems held after Rudd, Gillard and Abbott lost power. The review concluded "an inability to manage the business of government, and a failure to develop and communicate a persuasive narrative to voters – a failure that fed perceptions that it was a 'do nothing' government. The report argues these problems were entrenched from the beginning. They can be attributed to the lack of 'a satisfactory transition to government plan' and excessive centralisation within a defensive and cautious premier's office that distrusted the capacity of ministers and sought to limit and constrain their autonomy by imposing centralised control and approval processes."[lxxxix] Such a 'siege' style of management inevitably leads to a stasis in decision making, poor morale and a lack of cohesion among the leadership team.

The danger in inscribing a critique is that the bad comes to vastly outweigh the good, which is not a reflection of where we are as a nation. And yet, one cannot in conscience acknowledge that we need do nothing and will maintain our course. We are, in some ways, haughty and indolent, as a society which trades on its past has the alternative to be. We lack the hunger and determination that the 'up and coming' challenger might have before a title fight against an established incumbent.

Of course, as a nation and a government we can follow our current course, nip and tuck at the edges, and rely on the odd stint of good leadership to get us through. We can continue to have discussions about tax reform and other key issues of the moment, and ignore the elephant in the room – our out-dated system of government, which is focused almost solely in the short term.

I've asked myself repeatedly, 'what will happen if we were to do nothing?' If we blindly trusted in the hope that economic conditions turned in our favour, it is likely that we will be disappointed. If economic conditions were to improve, it is no guarantee that Australia will return to economic prosperity. A stark feature of the 'doom loop' is that we have to find our own way out, to acknowledge the need for a long term framework for governing.

If global economic conditions deteriorate in the short term, and we don't make substantive changes to improve our budget balance, we don't have the financial levers (a budget in surplus, higher interest rates and higher commodity prices) at our disposal that we had in 2008. The likelihood is that, without such levers to pull, we would be headed for an economic tsunami – higher debt, greater joblessness, and a reduction in living standards. The disaster that some forecast we need to have, may in fact be upon us sooner than we can imagine.

We need to face a few facts. Acting as China's quarry was great while it lasted, but the past is unlikely to be repeated with its former buoyancy. Materials such as iron ore are heavily commoditised, and aside from subtle quality differences, we have little competitive advantage in a global market. We will always perform a role as China's quarry, however we need to look beyond commoditised materials to new, strategic ways to add value for other nations, and in turn create sustainable value for ourselves.

From a political standpoint, if we were to do nothing, we will continue to flip-flop, as we increasingly come to the realisation that even the best leadership will not get us through when the system is sub-optimal. We'll continue to change horses, and try new alternatives, such as Palmer United Party and the Xenophon Party, but eventually they'll all let us down because of the archaic framework we insist they continue to work within, or simply because they were set up to fail.

We may not be prepared to accept, or even discuss it, however there is ample evidence to suggest we are in, or entering the 'Doom Loop'. The signs of macro social, economic and institutional tension are apparent.

Our electoral cycle and leadership churn dictate that, rather than the Collins 'flywheel', gaining momentum as change and performance takes hold, we are doomed to continue being the metronome, rocking backwards and forwards without purpose other than keeping time, watching other countries progress, while our global competitiveness slowly but inexorably erodes. It is avoidable, and we can thrive. But we have to do something about it.

Doing nothing to resolve the structural issues we face would be less demanding, however it is not an option. Our government, and the people who drive our institutional systems, have effectively become institutionalised by the culture of those same government systems. The car is driving us, rather than us driving the car.

We see this now more than ever - in order to be accepted within the political hierarchy, politicians and public servants largely tend to conform to the way they are expected to act and behave by the people around them. The more value they are perceived to deliver, the more the organisation will be prepared to accept their actions and behaviours and the more influence they will have over what's expected of others, thereby perpetuating the culture we have, by and large, in public service today. When failure occurs, deficiencies in the system tend to be blamed; institutional incompetence becomes the substitute justification for personal responsibility.

While Machiavelli reminds us that change is not easy, it is the option we have to embrace as a nation. "It ought to be remembered that there is nothing more difficult to take in hand, more perilous to conduct, or more uncertain in its success, than to take the lead in the introduction of a new order of things."

We have to, through disciplined thought and action, find our way off the 'doom loop'. We need to change tack, change our approach to governing, change the organisation, and change some of our key mechanisms of government.

Change will not be easy. There would be many willing change to fail – the vested interests which enjoy an unwarranted seat at the table, and those for who change would be personally negative, are just a few examples. We must seek change nonetheless.

# Part B

# Getting Australia 'Off the Doom Loop' – The 'What'

# 9. Effective Governance

*"In politics, half your time is spent dismantling the legacy of the previous blokes. You know, you defund their programs, you kill 'em, you rename 'em ..." from 'Hollowmen, Season 2, Episode 2, Working Dog Productions*

The subject of governance has become very topical in business. In government however, the concept of governance has received comparatively little airplay, although government is, to all intents and purposes, the very model for governance frameworks. Dr Lynda Bourne[xc] describes the objective of sound governance (acknowledging earlier adaptations) "to encourage the efficient use of resources and equally to require accountability for the stewardship of those resources. The aim is to align as nearly as possible the interests of individuals, the organisation and society". Given the gaps we have already discussed, there is scope for improvement.

Australia is fundamentally blessed with a governance system (defined most basically as the setting and exercise of authority) which is the envy of most nations. Governance is not a core issue, however in any change of the magnitude being considered here, maintaining governance is a key risk, and therefore needs to be considered up front. Whatever institutional reform might take place, the importance of maintaining the integrity, efficiency, egalitarianism and effectiveness of our core institutions cannot be overemphasised.

**Culture and Accountability**

That does not mean there is not room for substantial improvement in the effectiveness of governance. The right to vote, the right to peacefully follow your religion of choice and other similar rights of freedom, an independent judiciary – these are basic rights we enjoy, enabled by good governance, and occasionally take for granted. Considering the functions of governance below, the areas of greatest opportunity for improvement are in culture and accountability.

Don Argus, reflecting the insights of Jim Wolfensohn, contends that the efficiency of our government, justice, financial & social systems is critical to our international competitiveness, and yet they are not subject to the market, customer and audit scrutiny of business.

Culture and accountability starts with the parties. If political parties are part of our future governance system, they require dramatic overhaul. To this day, the revenue base, principally donations, of political parties remains a dark art, no better illustrated than by Clive Palmer's party being propped up in part by a dying business owned by him. An investigation is not only required into Palmer but the funding of all political parties. Political parties should be subject to the same oversight as government departments and financial institutions. Many branches and states of political parties today continue to be run as personal fiefdoms lacking any of the effective governance that has been applied to other organisations.

There are significant limits though to how individuals and society can communicate alignment with government. It is questionable whether the democratic system in general has the necessary input to ensure accountability for the stewardship of resources. It is available reactively through the judicial process, however there is scope for increasing proactive alignment. This might be achieved through a board type arrangement, in preference to a President (were we to become a Republic) of appointed eminent Australians across a diverse range of backgrounds which helped to steer values, strategy, planning and policy in a non-partisan direction.

As mentioned earlier, Australia has become the easiest democracy in the world in which to stage a bloodless coup. Surely we need to make this a little harder to do going forward, or establish some mechanism for electoral involvement, or some equivalent governance measure. There is cost in instability.

### First National Interest, then Political Interest

Placing national interest ahead of political interest is the core test of governance for leadership, and is where governance mechanisms require strengthening. The simple question, 'is this work in the long term national interest?' honestly answered, would circumvent significant unnecessary or poorly focused legislation and negotiation.

In a political system dominated by two major parties, independence of thought is difficult to achieve where policy is foremost. This is precisely why the development of a non-partisan long term planning mechanism is not only an appropriate marker for government, but enables a higher level of governance.

The election cycle, and the separation of strategy and implementation are key current issues, which are dogged by lack of a long term lens and partisan conflict. One suggestion which requires careful consideration is how we can take strategy development away from government, apply a long term lens to it, and make government responsible for the implementation of strategy.

According to Bourne[xci], the six functions of Governance are:

1. Determining the objectives of the organisation;

2. Determining the ethics of the organisation;

3. Creating the culture of the organisation;

4. Designing and implementing the governance framework for the organisation;

5. Ensuring accountability by management;

6. Ensuring compliance by the organisation.

The issue from a governance perspective is that in businesses, "the governing body appoints, provides direction to and oversees the functioning of the organisation's management and makes the 'rules' the organisation's management and staff are expected to conform to" while "management's job is to achieve the objectives of the organisation; working within its ethical and cultural framework, whist complying with the 'rules' and providing assurance back to the governing body that this is being accomplished." In government, we effectively have the same body performing both functions, which does not conform with a robust governance environment. The challenge is to provide separation.

The Australian political system can manage governance across each of these six functions more effectively. In the mind of the electorate, our objectives and culture are unclear, while ethics are being managed, it is not clear that we are managing ethics, or the optics of ethics as we should, as evidenced by Bronwyn Bishop's helicopter ride and the consequences of that event. Poor ethical choices have become commonplace among a minority of Australian politicians. The alternative approach is to establish the culture we want in government, appoint leaders who reflect that culture, and ensure the leadership team is aware of its accountability for maintaining the desired culture.

**Potential Governance Reforms**

The governance framework is haphazard. For example, in terms of audit, government does not have the same level of audit requirement as public companies, and yet the public scrutiny on government departments and entities should instinctively be greater.

Potential reforms available to Australian institutional governance include (but are not limited to):

I. Refining and digitising institutional processes, with particular focus on creating more uniform operating platforms, which increase digital security; government is as good a place as any for a technology 'innovation revolution' to begin
II. Making government, legal and financial institutions more 'customer' friendly. Our health system has been designed by experts, however its complexity reflects a lack of developmental involvement by users
III. Devoting greater resource to improving and standardising process and control, monitoring & policing
IV. Utilising available technology more effectively
V. Determining a governance model for managing innovation
VI. Improving the succession planning process to develop more capable leaders

Each of these initiatives is considered in the following chapters.

The significant requirements of company directors in the modern era, and penalties for beaches of fiduciary responsibilities should be extended to 'directors' of all organisations, including political parties and unions. Where directors are not in place in such organisations currently, they should be appointed.

The current process of budgeting, a core governance issue, is fragmented and disjointed. Surely the most effective form of budgeting involves an integrated process across all levels of government. Despite its clear complexities, integrated budgeting across federal, state and local government (assuming all levels of government were maintained going forward) provides the most concise platform for effective decision making and reduced bureaucracy.

**Practical Diversity**

At a time when company boards are seeking to maximise the diversity of experience, backgrounds, and skills of boards as a means of managing independence and governance, Australian political leadership seems remarkably vanilla in terms of diversity. Clever, diverse, practical, independent thought is a hallmark of effective legislation we need to be constantly striving for. This is, in many ways, more important than achieving gender diversity, although increasing gender diversity will undoubtedly contribute. If government has a 50/50 gender split in five years, retaining the same blend of lawyers, unionists, and political apparatchiks, we will have gained little in terms of practical diversity.

Boards are finding that there is an established link between increasing diversity & improving governance, and there is no doubt this rationale can be applied to institutional governance. Separating strategy development from implementation would increase the diversity of governance resource.

Ensuring independence of board and management is a key function of company governance. While various branches of executive government provide some independence, as does the separation of legal powers, a key role of governance going forward is to minimise the exposure of special interests in the political decision making process. Increased focus on the governance framework for our country will ensure greater independence, and in particular a heightened level of partisan and special interest oversight to provide improved overall governance.

**Governance as an Export Capability**

Our established and respected governance regimes offer an opportunity to become a global centre of excellence for governance, which will become a currency of increasing relevance in a global society seeking greater humanity and equality, reduced corruption and hegemony.

Governance training of government leaders should be a priority. The Australian Institute of Company Directors runs a Company Directors Diploma which should be mandatory for all governance roles in business and government. Similarly such training has export capability, albeit governance would need to be customised to the nation where training might be conducted.

**Compliance versus Risk – Governance Options**

We appear to have developed an unusually risk averse compliance environment, in the context of our 'have a go' culture. I'm not suggesting this is necessarily bad, simply that it appears to have become counter to cultural values, which can create frustration.

Our attention as a nation needs to be on the size and effectiveness of government – what size do we need our government to be now and in the future – until now, such ideas have been more or less taken for granted or considered too entrenched for change to be considered possible. Given our current needs, new technologies, social changes, etc., how can we deliver a step improvement in the effectiveness of government? Having additional layers of government is no guarantee of increased governance, and, as we've stated, the opposite is likely true – it can feasibly reduce governance. An alternative structural proposal is that a non-partisan 'governance' board or committee could more effectively substitute for the governance functions of the Senate, at the same time separating strategy development from execution and enhancing governance. This idea will be discussed in more detail later.

A common plea among company directors and social leaders is that we appear to have created a 'culture' where our overwhelming response to something going wrong is to legislate against it, rather than considering alternative remediation measures. Such response is typically driven by special interest groups, fuelled by the media, setting up a Pavlovian self-serving legislative response by politicians to act, or being seen to act.

The management of risk versus compliance cost is an ongoing balance for any organisation. The cost of injury is high and adversely affects culture. I've always seen safety as a barometer in companies for discipline. Those companies which managed safety well (low injuries and a disciplined cross-company culture) typically performed better relative to their peers across the rest of the business as well. Across a multi-tiered system of government, one of the key governance issues is the bureaucracy surrounding the management of risk. We are now over-legislating and under managing individual responsibility, and across three tiers of government, there is strong evidence the management of risk is immobilising decision making and productivity. If there was a safety dividend from this bureaucratic approach to compliance, it would be supported without question, however the management of risk has descended almost to self-preservative farce.

An improved, streamlined, simpler regulatory regime for all national third party assets, including rail track, electricity and telecommunications infrastructure is a key governance improvement to ensure the cost, quality and service performance of these assets. The cost of accessing such assets is paramount to our competitiveness, and there is no room for private or public rent seeking. There is also a need to enable long term, appropriate investment to maintain the efficiency of these networks. The efficiency of third party and infrastructure assets is being adversely affected by excessive, multi-level government oversight.

## An Alternative Model for Federal Governance

Figure 13 above summarises a proposed alternative model supporting sound government decision making. We currently have no forum for

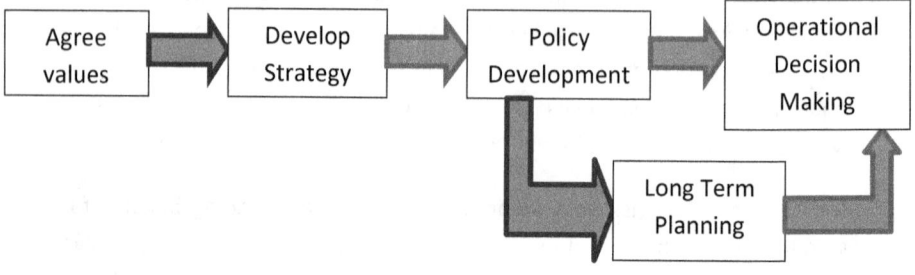

*Figure 13 – A proposed alternative model to support the process of government. From a government perspective in Australia, it appears as though only Policy Development is carried out, while the other components of this model are generally not.*

agreeing national values, no framework for strategy or long term planning; day-to-day operational decision making is largely based on adherence to policy, which typically suffers from a lack of delineation because it has none of the supporting frameworks to rely on. This framework needn't be bureaucratic, although it has to have appropriate governance to provide non-partisan outcomes.

Finally, transparency is a visual sign of the need for governance improvement. There appears to have been a stark contrast between how transparent our leaders believe they have been, and how the electorate, their stakeholders believe they have been. The ability to communicate well with stakeholders is a characteristic of sound governance. Leaders and governments can do amazing good work, however if they fail to miscommunicate or poorly diagnose their audience, that good work loses its effect. Part of the issue of recent times is that communications has been delivered by political operatives. While this is necessary from a party perspective, a non-partisan lens should also be applied to the leadership narrative.

There are undoubtedly risks in reducing layers of government, and the challenge is to find the appropriate balance between effective governance & risk management. The counter argument is that we can actually improve the level of governance by de-layering the institutional framework. Multi-layering processes and controls to build defence against risk is one way of addressing excessive bureaucracy and increasing visibility of decision making processes. The risk of reducing the layers of government may be lower than maintaining the current regime, which appears to be stifling effective decision making, and making it difficult for us to compete in the global marketplace, which is itself an issue of ineffective governance. If unnecessary layers of government simply reinforce poor decision-making (for example, through groupthink or confirmation bias), they not only don't add value, but destroy it.

An effective, well regarded governance structure, or series of checks and balances, is vital to effective government and our international reputation, as other nations assess the sovereign and legal risk associated with doing business with and in Australia. Our approach to social stability and economic sustainability will form the basis of Australia's 'storefront' to other countries.

As Lord Acton remarks, "No nation should ever rest on its political or institutional laurels ... Indeed, the history of liberty is far from finished; it is high maintenance and its growth is never certain." Doing nothing is not an option.

One of the fundamental roadblocks we face however is that inflexibility is entrenched in our Constitution. We cannot engineer fundamental change without constitutional change. Constitutional change requires double majority support in a referendum. A referendum in turn requires the majority support of Parliament. To achieve a parliamentary majority on questions of national significance requires considerable negotiation and compromise. All of these steps water down change to the point where implementing change becomes 'too hard'.

We need to ensure our governance framework provides the ability for rational change in the public interest not to be 'too hard'.

# 10. Values & Culture

*"Culture eats strategy for breakfast" (Peter Drucker)*

Morgan Guerin is an elder of Canada's First Nation people, the Musqueam, who have inhabited the greater Vancouver area for several thousand years. Morgan's quest is to retain the strong culture of the Musqueam people in modern life. The Museum of Anthropology at the University of British Columbia in Vancouver provides a fascinating insight into the journey of the Musqueam, which is determined to hold onto its traditional philosophy of kinship going forward, rather than become absorbed by what has gone before,. "If we lose our culture, we're just another municipality, and that's not who we are. Our grandparents fought to keep these things here, and it's not our place to give up that fight."[xcii]

However, the fight Guerin refers to is not violence, but rather a spirited effort to retain traditional culture and values among the modern day members of his people, young and old. They do it through storytelling, bighouse ceremonies, and education, and, to all intents and purposes, appear to be doing a wonderful job of preserving and sustaining their extended family culture.

Closer to home, Peter Cosgrove in his Boyer Lecture series in 2009 referred to the importance of establishing a strong, vibrant 'ethos' – the ethos of "shared risks, shared goals, shared grief and shared glory", which establishes a communal sense of pride and confidence.

The importance of a clear, national identity should not be ignored. It establishes clearly what type of community we want to be, "valuing a common approach to life rather than common ethnic origins".[xciii]

There is an irrevocable relationship between culture, strategy and performance, whether at the individual, company or national level. Culture though is the glue, the means by which people understand where they fit, everyone is accepted for who they are, and where people are motivated to make a meaningful contribution, clearly understanding how that contribution makes a social or economic impact. Culture provides the impetus for teamwork; the sum of the whole greater than the sum of its parts.

**Do We Appreciate What We Stand For?**

The greatest impediment to strong culture, based on significant experience, is poor communication – the inability to establish a compelling narrative, the failure to ensure buy-in and bring stakeholders along for the ride, the letdown associated with not clearly signalling the fit between bad news and the narrative, the failure to be direct and honest. Communication, in all its facets, is what drives strong and poor culture in any enterprise, large or small.

Social commentator Hugh Mackay illustrates that a moral framework can be as straightforward and basic as taking "the rights, the needs and the welfare of others into account", which will "increase the chance that others will do the same".[xciv] Eva Cox, in the same book writes "we need to put in a lot of work on developing the connective glue of society, to revive that sense of connectedness." It is politics, at the highest level, which provides that glue.

One output of the group working on the economy at the 2020 Summit, held in 2008, was to establish a 'national ambition':

> 'Australia should be the best place in the world to live and work. This will require urgent action to increase economic capacity through the creation of a truly national, efficient, inclusive and sustainable economy, supported by seamless regulation.'

This is as close as I have seen us come in recent times as a nation to a clarifying statement of direction, albeit this statement is made with specific emphasis on the economy.  A unifying statement is, despite the management-speak and 'weasel words' (to quote Don Watson) involved, important to our understanding of direction and purpose. The longstanding argument in favour of a Bill of Rights has merit, because as Lowitja O'Donoghue comments on the constitution, "It says very little about what it is to be Australian."[xcv] The culture of Australia, for many years our global calling card, seems to be now almost inert.

Values and culture, well managed, are the drivers for organisational outperformance. They enable strategy to 'make sense' and ensure alignment between strategy development and execution. The very best organisations and businesses build their organisational framework around a clear, coherent identity – emphasising just a few distinctive capabilities which are aligned with their ability to continuously deliver for their stakeholders. The depth of this challenge is that few organisations govern values, culture, and capabilities in a sufficiently disciplined way to enable this outcome.

When we have the unusual situation where the Attorney General, Sen. George Brandis recently argued that Australians "have the right to be bigots", it becomes obvious that our values infrastructure is letting us down, particularly as we are fighting to assert strong views against racist behaviour. While Senator Brandis' stance is technically correct, we shouldn't have to have the discussion if our values framework is in place.

Ian Coller[xcvi] wrote poignantly about French values, which have been well communicated over many years – 'Liberty, Equality, Fraternity'. In the wake of the Charlie Hebdo massacre, a man among the crowd observing a minute's silence at a memorial was asked what he was thinking. He said he was staring at the words on the column before him - Liberty, Equality, Fraternity. Coller, in the context of France's ability to embrace multiculturalism, suggests these are not just French values. 'They belong to everyone. They are not easy, nor are they unstained by violence. Heads on pikes, the guillotine, wars, revolutions: it took a century of struggle for French people to agree on these words. They were almost lost in the brutality of colonial oppression, in the dark years of the German occupation and the anti-Semitism that some French people – including, sadly, many Muslims — perpetuate even today. We must confront the past in its richness and its ugliness. France has never been the postcard fantasy of cheese and baguettes.' France has retained these core values through its heritage and they still resonate strongly for the French today even though shades of history did not support those values. France is, most agree, a more unified nation for this ongoing echo of core values.

Actor Deborah Mailmen's wish is also simple – that her grandchildren never experience, or even know the meaning of the word racism. So simple, but so much work to do as a nation.

Values and culture provide a sense of belonging and identity. They should have more importance and impact for nations, including ours, than the emphasis placed on them. Clarifying what we stand for allows us to be better understood internationally; we will become easier to work with if we can spend time conveying a clearer view of who we are and what we stand for.

It was no coincidence that Malcolm Turnbull mentioned culture in his first address to the Australian people as incoming Prime Minister, although it is perhaps surprising we have not heard substantively about values and culture from Australian leaders previously. That's not entirely true, because various leaders have mentioned values, however none have sought to institute a values or culture based approach to national leadership. As a country, we need to have the culture discussion, directly, with some urgency, fully, and inclusively, particularly as the immediate threat of terrorism evolves. Values and culture must come to mean more than words; after all our values are what unites us as Australians, although the nature of what it is to be Australian has altered substantially over time, impacted by multiculturalism and globalism.

Why is such an approach necessary? Because, for example, terrorism of any kind should never be acceptable to Australians; we need to understand collectively the importance of embracing Muslims as a vibrant segment of our diverse community, while simultaneously managing the terrorist threat assertively.

**The Impact of Values and Culture on Outperformance in the Long Term**

Leinwand and Mainardi[xcvii] conducted a study of an elite group of extraordinary enterprises over a number of years. They found that while success does not come easily even for the best performing businesses, these five organisations worked unconventionally in certain ways (refer figure 14)

These companies are able to outperform in the long term because they seek to sustain a culture which drives this outperformance. They commit to a corporate identity and retain that identity beyond the turnover of people. They build capability which converts strategy into everyday action. Such capabilities can be held as true for government and nations as business; in fact many of the businesses Leinwand and Mainardi analysed are global and multi-cultural in character.

| Conventional wisdom | The unintended consequences of conventional wisdom | The alternative: unconventional acts |
|---|---|---|
| Focus on growth | Getting trapped on a growth treadmill: chasing multiple market opportunities where you have no right to win | **Commit to an identity:** Differentiate and grow by being clear-minded about what you can do best |
| Pursue functional excellence | Striving to be world-class at everything but mastering nothing; treating external benchmarking as the path to success | **Translate the strategic into the everyday:** Build and connect the cross-functional capabilities that deliver your strategic intent |
| Reorganize to drive change | Falling into a habit of organizing and reorganizing: trying in vain to change behaviours and create success by restructuring alone | **Put your culture to work:** Celebrate and leverage your cultural strengths |
| Go lean | Cutting costs across the board: starving key | **Cut costs to grow stronger:** Prune what |

| Conventional wisdom | The unintended consequences of conventional wisdom | The alternative: unconventional acts |
|---|---|---|
| | capabilities while overinvesting in non-critical businesses and functions | doesn't matter to invest more in what does |
| Become agile and resilient | Constantly reacting to market changes: shifting direction in the misguided conviction that if you listen hard and act fast, you will survive | Shape your future: Reimagine your capabilities, create demand, and realign your industry on your own terms |

*Figure 14 - Five management practices represent an approach to strategy that underpin consistent enterprise outperformance, based on a study of exceptional enterprises. Source: 'Creating a Strategy that Works'*

The stability of leadership is an important component of outperformance. The churn we experience through government leadership, both through elections and party ructions, cannot provide a foundation for sustainable outperformance.

**Country-level Culture**

The term 'culture, like 'values' has become a 'buzzword' without many understanding what culture really means or requires. As Dr Simon Longstaff, Executive Director of the Ethics Centre notes, "all culture is built on a foundation of ethics"; it is the product of the 'good and bad, right and wrong' decisions and actions that people take on a day-by-day basis – "ethics …

underpins all human choice and thus all that we make and do."[xcviii] As a nation, our challenge is to ensure that we are continually striving to ensure we are collectively optimising the number of 'good' and 'right' decisions we make.

Whether we like it or not, Australia is a small (yet influential) player in a large, competitive, dynamic global society, and our future as a nation, as well as individuals, is to embrace this dynamism and competitiveness. So, how do we perform in the five practices in Figure 13? Some will say that it is unrealistic for a nation to be considered in terms of best practice in the same way as a company, however these five practices are as aspirational for us as a nation as they are for any company. These are the skills that, in Porter's terms, can separate us from other nations in supporting economic growth.

It is all too easy for us to isolate specific incidents, or even a small pattern of incidents, and point to poor culture or identity as an issue. This is particularly difficult in a national context, as significant geographic diversity, social complexity and differences constitute our collective national culture. Culture should not come with a 'one size fits all' mindset. Culture however offers great directional power in setting standards, strategy & planning for a group of people, large or small. It rebuilds trust, not only between our politicians and the people they serve, but between our nation and other nations.

Translating the strategic into the everyday is what betrays most governments and companies. The multiple tiers of government renders it that much harder to translate strategy into meaningful capabilities, such as energy and other infrastructure, red tape reduction, transaction costs and the like. Were we able to develop strategic national capabilities which support our focus on innovation, dynamism, and competitiveness, we would be better positioned to grow sustainably.

The social and economic cost of misunderstanding or misinterpreting public policy is likely enormous, as the Abbott government in particular will attest. For all the new Government's responsible effort to deliver budget repair, the 2014 budget was broadly criticised and rejected, in part providing the platform for Abbott and Joe Hockey's demise fifteen months later. The ability of government to establish a simple, clarifying message has significant benefits – it provides consistency and purpose to messaging. While image manipulation is seen as spin, relationship management is a craft essential to forming an appropriate, effective and honest message. The minute that message is not perceived as honest, the damage is severe and credibility difficult to retrieve. The electorate, unsurprisingly, does not react well to continual policy change, particularly when the values and strategy underpinning these changes is unclear.

This potential for damage is now greater than ever; the impact of bloggers and social media, whether right or wrong, can distort messaging, pierce financial black holes and destroy reputations and credibility in minutes and hours.

Many will question why a collective national set of values is necessary, let alone vital, as I am implying. Businesses and other public bodies have managed culture through values with varying degrees of success for many years. Those that have done it poorly have provided a set of slogans not genuinely believed or supported by their employees or stakeholders. Those that have done it successfully will attest to the results. In a government setting, values provide a unifying call to arms, a clarification of individual responsibility, and a common moral compass. Abbott's mantra, "we will end the waste, pay back the debt, stop the big new taxes and stop the boats" are not values.

At a national level, most of us identify more with our country than we do any other unifying body, including our employer. We watch our national teams compete with fanatical interest, and we maintain the respect of our national holidays with fervour. The sum of the whole is, in this situation, undoubtedly greater than the sum of its parts. A common set of values can only enhance our culture, society, and international standing.

It would be vital that we ensure greater bias is afforded to education in citizenship and constitutional knowledge in schools across the nation, to ensure such values continue to be embedded. It is the learned behaviour underpinning domestic violence, reliance on drugs and welfare which has to be unlearned at school and transferred to homes.

A key output is not simply to agree a set of values, but to engage the constituency across geographical and social groups, to have direct conversations about the values that drive us, to distil the output into a simple message, and to educate Australians accordingly. Values will only be effective though if the leaders of the day are true to them, day in, day out. Successfully done, this can provide a remarkable resonance between political leaders and the electorate.

The key with values is that, once defined, must be reflected in the talk and walk of leaders in everything they say and do. Values and culture have been equally abused in recent times. Tony Abbott's apparently ad hoc reference to 'Team Australia' for example provided no real definition of what 'Team Australia' was or stood for, besides arguing that Islamist fighters returning to the country were not welcome. 'You're either on the team or …' is no way to establish a solid values-based culture.

The 'tall poppy' syndrome is a clear example where our culture has become self-defeating. Who, for example, could be looking forward to being named Australian of the Year in 2017 given the criticism levelled against the last three winners, Adam Goodes, Rosie Batty, and David Morrison. All fine, accomplished Australians who should command our respect, each has received unfair, and in some cases jaw dropping abuse from commentators, the media, and the public. We have to celebrate this honour, not look for some hidden meaning behind it.

**What our Collective National Culture Might Look Like**

Can we have a collective Australian culture, and if so, what would that culture be? This is a discussion which has frequently taken place formally and informally, but has seldom been conclusive. It is important we hold this discussion inclusively, as problematic as it might be, and agree what we stand for and what we don't. How can politicians otherwise implement sound and considerate strategy and policy?

In discussion with a broad range of Australians, some of the values and propositions that have been articulated to me include:

- Energy & passion
- Diversity, of gender and race, is already a relative strength, but openness to ideas, cultures and people is vital if we wish to retain this strength.

We are against terrorism; we are for cultural diversity; encourage inclusion
- Perseverance & determination
- Integrity & respect
- Communal compassion & empathy; social inclusiveness and equality are not only important, they are fundamental to our national development
- We crave personal freedom, however a function of freedom is personal responsibility; we must accept that with freedom comes responsibility
- Calling out wrongdoing, including domestic violence, bullying, discrimination and racism
- Celebrating, not denigrating. Have fun and celebrate our successes both collectively and individually
- Actively supporting the less fortunate; community service should be aspirational for Australians
- Sense of society and citizenship
- Challenge unnecessary bureaucracy and duplication of effort, wherever it confronts us, be it in society, business, or government. We have to be constantly challenging ourselves – how can we do/be better?
- Our land is our strength and competitive advantage – we must nourish it, support the future of our land & those who work and protect it
- Encourage our people to reach their potential by playing to their individual strengths, particularly where they are aligned to our strengths as a nation
- Encourage talent and entrepreneurialism
- Talk straight. As Don Argus wrote, "… A vision without trust becomes an empty slogan. Trust binds people together, creating a strong, resilient organisation. To build that trust … leaders must be predictable & they must be prepared to share information & power. The goal should be a culture of candour."[xcix] We have become too afraid to say what needs to be said.
- Take risks but manage those risks

How strong is our current state culture? What would the effect be if we sought to shed our state culture, perhaps in favour of increased national culture or a more local culture? These are questions that would be asked if we considered transforming our institutional structure and 'doing away with' our state institutions. There is no doubt, to varying degrees, that we feel a state connectedness. This appears to be strongest in Western Australia and Queensland.

Simplification of our federal structure provides an opportunity to develop a strong local connectedness and culture – the village culture, which potentially drives greater cultural awareness because it is more localised in nature. We see this right across the country now, more particularly in regional towns and cities, in places like Newcastle, which found innovative ways to revive the city structure after the earthquakes, and Winton in Queensland, which is working tirelessly to do what it can to encourage industry and tourism despite, and in spite of, local catastrophes including the drought and the destruction by fire of the Waltzing Matilda Centre. Values and culture would be different under a different structure, but they would harness a more positive, unifying Australia.

Having travelled extensively in recent years, I've been fortunate enough to have the opportunity to ponder Australian culture in the context of how other nations reveal their culture. It seems in some ways as though our 'Aussieness' is not so strong as it once was, in part because we are striving for diversity. This is not a bad thing. It is important we continue to encourage our diversity, as this is the Australia of the now and the future. However, we should not leave the past behind altogether either.

**Historical Context of Australian Culture**

The question we need to answer is 'what do we want the people of our country to be known for?'

Australia's culture has contributed to our place in the world. It was the culture of great Anzac spirit which epitomised the first World War, the 'can do' attitude and integration of migrant labour which built the Snowy Hydro scheme, the Sydney Harbour Bridge & the Opera House, which became emblematic cultural symbols. Our courage, larrikin attitude & bravery became symbolic through the Second World War, and our post war growth was driven by a spirit of candour & action. Australians are very welcome as travellers around the world, a testament to the value of a solid culture and reputation internationally.

It is though our culture moving forward which we must define and model. Undoubtedly based on our short but rich history, this culture will propel us forward.

**Showcasing our Culture**

Horne described the need to 'tell our own stories'. We have a fascinating blend of social, musical and cultural heritage, which can be showcased more extravagantly, particularly as tourism becomes one solution to a post mining boom economy. Other countries do display their heritage and culture very well, often a philanthropic legacy of a wealthy entrepreneur. The EMP Museum in Seattle, which provides a modern exhibition of popular music, science fiction and pop culture, with emphasis on local content, is one such example.

Australian home grown culture is rich with stories and characters. Our tourism would benefit substantially if we showcased the musical history of home grown Australian talent since exported globally, such as its bands (ACDC, Midnight Oil, Cold Chisel, InXS, Divinyls, Mental As Anything, and the list goes on), actors (Cate Blanchett, Geoffrey Rush, Russell Crowe, Hugh Jackman and so forth), not to mention our artists, animators, cinematographers, poets, etc.? Being a music/pub scene tragic of the eighties, it seems to me we can do a better job of celebrating our recent history, which has been exhilarating in many respects. Celebrating our 'Australian-ness'. Towns such as Beechworth, Silverton, Derby and Longreach display our history and culture beautifully, and are worthy of a family trip if you can allow yourselves to miss the beach for one family holiday. Regional Australia, while now holding only a small percentage of our population, provides the most apt reminder of where we've come from.

'How solid is Australia's cultural foundation?' is a question we need to ask ourselves. A stronger cultural identity would more effusively celebrate its bush, music and other hallmarks of our heritage. We are a relatively young nation, with a clearly defined background of persistence and courage overcoming hardship. Our culture is teetering however in some social spheres - domestic violence, racism, sexism, poor modelling behaviour by sports stars, and union corruption, which are social blemishes we have to address assertively. We appear to have lost some of our national confidence, our mojo, which was at its memorable azimuth when we won the America's Cup in 1983, or the closing ceremony of the 2000 Sydney Olympics.

The research outlined by Deloitte (refer Figure 20) affirms that tourism is an industry which will create jobs and growth, and requires investment. The side effect of showcasing our culture, is not only that we can celebrate that history and culture ourselves, but profit from visitors from other nations who also want to experience and understand that culture.

**'Playing the Long Game' on Key Social Issues**

More recently though, our culture seems to have become 'muddied', and we appear to have lost the confidence that typified us previously. We have further earned something of a reputation as a nation of 'knockers', who cut down the tall poppy rather than applaud them.

The absence of a clear set of values is reinforced by the rise of anti-immigration groups and facebook pages which target immigration and racial groups, when terrorism is our true enemy. This is why our values need to be clear about what we stand for, and don't stand for, or stand against. As the world becomes closer, via the internet and faster, easier travel, the risk is for increased, more violent collision between competing value systems.

In a world where ethnic and religious differences without boundaries form the basis for acts of terrorism, we need to return to clear values which ensure animosity is not generalised, but focused specifically on those individuals, regardless of race or religion, who are not willing to conform to our values – a battle against terror, not a battle of race or ethnicity.

What we cannot stand for is socially intolerant behaviour, either within the family or social groups: in reality, any behaviour which is counter to the national values we agree to. We must be scrupulous in ensuring any such behaviour is called out. Not wanting to 'dob on your mates' is no longer okay. We all have an obligation to confront inappropriate behaviour. This is the courage which will reinforce strong and resonant culture.

There are specific subjects we need to attend to in defining what we stand for. While Australia has improved in its treatment of indigenous Australians, and symbolically apologised for the sins of the past, we need to ensure our values include the enablement of freedom and dignity for Aboriginal Australians. We cannot set values of freedom and equality without seeking a society which is inclusive of those who owned the land when first inhabited by white Australians. The remedy is not money, but rather a commitment to inclusiveness, the right to self-determination, education and other practical assistance which enable indigenous communities to regain their pride and self-esteem, and contribute socially and economically to our nation.

As to our future, a zealous approach to our environment is important to future generations. This goes beyond policy to a fundamental assurance that we will protect and nurture the environment. This should not be the mandate of the Greens but of all Australians who aspire to leadership.

Australia is a minnow on the global stage, and yet we have much to offer. Our country's soft power and regional influence comes from our relative stability and willingness to provide support where needed. We have however developed some sovereign risk associated with capital flows and reputational risk due to our recent political instability, some poor and reversed decisions, and our failure to deliver approvals and major projects within time and cost budgets. There is also no room for politicians such as Pauline Hanson and groups such as Reclaim Australia, who are damaging our reputation, despite representing the views of the minority.

Don Argus' 'letter' to our incoming Prime Minster, Malcolm Turnbull noted, "A vision without trust becomes an empty slogan. Trust binds people together, creating a strong, resilient organisation. To build that trust ... leaders must be predictable, and they must be prepared to share information and power. The goal should be a culture of candour." Trust comes from setting a standard, and meeting that standard, time after time.

Diversity is an area of discord for us as a nation; we need to do what we can to put dissent to rest. Diversity is not a barrier to national unity, as certain elements of society may claim. Nick Bowen[c] perhaps poses the debate most succinctly, arguing that diversity supports the development of our national identity. New citizens, despite the hardships they often face when settling in, 'will readily tell us what attracted them to our country, and in turn what we need to develop – they'll praise our optimism, the new found freedom, the opportunities, our sense of egalitarianism, the relative safety', and so on. As Bowen concludes, "they can define the national identity because they came here to embrace it."

We can undoubtedly develop a set of values we can express as a nation, and maintain with ongoing engagement with the community. They won't reflect the views of every Australian, but they can reflect the views of most, and provide a benchmark. An advantage of setting clear values is that these ideals form a basis and rationale for sound decision making, so long as the electorate see those values evidenced in the words, actions and decisions taken.

**Attitude towards Politics and Politicians**

Unfortunately, in the absence of sustainable government process, successive governments have been 'mythologised'[ci], however whereas O'Neill suggests this was an issue for the Abbott government, it has in fact been an ongoing issue for governments since Kevin Rudd was elected Prime Minister. It has become a systemic issue rather than an issue of personality; yet another symptom of a failure to plan appropriately as a nation. Rudd, Gillard, & Abbott, like Howard & others before them, were all outstanding Australians in their own way, otherwise how could they reach the pinnacle of Australian political leadership. However, like all of us, they are also flawed, these flaws magnified dramatically under the spotlight of leadership.

Our attitude towards politicians needs to change. It's a tough, 24 hour per day, 7 day per week, always on display 'gig', where mistakes and errors in judgement are constantly under the microscope. We need to treat our politicians with respect, ranking them somewhere above used car salesmen (apologies to all the used car salesmen!). If we set appropriate expectations for our politicians, the outcome will be that we will think better of ourselves as well.

In media interviews, journalists are increasingly entering the 'kill zone', seeking salacious factional 'gossip' when politicians are trying to make points on policy. That may be what the media perceives the public wants to hear, but it does nothing to contribute to the national interest.

It is this relationship of trust, of voters losing trust in politicians, which has to be regained. Building and supporting a culture where values are at the head of a governance hierarchy will help to rebuild trust. The lack of mutual civility and respect shown by politicians is not the modelling of values we want to see from our leaders. The ABC, despite its differences with government at various stages, has probably been best at 'depoliticising' the image of our political leaders, with television programmes such as Kitchen Cabinet and Q&A providing a more human insight into our political leaders. Understanding our politicians through a lens besides the media grab is important; it reminds Australians that our leaders are as human as we are.

Pulitzer Prize winning commentator George Will summarised the atmosphere poignantly. "The cry for leadership goes up from millions who wouldn't recognise it if they saw it, and would reject it if they did!"[cii]

**The Benefits of Robust Culture**

We should not get ahead of ourselves - Australia is not a future super power. We want to be a niche player – nimble, savvy, insightful – a 'go-to' player. Our cultural emphasis should be on developing our reputation in humanity and governance. In developing our governance culture and processes, we have the opportunity to stand apart in the world, and to develop a new export based on strong social values. Values support the development of responsible social relationships.

The development of values, established with consultation, and adhered to by our leaders, will add greater transparency for government and communal unity of purpose. Its value though will only remain while there is electoral clarity about the contribution these values make to happier lives and economic prosperity. Values can provide a sense of belonging and purpose to those who otherwise might struggle to find either. They provide a persistent sense of direction, and increase the authenticity and integrity of our decision making processes.

If, and once we can agree to a set of values, a significant advertising campaign would be required to reinforce what those values are, and what they mean. Canada is currently investing in a significant media campaign, educating people to call out domestic violence, bullying and other inappropriate social behaviour, using sporting heroes to reinforce the messaging. Australia is campaigning on some these principles, although the message is inconsistent from state to state.

Values are next to useless, and in fact damaging, unless led strongly and consistently by example. This will be one of the greatest challenges if we elect to proceed to develop a values based culture.

While there is no doubt Australians are a conglomeration of diverse 'tribes', from the original owners to recent settlers, forged differently, from miners in Western Australia to farmers in North Queensland, differing in style between the suburbs of Sydney's north, west, east and south, there are opportunities to unite under a banner of common values and culture, to help us to become more unified and cohesive as a society.

# 11. Strategy

*"All men can see these tactics whereby I conquer, but what none can see is the strategy out of which victory is evolved." (Sun Tzu)*

One of the key issues for leaders of all nations is similar (and probably more difficult given the media focus) to that faced by business leaders – maintaining attention to strategy when tactical issues confront the leadership daily. Zelleke and Zorn are of the view that country leaders, like many leaders of businesses are more absorbed in the 'here and now' than operationalising strategy. "Crises from all corners of the globe come flying at presidents, and these shouldn't be managed on an ad hoc and best efforts basis. Washington's actions should be informed by a strategic concept in which a president has conviction and confidence—derived not from in-the-moment intuition, but from first-rate strategic thinking."

We need to be able to find a way to ensure our leaders can be focused on strategy even when it is difficult to do so. That is when the dividend of leadership pays off.

**Separating Strategy Development from the Day-to-Day**

Zelleke and Zorn question how a process which retains the leadership focus on strategy might look. In responding to this conundrum, they suggest this process should create space for the leadership "to step back from the crises du jour: to raise questions rarely asked, challenge unexamined assumptions and "sacred cows," draw on the best data from varied sources, hear unconventional perspectives, think creatively, reflect, and prioritize." Perhaps it might reflect the Bill Gates approach, taking a day out each fortnight to 'think about the business' – accepting the importance of devoting regular time to 'the long game'. Zelleke and Zorn advocate the development of a 'Chief Strategy Officer' for the United States government. A not dissimilar approach will be proposed for Australia, distinguishing the functions of strategy development and execution.

Many outperforming nations are now devoting significant resource to the development and operationalisation of strategy. Singapore, for example, which successfully blends free markets with authoritarian leadership, has devoted impressive attention to national strategy, employing diverse teams — individuals with backgrounds ranging from computer science to fiction writing — to think rigorously about alternative futures and analyse data for signals about national risks and opportunities. The city-state's Strategic Policy Office, located in the Prime Minister's Office, is employed to think towards the future, communicate the plan throughout government, and create useful decision-making tools. South Africa is a further example of countries which have devoted effort to, and formalised their country strategy. The South African government similarly has developed a national plan to 2030, with the requisite rallying cry, "Together we move South Africa forward".

Other countries have come to understand the value of country level strategy. Besides China and Singapore, the Irish Government designated the title of National Development Plan to a scheme of organised large-scale expenditure on (mainly) national infrastructure. The period covered by the seven-year plan ran from 2000 to 2006. A second National Development Plan ran from 2007 to 2010 (spending €70 million a day every day during this period). The main elements to the original plan were the development of a national motorway network between the major cities in Ireland. The upgrading of the rail network was a secondary scheme.

In November 2011, the Irish Government announced that the National Development Plan was to be succeeded by a Capital Investment Plan. This scheme began on 1 January 2012 and is currently running until 2016. A second Capital Investment Plan is to run from 2016 to 2022.

The World Bank has developed a more strategic approach to assisting poorer countries, referred to as the Country Partnership Framework (CPF). Taking a more systematic country-driven model with the goals of ending extreme poverty and increasing shared prosperity in a sustainable manner, they are utilising more evidence-based mechanisms (such as the Systematic Country Diagnostic (SCD)) to gather data, set and implement these strategic goals. Similarly, the Inter-American Development Bank (IADB) has worked in conjunction with over 25 nations to develop a concise country strategy, establishing strategic priorities across areas including social and productive inclusion and protection, health, education, the labour market, infrastructure, transport, water and sanitation, energy, sustainable cities and urban development, security, institutional capacity, public administration, fiscal management, natural resource management and climate change, environmental and rural management, development through the private sector, productive and capital market development, science, technology, and innovation, and tourism.

While the needs of poorer nations are more basic than ours, the need for strategy is not. The systemic approach of such entities to strategy ensures engagement and unity, paves the way for focused plans, and provides a benchmark for accountability with a focus on the long term, which our nation would surely benefit from.

Australia has enormous resources available to support long term strategy development – the Australian research Council, Australian Bureau of Statistics, and the Australian Academy of Science for example. We fail to appropriately utilise these bodies because we structurally defer to the short term in governance, progressively reducing the budgets of these bodies when we should be utilising their capabilities to support effective long term strategy. It rarely suits government to consider paradigms beyond the election cycle. The disconnect between documents such as the Australian Academy of Science 2050 report and government policy is defining proof.

The questions, factors and scenarios raised around the overarching question of the Australia 2050 process, 'What is our realistic vision for an ecologically, economically and socially sustainable Australia in 2050 and beyond?' simply cannot be faithfully answered and implemented within election cycle governance.

While most countries appear to have a national security strategy (many are in fact available online), relatively few appear to have an overall formal or published national strategy, and then what's more, proceed to implement policy according to that long term strategy.

## The Simplicity of Strategy Applies to Government Too

Steve Bowman[ciii] provides a definition of organisational strategic planning which is quite appropriate for nation strategy by its very simplicity - 'the top four or five things that the board agree have to occur over the next 2-3 years. These four or five things have to position the organisation so that it is delivering against its (promises) and creating the future for the communities that it serves.' On a national basis, our horizon needs to be greater, however we don't necessarily need to defer from a simplistic approach. It is more difficult as a nation to consider a timeframe for strategy development of 2-3 years, although this is the typical time fence of current planning.

A perhaps less erudite quote claims failure in strategy to be either, 'those who thought and never did, and those who did and never thought.' I am sure government strategy in recent times has failed in both ways. Strategy, while core to business, is seldom mentioned in government, although it is first among equals so far as development of sound policy goes. After all, what is the vested interest for government to consider strategy when it has no commitment beyond the next election and its stakeholders are mired in the short term?

The marvellous feature of strategy, particularly at a nation level, is that it validates the core government agenda, and while it is not intended to provide a policy catch-all, well enunciated strategy provides clarity for all constituents.

For any organisation, strategy is essential to underpin the assumptions for longer term planning & budgeting; a budget without strategy is akin to trying to estimate the cost and to build a house without knowing the foundation on which it is built, the materials we will use and the number of rooms. Our country needs to have concise, publicised (as far as reasonably possible) plans on which we can base our fiscal plans. Debt targets are a key component of such planning, and the fact we've not set these debt targets in the past is a contributor to our current debt/GDP ratio being excessive.

Our national approach to strategy is counter-intuitive, in that while it should be the most visible, and is possibly the most important mechanism to guide progress, it is more or less invisible, and does not appear to be affiliated with day-to-day action. What we appear to have instead is a loose-ish set of policy guidelines across a range of portfolios which appear to lack integration, but are established to tie in with budget guidelines.

While views of the Kevin Rudd/Wayne Swan spending stimulus in 2009 diverge dramatically, largely based on partisan points of view, the stimulus is widely regarded as panicked, ill-conceived, unnecessary and a poor application of public funds. The fact the government of the day took such action, albeit under turbulent global economic conditions, highlights a failure of strategy, which would have shown that Australia at the time was positioned in the appropriate industries and had financial indicators (low debt, low interest rates, low unemployment) trending appropriately despite the issues faced by the wider world. It was a prime example of policy 'on the run' when sound strategy was needed.

Sensible policy development requires a strategic, long term framework. This is the link which has been missing in Australian politics – the clear enunciation of the four or five key areas and objectives which are of highest importance to our nation. It would be difficult to achieve under the current institutional structure, however it is vital to good government. Whether this role in Australia is an individual or a group of people, there is a leadership vacuum which needs to be filled. Besides Treasury, there is a lack of coherent, holistic perspective, to enable the status quo and assumptions to be challenged, and to "identify blind-spots" such as the mining downturn in advance.

According to Zelleke and Zorn, apart from the President (in our case the Prime Minister and perhaps the Cabinet), no one "actually 'owns' the responsibility to orchestrate whole-of-government strategy", which becomes more difficult when the Prime Minster and Cabinet are responding to crises on an ongoing basis the role of managers, not leaders.

Over many years of study and working in business, a cogent piece of strategic advice once presented was from an American entrepreneur and mentor Jerry Goldress. I'm not sure if this advice is original to Jerry, however it is as applicable to Australia and our place in the world as it is a small/medium business. The advice also shows that strategy can be simple and straightforward, in fact should be so. Jerry's advice in developing strategy was, 'find a niche, build a barrier'. That advice remains as appropriate today to our country as 10 years ago when I first heard it. Australia is a niche player in the world; if we adopt policies and strategies which follow this advice ie. find the 'nooks' where we can establish longer term advantage, then build barriers around those such as infrastructure, ease of doing business, centres of excellence, access to funding, etc. which enable those niches to be creatively aggregated on the world stage. Many of the Deloitte 'growth industries' (as per figure 19) are effectively niches, although with considerable global scale.

It is vital we understand our strengths going forward, educate and develop towards those strengths, and build infrastructure (not necessarily 'hard' assets but also delivery frameworks) to ensure we distribute and deliver those strengths globally. This cannot be achieved in a three year election cycle with no guarantee that strategic outputs won't be dumped with a change of government. There is little incentive for government to work for the long term. This is a fundamental weakness of our current democratic system, compared with governments such as Singapore and China.

It is time to formulate a process for action across the highest priorities among the best 'ideas' or policy areas above, in a way the population can follow, contribute to, and understand progress. It is time for government to acknowledge this need and work to establish a process which enables us to become, as a nation, more nimble, flexible, with a focus on outcomes.

Government must consider and apply strategy, rather than just policy, as business does. The last word on strategy goes to Warren Buffett, and it applies to government, although his words are intended for the managers of his businesses. "... widen the moat, build enduring competitive advantage, delight your customers, and relentlessly fight costs." Australia must, as a nation, widen its moat (not to protect, but to grow), support the development of enduring international advantage, make citizens not politicians the centrepiece, and relentlessly fight waste.

**A 'Stake in the Ground'**

As a proud Australian, I am seeking to understand how I am aligned to my country's future, and how we can best prepare our children for their future, just as employees (generally) seek alignment to their company direction. Of course, we each need to find our own way forward, however it helps to have some insight into the overall strategy. Because we are so different, that strategy needs to be clearly and consistently enunciated, straightforward, and provide a clear call and path to action. A strategic plan for our country would include as requisite elements:

1. A core, contained focus on just a few key initiatives and outcomes – we can't be everything to everyone, and will fail if we try to be, a point our major parties will do well to remember;
2. A simplicity which is understood by, and resonates with the electorate, reinforced by clear annual and long term objectives. The strategic plan would oblige bipartisan support, moderating this continual pointless, petty partisan banter – 'only we have a plan; they don't have a plan';
3. The strategy would enable the strategic to be converted into the everyday (refer figure 13), explaining how action to develop capability underpins strategy and supports planned growth;
4. Such plans are obliged to retain flexibility to take advantage of opportunities and 'environmental' changes as they arise;
5. A scorecard formulated to lucidly track progress for public disclosure

As Zelleke and Zorn outline in an article discussing US national security strategy, but equally applicable to overall national strategy, "A serious national strategy would start from a cold-blooded assessment of the global landscape, and of the most likely (but unknowable) futures that may emerge. It would also start from an equally dispassionate assessment of the nation's capabilities—its strengths and weaknesses—and how these may plausibly change over time.

This approach emphasises that we cannot make substantive change across all areas simultaneously, and must be clear where our priorities lay, as hard as this is for groups with specific interests in what may not be included in these priority areas.

**Doing a Few Things Consistently Well**

Strategy works most successfully when leaders prioritize ruthlessly among the many desirable policy goals; as strategy scholar Richard Rumelt expresses, "good strategy works by focusing attention and resources on one, or a very few, pivotal objectives whose accomplishment will lead to a cascade of favourable outcomes….". A genuine strategy would address head-on the inevitable hard choices and trade-offs to be made in the pursuit of the most-high value objectives; as strategy guru Michael Porter has emphasized, the essence of strategy is choosing what not to do.'

So, what would that cold-blooded focused assessment yield for Australian national strategy? Australia's competitive advantage lies in our diversity, our nimbleness and flexibility. It lies in our primary sector and the services sector. It does not come from satisfying the mass market or in manufacturing consumer goods. It comes, for example, from prioritising and supporting the top 25 'growth industries of the future' determined by Deloitte (refer figure 19). It comes from focusing on a few key priorities now, and providing internationally competitive conditions to compete, grow and flourish. It is this type of 'commercial' approach which will start the required momentum. National competitive advantage, as for any other competitive advantage will come from being first to market, being innovative & disruptive, and executing on strategy faster than other nations, then continuing to improve faster than other nations.

Perhaps that assessment might point us to the great rural wealth which is being eyed by other nations, but appears largely unloved to us. Agribusiness is number two in the top 25 growth industries of the future in the Deloitte review. Unfortunately, the sector is also going through some of the toughest climatic conditions in some regions, with for example, some of our farmers going through the worst drought conditions of our generation. They've de-stocked and deferred operational maintenance (such as fencing) to survive. They are conserving cash to pay debt and personal expenses. However, this leaves them nowhere to go when conditions improve. Their capital will have been deferred to interest payments, there will be no cash to re-stock and enable running repairs. And so their only option becomes to liquidate at the highest possible price. While Asia generally might regard us with some disquiet – a great place to invest, but with relatively poor infrastructure, and an inability to develop our prize assets – they understand in many cases the value of our land assets better than we do. They regard our farming land as an investment in the future, an opportunity to capture the supply chain for their local market, which is growing and drifting towards the middle class.

They understand the long term impact of the relaxation of China's one child policy. Unfortunately, the environment we've created for farmers does not allow them to prepare for these changes.

Our strategic treatment of our number two growth industry showcases our short term myopia. Raising the profile and capabilities of Australia's regional centres has to form a cornerstone of our long term strategy, because we simply can't afford to continue piling people into our major cities without consequences. People will only relocate to regional areas if we give them an incentive to do so – improved infrastructure (including technology), greater certainty of employment, improved security and a family-based way of life.

Overseas investors might choose to take advantage of such weakness by directly investing in areas where they perceive the future value to be greater than we do, or alternatively, regard the risk as too great and choose to invest capital elsewhere. It might highlight what we've known and yet failed to fully capitalise on for over half a century; that we've failed to adequately develop the northern Australian economic zone. There are many considerations, but one that escapes us is to make an investment now for a yield twenty or more years out. The issue is that we invested these funds politically through stimuli including an economic 'sugar hit' in the form of a 'cash bonus' back in 2009 when the strategic value of those funds would have been better utilised on purposes such as helping our struggling rural sector, identified as a growth industry of the future, off the floor.

Strategy becomes the enabler, and sets the sounding board for any policy that follows. It provides ready benchmarks that policy must meet. The other advantage of developing long term strategy is that it enables us to develop lead indicators of performance in those areas we are setting strategy. So much of our nation's reporting is lag, providing no opportunity for coherent response. It is too late to jump out of the way after the bus has already hit you!

## Strategy Provides the Narrative

Consecutive leaders have, in the words of George Megalogenis[civ] "shown a Howard-like inability to stay on any one topic long enough to ensure they are taking the people with them."

Strategy is the platform for government narrative and messaging. It reduces the potential for confused and sequestered communications because the government strategy is clear and visible. A continuous theme of politics has been the mixed and confused narrative from our leaders because our core objectives are not clear or understood. A sustainable budget position has to be our key strategic plank. This enables government to establish a narrative about the consequences of not progressing this objective, and can then come to decisions about the action that needs to be taken.

This is where partisan politics becomes an issue for our ability to make effective, agile decisions. Neither party is unified, despite their protestations otherwise. The interests of the party and their sitting members are frequently different, particularly when it comes to making difficult decisions. Again, the budget is a case in point. While there is a clear need to increase revenue and reduce expenditure, this requires unpopular decisions. Unpopular decisions can cost votes, which threatens the seats of party members with small majorities. This promotes internal party discontent, leading to negotiation, which ultimately 'waters down' decisions. Vested interests placed ahead of the national interest.

Only a coherent, long term view of our future enables us to make optimal financial decisions, when & where to invest in infrastructure, the useful life cycle of existing assets, and the optimal time to recycle assets. Long term planning provides the ability to develop equity for future investment, rather than fuel growth on debt alone. It enables us to plan for & smooth turbulence to an extent, by storing the income of good years in preparation for tougher periods.

This is where strategy is counter-intuitive with the process of government. Strategy should be considered on a cycle, I am suggesting of about fifteen years, consisting of five year segmented rolling plans. This is why strategy development needs to be separated from government; we have no hope of developing sound strategy through the election cycle (refer Chapter 10 for more detail).

We need to then look at how we can best invest in the infrastructure underlying this advantage to deliver best capability – our broadband, our freight and people movement systems, research environments, knowledge and data warehouses, economical power, all contribute to our competitiveness and provide a platform for growth.

Our attention to our research and innovation structure remains important. Like any good organisation, it is vital we retain an up to date register of the nation's intellectual property, regardless of ownership, as a means of managing the best national outcomes from this IP. Further education is needed to understand the enormous value of our intellectual property. Our current research & innovation effort is fractured. You need look no further than the phenomenal effort devoted to cancer research and other significant health issues in our country; how much can we progress this work by bringing together the disparate effort across our nation to deliver synchronised outcomes and, hopefully, a cure? CSL, Cochlear and Resmed are just a few of the significant enterprises which have been built on Australian research.

Whereas our emphasis has been on digging up the ground, we need to turn towards 'smarter' industries, while getting smarter at those industries. We have to seek to add value to whatever raw materials we can; rather than simply shipping raw product offshore, there are niches available to add value, particularly in food ingredients & rare minerals, for example. Michael Porter expressed the same sentiment in a different way, "ultimately, the only way to sustain a competitive advantage is to upgrade it."

Strategy was relatively easy for Australia twenty years ago; China was establishing itself as a world power; it needed the resources we held in abundance, and we simply thrived on the back of increased demand. The only problem with this strategy is that history has proven these growth streaks do not run forever, and our Plan B failed (to avoid putting all our 'eggs' in the China 'basket'. Now, as China's economy undergoes the inevitable slowdown, our flank - our focus on China as a trading partner & our relative lack of strategy is revealed.

## Structural Separation of Strategy Development and Implementation

As Peter Costello observes, "we need to have good government in order to do well, and if we don't have it, it will catch up with us."[cv]

Zelleke and Zorn[cvi] proposed a Chief Strategy Officer role be adopted for the US, an adaptation from the corporate sector. They describe this role "not a Kissingerian 'grand strategist,' but rather a process-focused individual charged with owning and managing the strategy formulation process".

In Australia, this could fall under the jurisdiction of a Strategy Office, if such a team was established. Strategy development would be separated from strategy execution under this proposal. The role of a company board is to set strategy, maintain governance & monitor performance. While governance would not be a core responsibility in relation to any board to government, there is food for thought in establishing a non-partisan body to set strategy and monitor performance, with government's role becoming the operationalizing of strategy (refer Chapter 12).

Separating strategy development from implementation provides one other very important benefit in terms of governance. It offers a further governance benefit in terms of the separation of powers for government, preventing some of the 'pork-barrelling' and vote buying driven by investment today.

The same clarity of purpose can be applied to each portfolio – the questions to be asked are 'who are our stakeholders?' and 'how do we create value for those stakeholders?' A strategic time fence enables these questions to be clearly enunciated for incoming government ministers, to ensure the road being taken is the right road, in the long term national interest.

The final word on strategy is best left to a German proverb – 'what's the use of running if you are not on the right road.'

## 12. The Planning Conundrum

*"Those who are victorious plan effectively & change decisively. They are like a great river that maintains its course but adjusts its flow."  (Sun Tzu)*

Having established the vital role of strategy, we now have to consider how we can convert simple strategies into extensive plans which drive unified, cohesive government action.

Few of us have had the opportunity to sit in on a Cabinet meeting. Cabinet is the pivotal planning mechanism for the nation, bringing ministers across the range of portfolios together to present bills and resolve issues. "Cabinet's role is to direct government policy and make decisions about national issues. Cabinet ministers spend a lot of time discussing current national problems and how these can be solved."[cvii] It is effectively the corporate equivalent of an executive meeting.

**Converting Strategy to Plans – Playing the Long Game**

The world seems to be speeding up, and not always for the better. We appear to have an obsessive focus on the here and now. In just one of many examples, Seek shares were recently 'slapped around' after a profit result which did not meet expectations. There was nothing wrong with the business; the company were clearly investing back into the business for the longer term. Shareholders who sold at the time will be disappointed; the share price is now more reflective of this investment.

The same issue confronts us as a nation - how can we, as a nation, plan for the long term future, when political decisions are driven by media and three year election cycles. The greatest visionary leader in Australia today could not hope to persuade and galvanise 20+ million Australians of various ethnic, social, religious & demographic backgrounds to a long term plan, nor could we implement the necessary change to achieve such a strategy the way we are currently organised.

Central planning is seen by many as the domain of socialist regimes, a means of maintaining control. However, if the scope of planning is clearly defined, it can propel momentum; the benefit of unified effort.

The realisation in business over many years that strategy development is in fact relatively more straightforward than strategy implementation is at the foreground of any mechanism to develop long term action plans. Although business has a catalogue of issues in implementing strategy over recent years, the reputation of government in implementing strategic change is considered less favourably. Policy and implementation have always appeared to be somewhat divorced. One has only to consider the litany of failed policy outcomes of the recent leaders, the Rudd era mining tax, grocery and fuel watch; from Building the Education Revolution, which exposed massive rorts, to the pink batt scheme, resulting in unnecessary deaths, underline a lack of capability to ensure implementation is managed appropriately. The Abbott government failures to finalise and implement Medicare co-payment and its signature parental leave policy merely prove that inability to implement is a government issue rather than an issue faced by either party.

My proposal is that we establish a planning framework, aligned with strategy development, which enables planning to be considered in the long term. Planning would become an activity independent of government, overseen by a non-partisan forum, enabling planning to be similarly elevated independent of the electoral cycle. Preferably this forum would have a fifteen year timeframe, with rolling periods of review, perhaps along the lines of:

- Years 10 - 15 out – a greater component of 'blue sky', a long term agenda, identifying projects of national interest, and understanding the global landscape of that timeframe
- Years 5 – 10 out – bringing flexible plans (without commitment) before the nation, understanding the appetite of the nation (stakeholder management), considering referenda, and developing supporting implementation frameworks, preparing to lock these plans
- Years 0 – 5 out – plans for this period are 'locked and loaded'. The role of government then becomes the implementation of the agreed 5 year plan, with an elevated approval process required to

authorise changes, with the intent of improved and sustained implementation.

Henry Kissinger once talked about business, however his comments apply equally to the role of government. Supplanting 'country' for 'business' offers the following insight; "The ultimate task of a leader is to take his *country* from where it is to where it has never been. *Countries* operate by standards of average performance. They sustain themselves by practicing the familiar."

**Measuring for Accountability**

As an ordinary Australian, I see a significant (perhaps inordinate) focus on the annual budget, but very little visibility to horizons beyond, or other trending Key Performance Indicators (KPI's) of national performance. I'm confident they are there; we just aren't given the opportunity to see or reflect upon them. This is not to say that longer term planning is not happening; I think we all realise it is, however disciplined or haphazard the process may be. The point is, if done, that it is not visible to ordinary Australians. My suspicion is this due to lack of process rather than poor communication.

One of Australia's (and indeed the world's) greatest tidal waves is our aging population, yet we don't seem to be coherently preparing the infrastructure or skills required to support this massive social change. This issue will increasingly divert public resources and funding from education, infrastructure and other key forward programs.

Tony Abbott & the LNP (successfully) resorted to slogans such as 'stop the boats' because such narratives are among the few available to government to communicate with an uninformed electorate. Australians are crying out for clear, rallying (perhaps even bipartisan!) plans in the key policy areas of health, education, transport, etc., rather than the 1 year back, 2 years forward of the current election based cycle, which is clearly damaging us as a nation.

In Australia, we are cuckolded by the agenda & views of the few, with potentially significant infrastructure developments such as the Inland Rail Corridor between Brisbane & Melbourne, or track duplication on the eastern seaboard being delayed or perhaps not invested in, because of our myopic inability to establish a co-ordinated infrastructure plan. For the Chinese to demean our infrastructure is proof indeed that we are letting ourselves down with respect to planning.

Reform will not simply occur by increasing the election cycle, as the fundamental planning process has not changed.

### 'Plan on a Page' – Bolstering the Narrative and the Budget Process

It should be a requirement that each ministry produce a 'plan on a page' across its ministerial portfolio, which is distributed for the public to review, and provides a means of holding government accountable to the people to get things done. An annual review of the progress against the 'plan on a page' targets also provides increased accountability.

How can we currently expect Treasury to provide forward estimates which can be trusted when we don't have the strategic and planning framework behind it to provide the appropriate spending and revenue assumptions. If there is an election within a three year period, forward estimates will depend on which government is elected and what their election platform might be. The lack of budget accuracy is borne out by the budget deficit 'blowing out' in a form not foreseen by Treasury. How could they budget without the framework in place?

John Wanna has observed the historical issues which contribute to a dysfunctional budgetary system and the parlous state of the nation's current fiscal situation,[cviii] describing it as "an anachronistic system inherited from the Royal Budget (the King's Chest) – keeping all resources in one consolidated revenue account while separating expenditures from revenues."

As with most of our current system, there are historical reasons why the system works the way it does, however it would be extraordinarily difficult and inflexible to effectively manage what Wanna refers to as a "'magic pudding' fund against which all manner of claimants make audacious bids." He suggests that federalism further compounds this situation: "because federal governments want to spend their huge tax take to gain most exposure, while the mendicant states and territories continue to cry poor and have few other tactics than going 'cap in hand' to the Commonwealth for 'more funds", which results in the central budget institutions being out-manoeuvred by federal and state governments deals. Spending is ratcheted up as governments and special interests act as modern day Oliver Twists. Wanna further infers that "many of our public policies are irresponsibly demand-driven with few caps, so people enjoy goods or services and the Commonwealth pays the eventual bill." This explains clearly why we have an expenditure problem.

An excessive component of the federal budget is non-discretionary (Wanna suggests this is 85% of total spend, on entitlements, transfers, ongoing grants, etc) which can't be trimmed without a major fight in parliament. This is even more difficult based on current senate composition. Wanna further suggests that "we have enshrined a culture of compensation all-round (the "no discrimination" mantra) – and this applies to any changes in either entitlements or taxation levels."

It is nigh on impossible to develop significant budgetary reform under our current institutional framework. Even if the government managed to implement a rise in the GST from ten to fifteen percent and made the tax more inclusive across goods and services, our spending habits need to change, or an ageing population and increased health expenditure will demand pressure for a further increase to compensate for theses cost increases down the track.

**Driving Incremental Improvement**

The need for reform is a clear clarion call. Momentum for change has to be developed by driving small but symbolic incremental fixes which establish a climate for more far-reaching change, thereby highlighting the community benefits of reform. These may include a higher profile search for savings across all portfolios, improving government purchasing power across all levels, terminating unnecessary waste, or identifying new means for government agencies to find new or increased revenue streams.

Ultimately, there are significant economic as well as systemic benefits in transferring increased control to federal government to manage health and education strategy and policy centrally, enabling, for example, levies and charges to be extended more broadly and systematically, and developing a system more oriented to user pays. Wanna also refers to the European method of hypothecating (or securitising) funds to enable the provision of investment for dedicated public purposes. "A specific contributory levy, say, for pharmaceuticals would be set and paid into a hypothecated account which could only be used to pay for subsidised prescriptions, and managed actuarially. If people wanted extensive low-cost prescriptions, then the levy would be set to cover that level of spending; if people wanted less subsidised medicine then a lower contribution could be imposed. Hypothecated provision would compartmentalise these items from consolidated revenue, make them self-funding and annually balanced, making the job of funding and managing core government activities so much easier."

The dearth of solid forward information available to support the budget, and the complexity and variability of revenue sources contributes to a less empirical approach to budgeting, as explained by Wanna. "Each year accurate projections about economic growth are made which determines a fixed formula of revenue income (roughly 17 per cent of GDP); the expected actual revenue figure is directly transposed into a precise aggregate expenditure limit; no more, no less, it has to balance the revenue."

"The expenditure budget is then allocated on a stipulated formula basis whereby each major policy sector of public spending receives a prescribed fixed share; there is no bidding or lobbying for more funds, but agencies have relative autonomy to recalibrate their priorities within their spending envelope. They can shape their spending strategically. But the only avenue through which any budget growth can occur is if the economy as a whole grows; so agencies have enormous incentive to direct their thinking (and the majority of their funding) towards driving economic growth, from within their own budgets or in conjunction with other stakeholders."

This places context on the age old practice we discussed earlier of government departments ensuring their budget is spent at the end of the year, and the impact on budgets.

"Proposals to bring about systemic change to the traditional patterns of budgeting will be resisted by the conservative establishment and those that like the present dysfunctional system, or perhaps do well out of it themselves. But the public interest is not served by retaining perverse budgetary practices, or the perverse incentives that riddle the system. It is not served by sticking our heads in the sand in an ostrich-like mindset believing the problems will just go away."

This lack of ground-up proactivity in managing expenditure down is symptomatic of the apathy which remains in the public service today. Al Dunlap may not be the answer, however we have to take a harder, more commercial look at how our money is being spent. As Wanna concludes, "the budget will not correct itself on automatic pilot; and the longer it doesn't, the more we will pay in interest payments on mounting debt, the more our children will pay in years to come and the less we will have for today's areas of genuine need."

Of course, planning in and of itself is not an answer to all that ails government. Planning, done poorly can detract from, rather than add to, government by sending the wrong signals and disenfranchising those not involved. A planning environment needs to enable government to retain flexibility – changing plans is a fact of life.

A well-executed, whole-of-government planning process will provide greater certainty, and can then dovetail throughout government departments to provide a synthesis between portfolios and with the centre of government that would be difficult, nigh impossible to achieve in the current framework. It is a vital cog in an effective governance framework.

# 13. Managing Political Leadership Talent

*"We expected that good-to-great leaders would begin by setting a new vision and strategy. We found instead that they first got the right people on the bus, the wrong people off the bus, and the right people in the right seats – and then they figured out where to drive it." (Jim Collins, from Good to Great)*

In 2009, then General Peter Cosgrove surmised that Australian leadership was "patchy", occasionally 'out to lunch'. He noted that leaders fail for three reasons - a lack of competence, a lack of support or loyalty from those they lead, or a failure of integrity, and indeed a combination of the three may apply.

Ministry 'reshuffles' seem to be an ongoing slice of government life these days, whether due to retirement, indiscretion or the reasons for leadership failure summarised above. The role of Prime Minister and trusted advisors in this circumstance is to select the new look cabinet. The main factors in selecting a new ministry for either party cynically are favouring those who have provided support in the past or who are owed a favour, ensuring factional weighting, and ensuring state weighting. Understanding the strategic needs of the ministry, the complementary skills of department heads and the skill set needed in an incoming minister are, needless to say, lower on the list of leadership priorities. The processes of selecting and developing leadership talent are undoubtedly counter-intuitive. The outcome, inevitably, is that the wrong people occupy the wrong seats on the bus, often at enormous cost and opportunity cost to the nation.

**Leadership can be Lonely**

The capabilities of leaders, whether in sport, business, government or other field of endeavour, are arguably similar. It involves establishing a philosophy and set of values which resonates with those following you, implementing disciplines which are consistent with those values and philosophies, and using these to drive smart, enthusiastic, diligent effort in the right direction. The 'Win Forever' philosophy of Pete Carroll, coach of the Seattle Seahawks in the NFL is an example. His philosophy is that he, and those he leads, are in a relentless pursuit of competitive edge in everything they do. The values he reinforces in those around him are to respect every person and every opportunity, and, to get the most out of a team, every individual has to maximise their contribution.

Despite leadership selection typically being a test of popularity, leadership itself is seldom a test of popularity, but rather the ability to create and implement a vision, effective decision making and creating a high performance environment in pursuit of defined goals. Leadership requires the courage to doing what's right for the long term future of the nation, and not shying away from taking tough action in the short term if that is the appropriate medicine to ensure long term gain. And yet, in all democracies around the world, the key selection criteria in an election emerges as popularity! There is something quite wrong with a leadership selection process based on a popularity contest when effective leadership often necessitates making unpopular decisions. By and large, our political selection process has ignored best practice theory of determining attributes and selecting to achieve defined outcomes.

There are 2 core reasons why people decide to enter politics; either they want to genuinely contribute to society, or they desire power. Largely, it is the former. Either way, it is the system of politics that lets those people and the people they serve down. As former Prime Minister Abbott ruminated[cix], the biggest problem with his government was "people's reluctance to accept that short term pain might be needed for long-term gain," building a "resentment that someone, somewhere, somehow is getting a better deal" which becomes easy for self-interest to exploit.

As Professor John Keane has highlighted, we need to again produce "world class leaders courageously committed to the public good." However, this seldom happens by chance; we have to find people with the appropriate skills and capabilities, then prepare them for leadership roles, ensuring they are appropriately supported to lead with courage for the greater public good. The partisan duopoly does not provide suitable conditions to foster such leadership.

Today's political leaders are being 'trained' to be cautious, to not reveal their true views and feelings. We need look no further than the latest incarnation of Malcolm Turnbull. Is this caution in Australia's best interests? I'd argue not: we need leaders who are fearless, perhaps not in expressing their innermost views, but who will courageously prosecute the national interest, without the undue involvement of their party or vested interest groups.

Leadership loneliness can take various forms. There is the loneliness of leadership where you are not leading in the way you think is best, of not being true to oneself, and there is the loneliness of leading fearlessly. In my experience, fearless leadership is inevitably in the best interests of the entity.

**The Australian Political Incubator**

In 1882 Robert Louis Stevenson wrote, "politics is perhaps the only profession for which no preparation is thought necessary."[cx] While this is no longer true, it is unerringly still the case.

Our liberal democracy is guided by a team of (largely) 'career' politicians; relatively few Australians convert from having an opinion to raising their hand to contribute to the political leadership of our nation. Surely the nation would benefit from greater diversity in the ranks of our political leadership than the lawyers, unionists and political staffers which appear to dominate our leadership apparatchik.

The question is why would a successful, experienced leader be lured to life in politics, when we treat those who do devote their lives to public service with disdain. The arcade game 'Whac-a-mole' seems the best analogy to being in politics these days.

In contrast to the current period, we need to be able to deliver appropriately skilled leaders for election, then we need to ensure the incumbency of our political leaders, so that they have the opportunity to implement a long term agenda. That is not to say we won't continue to get some 'duds', however we need to manage the process rather than hope it happens the right way. Perversely, this can only occur if our selection and development processes allow us some assurance that those most suitable to lead have that opportunity.

In my experience, the most effective politicians are likely those who retain a nagging doubt about the political process, and who aren't carried away with the power of their position. Margaret Thatcher's political philosophy 'is founded on a deep scepticism about the ability of politicians to change the fundamentals of the economy or society: the best they can do is to create a framework in which people's talents and virtues are mobilised, not crushed".[cxi] In a company setting, this is similar to doyens of business, such as Richard Goyder, Gail Kelly and Kerry Stokes, whose great skill was to employ the best people, and provide an environment under which they flourished.

The selection process to become a politician is arduous and long winded. The path within the major parties goes something like this. The staging ground for future politicians is typically through the youth movement. Once you are involved with a party, you are typically exposed to the campaign trail, assisting political canvassing. Along the way, party members typically become aligned with a party faction, based on their beliefs and relationships. Running for pre-selection is the first test of your developing influence, although many pre-selection battles are won before they start; the lessons of 'running the numbers' and engineering factional support. If the factional battle is won, a candidate will go through the arduous campaigning process, which is a school of hard knocks – endless traffic stalls, doorknocking, and press fleshing. Very few campaigners win at their first attempt, and it becomes a test of will, persistence, and financial backing.

Julia Gillard gave us perhaps the most realistic perspective on the attributes needed to become Prime Minister, although the attributes she ascribes are counterintuitive to corporate leadership thinking. In an interview for Australian Story in 2006, some four years before she became Prime Minister remarked, "I'm not naive you know. I'm not Doris Day, who's just somehow parachuted into Canberra. I had to fight hard to get pre-selected. I had to play a factional game to do that. I had to count numbers, I had to make deals, and I'd do all of that again tomorrow if I needed to." While it may be easier to ascribe this to the difficulties of women trying to make it to the top, others including Tony Abbott have also clearly described their 'Battlelines'.

The political 'attack dog' class, while seemingly attractive in reinforcing partisan power, has little if any benefit for the national interest, and in fact can be harmful to our international reputation. It was perceived that Tony

Abbott made an effective Opposition Leader, although a less effective Prime Minister because he carried this tag. Chris Bowen, Christopher Pyne and Penny Wong, of the current cohort, will benefit by displaying their leadership credentials rather than their 'ranting' skills (as so beautifully described by Williams), the continual "tiresome parades of intellectual conceit" and "descent into simplistic binary views on politics and society."[cxii]

The conundrum is though, that while this process creates good politicians, it does very little to create good leaders. The development of political leaders appears to be a matter of luck rather than a matter of leadership development process. The succession planning processes of both major parties are quite ineffectual. The internal party selection process is largely clandestine, resulting in selection outcomes which are often not attuned to the electorate.

Candidates who don't 'toe the party line' though typically have a short and turbulent political career span, regardless of their abilities or attributes. I've got to know a number of able politicians who were punished for partisan non-conformance, even when following the wishes of their electorate.

The system appears to favour the loud and brash. Candidates such as Cory Bernardi and Doug Cameron for example are highly partisan and opinionated, but don't appear to reflect their relative constituencies, whereas more moderate and considered political thinkers, such as Steve Bracks, Peter Costello and Lindsay Tanner retire too early, before their true promise is delivered. We need to ensure our political processes protect the talent we wish to retain, and 'unload' those that aren't nurturing the national interest – get the right people on the bus, and the wrong people off the bus.

At a State level, candidates such as ('Plonker') Peter Dowling, Gordon Nuttall, and Milton Orkopoulos would simply fail to reach a position of representation under a more rigorous and disciplined selection process; under our current selection system, 'Plonker' even managed to be appointed to head a Parliamentary Ethics Committee!

We are failing to invest in finding & training talent to lead; to attract the best available talent to lead. Instead, we have capable people without the requisite leadership skills stepping up to lead. Make no mistake, every political representation role is a leadership role, whether leading the electorate, the party, the council or the country.

**An Assessment of Prime Ministerial Leadership Capabilities**

Evidence of learning, "the capacity to interpret and reflect on experience" is a key element Tiernan[cxiii] cites that recent government (the Howard government aside) has failed to incorporate in changed process, procedures, practice or culture. She goes on to note the key impediments to learning for Australian politicians, the pathway to government, an advisory model which deprives political leaders of the capacity to learn, and the nature of Opposition, which causes a leak of talent.

The table below (figure 15) summarises some of the key pre-requisite attributes for political leadership, and qualitatively assesses how our recent leaders have performed against these attributes. Of course it is a highly subjective assessment and open to controversy, however the table underscores that, like any other enterprise, leadership skills need to be matched to the situational environment. We need a more proactive and practical methodology for developing and selecting leaders.

The point is not to compare the various traits of recent leaders, but rather to develop a process which ensures leaders of the future are appropriately skilled and prepared for the mantle of national leadership. Attributes such as courage were seen as a feature of, for example, Hawke and Keating, although courage appears, unfortunately, to be valued somewhat less highly than it was. Courage is needed in our leaders now more than ever. We could discuss the weighting of these various attributes, and what attributes make an ideal Prime Minister until all the cows are in China. The point here is that we should be reviewing the character and attributes of current leadership candidates, matching them with the attributes we require, and developing our candidates of the future to lead, rather than just 'letting it happen'.

| Attribute | 'Ideal' | Abbott | Rudd | Gillard | Howard |
|---|---|---|---|---|---|
| Ambition | High | High | High | High | High |
| Confidence | High | Medium | High | Medium | High |
| Fearlessness, Courage (Unwavering resolve) | High | Medium | Medium | Medium | Medium |
| Humility | High | Medium | Low | Medium | High |
| Integrity | High | Medium | Medium | Medium | High |
| Ability to Communicate | High | Low | Medium | Medium | Medium |
| Ability to Inspire | High | Low | Medium | Medium | Medium |
| Capacity to Learn | High | Low | Low | Medium | High |
| Respectful | High | Medium | Low | High | High |
| Enthusiastic | High | Medium | High | Medium | Medium |
| Awareness (self & others) | High | Low | Low | Medium | High |
| Authenticity | High | Medium | Low | Medium | High |
| Decision making skills | High | Low | Low | Medium | High |
| Empathy | High | Medium | Low | Medium | High |
| Emotional Intelligence | High | Low | Low | Medium | High |
| Creativity, Agility | High | Low | Medium | Low | Low |

*Figure 15 - A qualitative appraisal of the attributes of recent Prime Ministers against a suggested ideal across key leadership attributes. The focus should not be on the assessments of each Prime Minister against each attribute, but rather a wider appraisal of what attributes we are seeking in a Prime Minister, to ensure we select the person with the most suitable attributes to lead. That said, this table highlights the perception that recent leaders have typically not been perceived to have the appropriate attributes to lead.*

Fairfax Ipsos polling[cxiv] identifies eleven subjective 'competencies' or indicators upon which it bases its leadership polling:

1. Competent
2. Has a firm grasp of economic policy
3. Open to ideas
4. Has a firm grasp of foreign policy

5. Strong leader
6. Has a clear vision for Australia's future
7. Trustworthy
8. Has the confidence of his party
9. Has the ability to make things happen
10. Has a firm grasp of social policy
11. Is easily influenced by minority groups

It is on the basis of such factors that we make a determination on which of the major party leaders will make a better Prime Minister, and yet, such factors have little influence on an election outcome.

An alternative leadership model is that proposed by Jim Collins, in what he refers to as Level 5 leadership the peak level of a hierarchy of leadership capabilities. Level 5 leaders employ a 'paradoxical mix of personal humility and professional will', display ambition, but for the enterprise rather than themselves, are compellingly modest and fanatically driven, display a workmanlike diligence for sustained results, and apportion success to others and blame to themselves.

Authenticity is a key attribute needed in our Prime Minister. It is interesting to watch the US election process, with the continued involvement of Donald Trump, who should realistically have no chance of becoming president, being positively polled because he is seen as someone with an authentic experience and mindset to resolve key issues in America. Without authenticity and integrity, a politician has little to offer, as Kevin Rudd found out when the private and public perceptions of his behaviour came to be seen as different. Nicholas Stuart[cxv] described Rudd as "a mystery wrapped inside an enigma – the further you go, the more questions you end up with." This description alone says a lot about how little we understand about our leaders.

That Rudd was able to project such a popular public persona during his ascendency to the role of Prime Minister, hiding the darker personality traits which were better known to those close to him, and which later became very public, emphasises an imperfect leadership selection process. That Tony Abbott was seen to be an effective Opposition Leader but unable to become an effective Prime Minister also highlights the different capabilities which may be needed to lead Opposition as opposed to leading the country.

If we were to apply this simple matrix across the Cabinet, the Ministry, the Director Generals of departments, down through state & local government leaders, we may get a different view of the people we are trusting to lead.

We need to accept that our leaders will make mistakes & allow them those mistakes; similarly we need to accept that our leaders will need to make unpopular decisions. We choose our leaders on the basis of popularity, and yet leadership is not intended to be about making popular decisions. In fact, it is often those leaders in business who make unpopular decisions at the time who time shows to be the best leaders.

Our leaders have to be able to think, act and lead at a higher level. In recent times, this has been impossible, in part as already noted due to media management, which has caused our political leadership to behave, it would seem, tactically rather than strategically.

Factionalism and political interest appear to be far too influential in political appointments. Joe Hockey's appointment as Australian Ambassador to the United States, when Kim Beazley was acknowledged as doing such a fine job is one example. The appointment of Bruce McIver, former President of the Queensland LNP to the board of Australia Post over a field of candidates who would have made a far more valuable contribution to the organisation is another of many recent examples where organisational benefit and appropriate selection process is subjugated to political interest and 'jobs for the boys'. It is poor governance in action.

The history of Australian politics is littered with progressive Governors and Prime Ministers; they are ambiguously the best leaders we have had. From Governors Macquarie and Bourke to Prime Minister Keating, across both major parties, we have enjoyed the greatest sunshine following progressive leaders. They were prepared to question the status quo and back their judgment, and typically had the courage to follow through on their conviction. On the other hand, our poorest leaders tend to be guided by the minorities, failed to develop or communicate a plan, and are likely focused on staying in power.

In politics, the Whitlam, Hawke & Keating eras are often considered in this light. As David Hill[cxvi] describes, the era of Governor Lachlan Macquarie was regarded as the significant period of reform for the colony of New South

Wales, a focus on exploration and development of town and inland infrastructure, and the creation of our first bank. It was probably Macquarie's most contentious reform however which caused his downfall and laid the foundation for the society we know today. Governor Macquarie sought to achieve emancipation for convicts who had completed their sentences or been pardoned, putting himself at odds with his superiors in London. He took the further step of seeking placement for convicts in senior government posts, which also placed him at odds with local aristocrats whose 'entitlement' was threatened. For leaders, being right doesn't necessarily mean being popular!

**Attracting Leadership Talent**

The inability of politics to unstintingly maintain focus on the national interest is one reason why we fail to attract the very best people to government leadership. While we could benefit by being able to attract our most talented people to a career in public service, their concern is that they 'don't want to get caught up in the politics'.

We have a lot of talented, capable people 'on the bus', however this may be as much by accident as good practice. If we consider the processes of attracting and retaining talent in the context of the transparency of such roles, I am often amazed that people will seek careers in public life at all. How often do we hear people say 'so and so is hopeless', then in the next breath 'you couldn't pay me enough to be a politician'.

Another is a lack of formal training. The Australian Institute of Company Directors and Australian Institute of Management offer base courses and continual learning for company managers and directors, and yet the more complex and diverse field of professional politics does not really have a qualification for up and coming politicians besides classical theoretical politics courses at university.

What is our current succession planning methodology for leaders, and in particular the demanding role of Prime Minister? How do we prepare our leaders for high office? We place more emphasis on succession planning for our business leaders than we do our national leaders – and yet we expect extraordinary performance under very difficult and transparent circumstances.

What would happen if we were able to entice some of our best business leaders to lead government – people of the calibre of Gail Kelly, Richard Goyder, and Allison Watkins, to name just a few – talented leaders who would score highly on the matrix above (figure 13). Running government is undoubtedly different, and should not be compared, to leading a business. There are however capabilities and learnings which can be applied.

In Nicholas Barry's commentary on Laura Tingle's quarterly essay,[cxvii] that "Prime Ministers now have the ability to dominate the government's policy agenda in a way they previously did not. However, this power is highly contingent on their personal popularity. Colleagues are likely to put up with a highly centralised approach if a prime minister has recently led the party to a major election win and is doing well in the opinion polls." This again points to structural institutional issues. Barry points to "a basic failure to properly think through policy in advance and expose ideas to debate."

The major parties are inclined to view outsiders and newcomers with suspicion, particularly if they are expedited to the level of representation; this is a contributing motive for newcomers to avoid entering politics. Both major parties principally choose their candidates from the ranks of the party faithful. The selection process highlights a lack of diversity which fails to reflect our social diversity; almost a closed shop in union parlance. Perhaps as Nick Bowen points out[cxviii], efforts to increase diversity should not focus only on gender diversity, but on increasing the diversity of ideas and opinions.

While both executive & political recruitment processes can be arduous, recruitment for office seems to be more based upon the ability to 'rise to the top' of party factional battles than to be the best available electoral representative.

**Public Service Leadership and Remuneration**

The Honorable Mike Baird, Premier of New South Wales at time of writing, gave the Garran Oration at the Institute of Public Administration national conference in October 2015. He noted the foundational contribution to federation and national governance of Sir Robert Garran, a trusted counsellor and advisor to sixteen governments of all persuasions over a period of thirty years after federation, and a significant influencer behind federation, advocating from town to town the need for national unification. Without the input of venerated public servants such as Garran, it is possible federation might not have taken place. Unfortunately, in the current era, the tenure of faithful party servants is sometimes less stable, a function of the grey line between sound advice and perceived politics.

In his oration, Baird expressed his desire that public service leaders are embedded with self-belief that they can enact change. To do so however, we have to revert to the past, returning to a 'leadership in the public interest' relationship between the public service and the executive arm of government, where public service leaders are confident to give frank and fearless advice, and, as Baird declares, to 'take risks', and where the executive government maintains a professional and communicative relationship with its public service advisors where the division expressed as 'that's for politicians to decide' is instead a conversation among equals.

Nor are we compensating our public service leaders appropriately. We seem to be living with out-dated remuneration practices in government - generous superannuation and expense entitlements should be dispensed with, replaced by market based salaries which enable us to procure appropriate talent. Why is it that the Prime Minister is paid the equivalent of running a medium business? We compensate with generous superannuation & other perks, but it doesn't make sense.

Why do we continue to remunerate politicians & public servants with anachronistic schemes such as defined benefits plans & allowances, while paying them less than what they are worth. There are more opportunities for politicians after service than the ordinary worker, and yet we pay them well beyond tenure. If a politician is good enough, he or she will find bountiful career opportunities after politics; if not, they probably shouldn't have been there in the first place.

There is a significant issue with public servant pay; why aren't people in public service remunerated in the same way other income earners are paid. Generally, politicians and public servants are paid poorly on face value, and yet it is difficult to compare because of bloated entitlements and superannuation. One of Prime Minister Turnbull's early initiatives is to change the terminology of entitlements to what they should be – expenses reimbursed on approval. This type of thinking needs to be taken further, because once we establish a level playing field for remuneration, it becomes easier to attract people to public service, not harder, which is the suggestion of those vested interests trying to retain their traditional entitlements. It is very hard to successfully appeal to constituents to bear some pain when they perceive an entitlement system inconsistent with that pain they are being asked to shoulder.

One benefit of removing the layer of politics between local and federal government is that it would provide a more natural training ground for political talent to develop in a controlled manner. Identifying and focusing on our best 'up and comers', with a customised leadership development plan would be another way of fostering our future political stars.

Leadership of public service departments also faces its challenges. Ministers and Heads of Departments require a relationship of mutual trust to ensure the effectiveness of departments. Increasingly, leading public servants face reduced security of tenure, and are viewed as partisan by ministers. In Tingle's Quarterly Essay, she notes a lack of historical knowledge as a key reason for Australian politics becoming "... not only inane and ugly but dangerous", citing a less balanced and effective relationship between the public service and ministers. The relationships here are as vital as any working relationships in our country; we require good, capable, emotionally mature people in key roles to enable frank discussion and sound decision making.

While not structural, improving the level of engagement between ministers and the public service leaders they work with is vital to ensuring effective government outcomes. It should be expected that part of a risk management approach from the public service is that they 'play devil's advocate' without fear of retribution, to ensure better policy outcomes.

Mentoring is a business initiative which can have great benefit for government. Although mentoring does take place in government, there is likely an opportunity to formalise mentoring frameworks for our key leaders. This might take the form of an Advisory Committee of eminent Australians who could meet with the Prime Minister (and other senior leaders as appropriate) regularly and provide non-political feedback and advice. Of course, this would need to be undertaken with the highest confidentiality.

The capabilities for great leadership are rare, and it leads one to take the view that the Prime Minister should not be limited to his own party leadership in the search for the most capable, unified talent to lead in Ministry. While utilising talent from the other major parties may be just a step too far, why is it not possible to appoint a ministry from beyond the ranks of the political elite? The best leadership talent available should be brought together to manage our country.

Managing our political talent requires greater emphasis going forward. The failure to do so in the recent past has created significant opportunity cost for the nation. There is too much risk in not ensuring the best people available to lead are positioned to lead, and yet the current process is akin to a lottery. Engagement with the Australian people will likely increase, unless we can develop government which ensures people that it cares for them, wants to know what they think, will enable them to grow, and will appreciate their contribution.

The development of such skills requires a significant forward investment in the development of leadership capability; there is a causal link between sustained investment in capability and sustained growth and competitive advantage. If we are to expect the best for our country, we have to decide the capabilities we seek in our leaders, equip leadership candidates with the training, skills and experience they need to navigate our society, economy and a dynamic global environment, and to support them to make wise, courageous and effective decisions.

# 14. Our Institutional Structure

*"All organizations are perfectly designed to get the results they are now getting. If we want different results, we must change the way we do things." (Tom Northup)*

Among Winston Churchill's numerous one-liners is this gem - "the only institution that successfully resists change is the graveyard".[cxix]

That our institutional structure requires change is indisputable. What we have to first consider is what we need our institutions to be and do going forward, before affirming the structure most appropriate to meet those needs. This should, for example, include a greater global context and a focus on technologies that were not even dreamed about when federation commenced. It should include a whole-of-government review of roles and responsibilities. There are substantial opportunities for reform of our core national establishment – our partisan, executive, government & legal bodies, based both on current best practice around the globe and by addressing current issues.

Acemoglu and Robinson[cxx] identify a link between the strength and stability of a nation's political and other institutions, and national prosperity, arguing that without good government, the incentive to create wealth dissipates. We know this to be true, reiterated by the underlying stability of our own institutions, however performance is not meeting expectations, attested to by government churn. The link between stability and economic performance is confirmed the world over, most recently detrimentally in Greece. China sees the rooting out of corruption and stability of its core institutional bodies as a determinant of continued economic prosperity.

Tony Abbott remarked in Battlelines, "Australia has states because it was the price of becoming a nation, not because the federation fathers thought an intermediate level of government was necessary to avoid tyranny or that some services were inherently better delivered by states." It is a shame (while not surprising), that while most Prime Ministers have criticised the state structure beyond their term, none have elected to tackle the issue while in office.

For Australians, one of our most common refrains is that we are over-governed. This statement is not intended to attack the many (largely) hard working men & women who represent us in government, however the fact is we don't need a three-tiered system of administration, which more often than not gets in the way of effective government. We could streamline our performance, decision making, agility and flexibility if we undertook the serious task of restructuring government, much as companies restructure, taking out layers, to reflect changing market conditions. We could further streamline processes if we instead directed our ingenuity to whole-of-government system re-design rather than the commercialisation of technology and innovation.

Delayering organisational structures has been going on for a long time, in response to the need to simplify and improve technology, increased competition, and the desire to reduce the cost to serve. Like it or not, government requires the same attention. We will witness in times to come a rash of cashed up, savvy, international businesses arriving on our shores to 'eat our lunch', both in the government and commercial sectors. Queensland Premier Campbell Newman's attempt to downsize the Queensland bureaucracy some years back, while brusque, was undoubtedly proper. Whether the approach was apt, and whether the narrative and methodology could have been handled better are questions in hindsight, however the need to downsize, regardless of the views of the Public Service Union was and still is necessary. Other states are now following the Queensland template, albeit learning from the mistakes the Newman government made.

Reducing the influence of 'special interest groups' in institutional decision making is an urgent priority. Vested interests create inefficiency in allocation of government time and funding, deliver 'fractional truths', and divert resource for unproductive capital. We need to direct resource on those segments of the economy which ensure growth and a return to a sustainable budget balance. Special interest groups create greater inefficiency in smaller countries such as Australia than larger countries, particularly when we have three levels of government available to lobby, enabling lobbyists to establish further roadblocks to unwelcome change.

The public recognises the need to consider carefully the institutional structure of the future for our nation; it generates much of the restlessness we demonstrate. Butler-Bowdon's observation of the deterioration of confidence in government in the US is just as applicable in Australia: "In the 1960's, 70 per cent of Americans said that they had confidence in the federal government. Today, with congressional gridlock, deficits, and increasing inequality, that proportion has dropped to 17 per cent." We need to have a focus on at least fifteen years out, rather than a myopic focus on six months to three years.

The governance stream at the 2020 Summit determined that federation required reinvigoration to enhance Australian democracy and empower government to 'work' for all Australians "by reviewing the roles, responsibilities, functions, structures and financial arrangements at all levels of governance (including courts and the non-profit sector) by 2020". They proposed doing this through a three-stage process:

1. an expert commission which reviews roles and responsibilities, then proposes a new mix of responsibilities,
2. a convention of the people, informed by the commission and by a process of deliberative democracy, and
3. implementation by intergovernmental cooperation or, alternatively, referendum.

Clearly reform is on the minds of many; it is the implementation of reform that will exercise our minds more ebulliently.

Among the potential institutional enhancements to be considered are some specific concepts across party lines and tiers of government.

**The Major Parties**

As stated previously, none of the major parties naturally reflect the views of ordinary Australians, and have not done so for many years; they constantly appear to be fighting amongst themselves for the middle ground, leaving an unclear position for voters as to what they stand for. They are promoting electoral volatility by widening the hollow.

In the event we don't seek to reform partisan democracy, we will continue to see what we have seen over the last thirty years – new parties will form, attract the votes of the disenchanted, but without an appropriate governance regime in place will become victims of their own growth, imploding over time as the Australian Democrats and Palmer United Party have done. The only variable will be the speed of their demise, a function primarily of their governance capability.

One reform alternative is to demolish the existing party structure and its factions, and start again. This approach has practical implementation issues, however it does provide voters with the opportunity to align their philosophy with their party of choice, in a 'partisan beauty parade'. This division may occur along the factional lines described earlier. The downside to such an approach is that existing parties would need to agree (which is unlikely) and we need to avoid factional influence (if by some vague chance they did agree). Would it not be interesting if we had the opportunity to redefine our partisan choices from first principles?

In a parallel dimension, the six new factions (Labor 'Progressives', Liberal 'Progressives', Labor 'Unionists', Liberal 'Conservatives', Greens, and National or Country Party) would have an opportunity to present their vision and communicate what they stand for. We would cast a vote, which would most likely end with a split parliament, and then see how the cards fell as each faction sought to influence power. My money would be on a coalition between the 'progressive' factions. The National or Country faction would probably return to its traditional (and arguably more powerful) position as a pressure group, and the conservative and union factions (the foundation members of the two major parties) would, in my view, die in time (unless they sought to review their policy platforms). This is just one potential, albeit unlikely possibility.

While this option retains partisan power, it provides an opportunity to realign party thinking, and to fill the gap between political parties and the people they supposedly represent. I believe we would see a more effective, unified government by combining the two progressive factions of the current competing major parties than we currently experience. It would force a re-consideration by competing voter 'factions' about how they would influence the political agenda going forward.

Alternatively, in the new world of social media, is there an opportunity for 'active' technology-based democracy to take over from political parties? The Pirate Party ran in Griffith the second time round, and has simultaneously been setting up 'shop' all over the world, seeking to establish 'a more inclusive and creative culture'. The Pirate Party describes itself[cxxi] as 'a movement based around the core tenets of freedom of information and culture, civil and digital liberties, privacy and anonymity, government transparency, and participatory democracy.

Unfortunately, such 'movements' have little alternative but to set themselves up along party lines, however there are greater opportunities for such groups to create a greater social crusade. The idea of 'participative' or 'active' democracy is in its infancy, and I'm not clear how it might work, but we need alternatives which bridge the gap between parties and people. It may include digital plebiscites, a means of gauging community interest across a range of policy areas. The ABC television program 'Q&A' has highlighted the opportunity to better harness and communicate instantaneous social media, both positive and negative. The challenge is to separate meaningful contribution from the flippant or personal aside.

As the Pirate Party states on its website, 'shared expression creates shared experience and values'. Such options should be seriously canvassed and openly discussed. No-one is looking for a 'Hail Mary' but simply viable, agreeable options which remove the 'dark side' of partisan politics.

Finally, political parties should be subject to the highest levels of financial rigour, reporting and audit, and the structure of the two major parties simplified to report aggregated donations and income sources. These are the people running our nation; there should be no places to hide.

Reform must seek to reduce the partisanship of government, because this niggling 'cancer' is destroying consensus, inhibiting decision making, and affecting the national interest. Throughout this chapter we discuss various alternative citizens' forums which may assist in reducing partisanship.

**Federal Government**

Michael Costello, reporting in The Australian in 2008[cxxii] opined, "heaven knows, we desperately need some serious long-term planning in this country."

To get the best from government, we need to build our capability in strategy development, and organisationally separate strategy development from strategy execution in government. So long as we retain electoral terms, the 'management' of the country won't deliver us the long term direction we sorely need.

It is difficult to sketch an organisation chart of Australian institutional leadership. My version of how we might structure government is crudely illustrated below (refer figure 16). Whether we operate as a republic or not is not, I believe, almost inconsequential for a revised governance structure. If we were to become a republic, the current role of Governor General would remain, with a different title and altered powers, simply no longer serving at the pleasure of the Queen if the change to a republic was consummated. More important is to structurally separate the long and short term planning time fences from the day-0to-day operation of strategy and government.

One option is to alter the structure to develop a Strategy and Governance 'Board' or group, which the Governor General (or 'Head of State' in the case of a republic) chairs. This Governance 'Board' would consist of (say ten) eminent Australians across a range of fields (suited to best develop broad social and economic strategy), appointed by bipartisan or alternatively judicial agreement to fixed five year terms, with one position rolling out annually to provide renewal, stability and continuity. The members of this Committee would have specified backgrounds in science, the arts, business, economics and entrepreneurialism, law, finance, human rights, indigenous leadership and similar appropriate endeavours to be able to contribute to national strategy.

The role of the Governance 'Board' would be to 'set the stage' for government, establishing the national vision, overseeing the development of long term strategy, mentoring government as they implement the strategy, and overseeing the strategy group, which would be responsible for developing national strategy and long term plans. They would also be responsible for establishing a path to approval of strategy with government.

The advantage of such a structure is that it allows our nation to be more attentive to the long term, takes the strategy development process beyond the election cycle, and ensures strategy is non-partisan and more closely aligned to the public interest.

Under such a scenario, federal government would be elected, as now, to take responsibility for the operationalisation of national strategy, policy and electoral cycle planning, with input from local council stakeholders (based on a reorganisation of councils below). They would become accountable for the delivery of the strategy, with specific measurable targets established across the government portfolio for each term of government. Elected representatives would have input and approval (as noted above) of the long term plans, to ensure they own the implementation agenda.

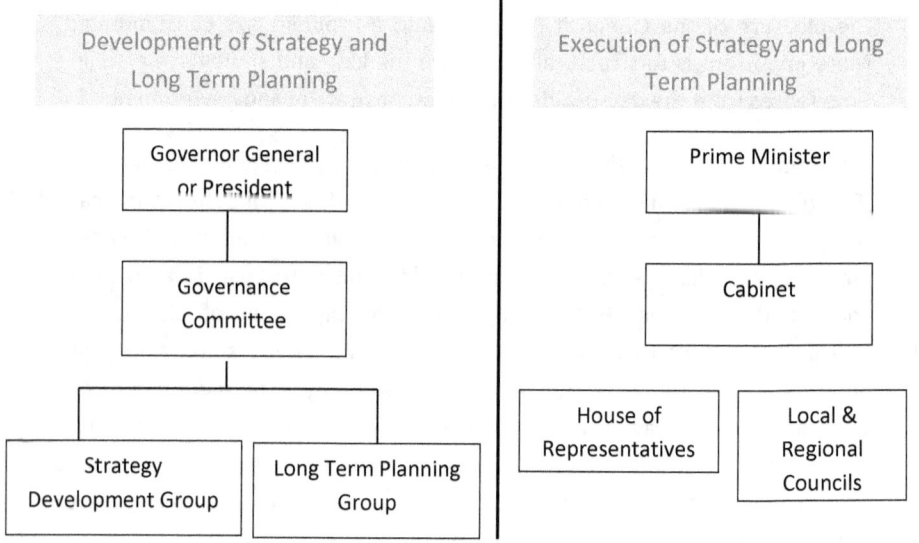

Figure 16 – An alternative organisation chart for federal governance

An alternative proposition is that one house is restructured to develop strategy, the other to implement, with joint sign-off of agreed strategy by both houses. Such an option though would be impractical in the current senate structure.

If we assume that one level of government is not needed in the long run, it would provide the opportunity for a common electoral boundary to be applied to all levels of government. Assuming the current number of federal electorates (145) is appropriate, this would form the basis of delineation at a federal and local council level. This would put an end to the continual redefinition of boundaries which currently results in confusion and often unnecessary cost.

A streamlining of our government is needed - to cut the cloth to size, and enable the integration between leaders to make decisions and actively implement strategy. We have probably never really needed, and now certainly do not need three tiers of government. Nor do we have efficient and effective integration between tiers of government or electoral boundaries, emphasised by the shambles operating as COAG (Council of Australian Governments). Consider an electoral area in western Queensland with which I am familiar, and which highlights this issue. The regional council in Longreach (an area of almost 41,000 sqkm incorporates Longreach, Ifracombe, Isisford and Yaraka), while the state seat of Gregory (covering an area of some 327,000 sqkm from Dingo to the Barcoo across and Muttaburra down to Quilpie, and the federal seat of Maranoa (an area of 731,000 sqkm stretching from west of Toowoomba to the Northern territory border and from the NSW border to north of Winton). There are more than a dozen local councils encroaching within the federal electorate, some having to deal with multiple state and federal members. It just doesn't need to be so complex, particularly when the federal member is covering an electorate of ¾ million kilometres! Integration of multi-tiered government boundaries should be based on the needs of the community rather than the determination of partisan support.

Based on this streamlined structure of 145 federal electorates, with one member elected to represent that electorate at 'federal council', and another member elected to run the electorate at a local level, to effectively implement federal strategy, deliver services & enact the budget, we would considerably reduce the cost of government while enhancing its effectiveness. The proposed structure would remove significant duplication in government departments, place greater autonomy in local electorates to 'act global, think local', and provide integration between federal representatives and local leadership. It would place the onus back onto communities to develop their talents and attributes, and lobby directly nationally where help is needed. Many local councils already lobby directly to federal government although they report to state government, underscoring the current inefficiency of our multi-tiered bureaucracy.

The Federal Government would take greater responsibility for setting national policy and managing the cost of government down, including the natural efficiencies which would come from initiatives including purchasing, standardisation, and enhanced interface, although local councils need not follow those guidelines unless agreed mandatory. The ongoing argument of cost management of health and education between state and federal

| Country / House | No. of Sitting Days |
|---|---|
| Australia – House of Representatives | 75 |
| Australia - Senate | 59 |
| New Zealand Parliament | 90 |
| US Congress | 157 |
| Britain – House of Commons | 177 |
| Britain – House of Lords | 138 |

*Figure 17 - A comparison of sitting days for parliaments in Australia, New Zealand, United States and Britain in 2015. On the basis of these numbers, the Australian houses of parliament sit for considerably less time than associated democracies.*

government would be dealt with greater clarity, without the spurious 'bogus' arguments about who is not giving who sufficient subsidy, while important funding is simultaneously extraordinarily wasted.

We need to have a house, a forum, of candid debate, on issues of relevance, and ensure there is appropriate sitting time for such debate to be held, within an appropriate framework and rules for meaningful debate. It is interesting to draw comparison between the sitting days of similar democratic governments (as per figure 17), and, while more debate is not necessarily better debate, the stark contrast remains between sitting days in Australia versus other democratic houses, before we even consider the quality of debate. We could not cogently argue that Australian government debate is of a high quality.

Review of the Senate is necessary and urgent, and certainly appears to be on the agenda – the question is whether it will go far enough. The most obvious recommendation is to replace the current Senate with either a proportionally representative chamber or a non-partisan house of review. The proposed non-partisan Senate structure, like the Governance Committee, might utilise eminent Australians across fields of endeavour beyond politics. They would be elected to one term only, ensuring a recycling of talent, and would require mechanisms ensuring diversity across class, gender, age, ethnicity, and area of expertise. It would provide a diversity of opinion and practical experience not available to our government under current arrangements, unless formed ad hoc.

We cannot continue with a Senate composition which fails to appropriately represent the Australian people. The current non-proportional composition was agreed to enable federation to occur, however it is no longer representative of our demographic and social mix. I love little Tassie (despite Jacqui Lambie) and South Australia (despite Sarah Hanson-Young) as much as the next Australian, however it is ridiculous that these states should have an equal say to New South Wales or Victoria.

We have to review the layers of bureaucracy which have been developed over time. We face substantial unnecessary red tape when regulations across federal, state and local council are combined in some cases and divergent in other cases.

The structure and function of the Prime Minister's Office (PMO) is critical to the delivery of outcomes and reform. The dysfunction of the Rudd and Abbott offices, regardless of where the fault lay, undoubtedly contributed to the downfall of each Prime Minister. Similarly, the function of COAG, which forms the foundation for Commonwealth-State relations also requires greater formality, to ensure agreements made between leaders are soundly and uniformly implemented.

Extending federal parliamentary terms to four years is a band aid fix which would enable government to start considering our national position more strategically, as well as signal to the electorate the need for stability. It would also conservatively add $200-300 million to the budget bottom line each saved election, and enable business to reduce exposure to the calm which seems to beset the commercial sector leading to each election.

Tightening the entry requirements for minor parties is another long overdue reform which has been placed in the spotlight by the Palmer United Party in recent years. We can't afford to have political parties fail the way businesses fail. The defection of elected party officials to independents, and the public financial duress of the Palmer empire highlight that there have to be clear governance requirements to support entry as a political party. While a duopoly is not in our best long term interests, we would be much better served by two or three other parties with the electoral clout to positively influence government, rather than thirty or forty candidates looking for their day of sunshine.

Implementation of a national dashboard (wouldn't that keep the consulting firms busy!) supported by a State of Australia speech (a State of the Union hybrid), outlining performance for the year gone, outlining commitments and forming the narrative for the year ahead would provide an accountability that we don't have in place currently beyond the budget. Right now, we have the budget, an encyclopaedia of promises and pork barrelling which suffers from the credibility gap of promises not kept. If we were able to establish a scene setting speech by the Prime Minister of the day, talking to performance and plans, supported by an auditable dashboard, it provides a window into more defined, open, and accountable government.

The tenor of parliament needs to be changed towards a house of meaningful debate. The reputation of parliamentarians has been in tatters, particularly since parliament was first televised. Politicians look thoroughly disinterested (when awake) and the quality of discussion is vapid and personal. For reform to occur, a number of changes are necessary, which may include, but are not limited to:

- Increasing the duration of parliamentary sessions (our parliament sits less time than most parliamentary democracies) and providing better definition of the topics to be debated

- Introduce rules to improve the quality of debate, including banning 'Dorothy Dixers' (what is the point when there are so many opportunities to debate matters of substance?). Allingham goes further, suggesting we abolish the charade that is Question Time altogether[cxxiii]. The image of politicians would likely improve somewhat were this notion taken up.
- Nick Bowen points to a British effort to reform parliamentary debate which involved reducing the amount of time the Prime Minister spends on the floor to a focused question time. After all, the role of Prime Minister is to lead, and this is best done away from parliament, allowing others to manage the day-to-day business of parliament, with the PM coming in to provide a decision point at an agreed time.
- Improving the professionalism of the leadership handover when government changes. When government changes unexpectedly, as happened in January 2015 in Queensland, handover occurs virtually overnight, the incoming government wearing the look of shock on their faces, and an outcome where the incoming government appeared to suffer paralysis in their decision making for some months afterwards. Surely in the modern era, this is one area where we can place the national interest ahead of party politics. The United States in comparison works through a three month handover, including bipartisan funding and comprehensive transition plans to ensure handover is effective.
- Nick Bowen also illustrates another simple but meaningful attitudinal UK reform being proposed, the use of names rather than titles in reference to other members of the parliament, an effort to personalise debate which has merit.

In summary, the focus of reform needs to be on returning dignity to parliament, and policy development rather than unnecessary defence and justification, which includes a review of the Standing Orders to reflect the behaviour we expect in parliament.

### State Government

Nick Bowen[cxxiv] conveys the story (told to him by industry veterans) of the effort some years ago to develop a national tourism campaign. The campaign almost faltered and certainly lost some of its effect as the states jockeyed for position. Deadlocked in negotiations on the fear that one state would fare better than another in advertising coverage, the compromise the state delegates arrived at was that no identifiable landmarks would be shown in the campaign, so that the Barrier Reef did not compete with Uluru or the Twelve Apostles. The campaign left potential international tourists wondering, as Bowen observes 'where the bloody hell were they'?

Such counter-productive attitudes remain deeply ingrained in the culture of state public servants across portfolios including health, education and transport. A core premise for simplification of institutional presence is the streamlining of government, which appears to have become mired in doing business with itself. A continual theme is the ongoing negotiation between government bureaucracies, which does little to add value for constituents.

Removing State Government is not a new concept, being first formally suggested in a Labor Party document in 1920, and was most famously articulated by Bob Hawke in 1979 on the eve of his career in federal politics. The Labor Party document even went so far as to lay out the (150) local council boundaries. Hawke reiterated clearly his view that "we'd be much better off without the states" at the fiftieth anniversary of the National Press Club in a joint discussion with John Howard. Howard didn't disagree, saying "if you were starting again, you wouldn't have (the states)."

Reducing a level of government will not be regarded as pragmatic by some, however respected realists such as John Button regarded it as totally appropriate 'in the new millennium'.[cxxv]

If removing a layer of government is deemed practicable, state government is the layer to go. In recent years, businesses have removed layers of middle management. While cost/benefit has been a driving factor, this simplification of structure has resulted in a streamlining of communications which has enhanced performance. Streamlining of government institutional structure should be reviewed and considered in the same vein.

The argument for state government is that they promote competition and political diversity, & that we've become attached to them, none of which are solid arguments in support of keeping state government. The argument that states diffuse power is both an advantage and a disadvantage depending on perspective; establishing appropriate governance enables this concern to be addressed.

Brutally put, the states are effectively extraneous, and probably an impediment to the development of Australia's national infrastructure. By way of example, when we should have a uniform dual lane rail track between our east coast capitals, we have a bits and pieces system cobbled together which inhibits efficient supply chains and rail tourism. We have thousands of unnecessary trucks running linehaul because we've failed to develop our rail infrastructure appropriately.

If state government powers were to be devolved federally and locally, a complex but not impractical change, it would provide greater autonomy to implement federal uniformity (where appropriate), while allowing regional differences to be managed locally. This would enable the federal government to establish more efficient operating models in areas including health, education, infrastructure, policing, energy, rural development, natural resources and other key policy areas. Considerable tactical and operational power would be devolved to a local level to implement national policy.

The most effective way for this to occur would be to amalgamate council boundaries and federal electorates into the 145 electoral boundaries now applied federally. Elections would then be held federally to provide a candidate to represent the electorate federally, and locally to elect the people responsible for local administration. Such a structure would enable more direct influence to rural and regional areas, and enable the operationalization of strategy to be undertaken moire effectively, customised to suit the needs of local constituents.

There is a need for increased consistency which the devolution of power to federal parliament will enable – common time zones across eastern states, common national public holidays; small matters in some respects, but important nonetheless. An integrated national public transport card – again, all possible if the framework is correct.

To this day, the states, whether they care to agree or not, remain entrenched and set in their ways, in spite of a range of progressive, effective, indecisive and enigmatic leaders. They continue to be highly competitive, and deeply suspicious of each other and federal government throughout the bureaucracies they maintain. State governments typically only unite when their amalgamated 'argument' with the federal government surpasses their enmity for each other. It is time for change.

**Local Council**

Thomas 'Tip' O'Neill (Jr), who became Speaker of the House in the US legislature, was advised by his father, a bricklayer and city councillor that "all politics is local politics",[cxxvi] a mantra he maintained throughout his career in federal US politics. While local councils have their issues, including poor governance and corruption, there is significant scope to increase the capabilities of our local government.

As mentioned previously, one proposition is that that the current 560 or so councils be aggregated into 145 councils aligned with federal electoral boundaries. Such aggregation provides better information federally and between electorates. An alternate option is to reconsider a plan designed and seriously evaluated by the Department of Post-War Reconstruction, which divided Australia into some 34 regions, with an underlying set of actions to upgrade local council functions and capabilities.

Greater homogeneity between councils provides the opportunity to establish performance benchmarks, such as cost per head, capital invested per head, proportion of electorate on welfare, etc. which in turn drives performance improvement. While there will always be differentials between say regional & city councils, establishing benchmarks is a transparent means of managing improvement. At the moment, there is little opportunity to compare councils on a like-for-like basis; this lack of transparency creates inefficiency. We cannot hope to counter claims of inefficiency until there is a more transparent mechanism for comparative measurement in place. This is harder with state governments acting effectively as a buffer, but would be much easier with the 145 councils reporting into a national federated structure. It further provides a methodical leverage point for establishing and reproducing best practice across these electorates/councils. Like it or not, a large number of those 560 councils are not viable, have not ever been viable, and will not ever be viable.

Such a structure provides perhaps greater opportunities for improved governance than the current structure, as federal oversight and greater transparency provide improved discipline in managing costs and service. 'Taking out the middle man' also imposes greater scrutiny on local councils, some of whom have suffered credibility issues in recent times.

**Legal Institutions**

Just as security was the prime mover towards Federation at the end of the nineteenth century, security is a key issue propelling reform now. Policing in particular is hamstrung by the different state systems and cultures. We are already seeing that the basis of conflict in the modern era is people of different ethnic and religious backgrounds asserting those backgrounds. We need integrated policing tools to identify and proactively address such social issues, rather than tools limited by state borders.

Accountable, public measurement is a prime reform needed to legal institutions. We need to find ways to manage service, cost and backlogs, so that the institution of the law becomes responsible for social as well as legal outcomes. This is difficult, as data should not of itself be the key driver of legal process. However, the development of publicised data which ensures the focus timely throughput and service will provide a concentration of attention beyond simply the technical aspects of the law.

**Financial Institutions**

A number of our financial institutions would benefit from having the same governance structure implemented as is in place at the Reserve Bank, including a board comprising a mix of independent and executive members, published minutes, and a code of conduct. These reforms would provide greater accountability and transparency to these regulatory authorities.

One of the Harper Review recommendations identified the need for a new body called the Australian Council for Competition Policy to be established, to advocate and drive reform and perform reviews of policy. The argument for a clear mandate on long term strategy will be discussed further; such bodies might be part of a broader focus on strategy and reform.

**Alternative Democratic Models**

The debate over Australia becoming a republic has lingered for some time now. However, the issue of converting to a republic is more ceremonial than advantageous. The benefits of becoming a republic are relatively small; there are significantly greater opportunities to improve our institutional structure; becoming a republic is relatively low in the hierarchy. The greater challenge is to achieve a more integrated, efficient and effective model of federalism. The republic issue belongs on the backburner for now; we need to solve the serious issues first.

There is an assortment of alternative democratic models which are in various stages of development, trial and use throughout western democracy. Most democracies are, to different extents, a representative democracy.

Most countries which operate representative democracies allow one or more of three forms of public political action which provide limited direct democracy – referendum (the ability to negate a law passed by the legislature), initiative (citizens placing a bill before the public and having it adopted, effectively bypassing legislative approval), and/or recall (citizen ability to recall a representative from office).

Compulsory referendum subjects the legislation drafted by political representatives to a binding popular vote. This is the most common form of direct legislation. Referendum empowers citizens to make a petition that calls existing legislation to a citizens' vote. Direct democracy provides citizens an extraordinary amount of participation in the legislative process by which laws are created by direct society consensus. This form of democracy is applied in Switzerland and grants the voting public a veto on laws adopted by the elected legislature.

The power of 'initiative' allows members of the public to propose specific statutory measures or constitutional reforms to government. As with referendums, the vote may be advisory or binding. Initiatives may be direct or indirect. With the direct initiative, a successful voter proposition is placed directly on the ballot to be subject to vote (as used in California since the 1970's). The California process has become more flawed as it has become increasingly 'professionalised'. Switzerland utilise indirect initiative for constitutional amendments.

The power of 'recall' gives the public the power to remove elected officials from office before the end of their term. I'm not aware of a modern democracy in which this power is currently available.

The concept of 'deliberative' democracy is being trialled in Australia, and is an innovation proposed by the New Democracy Foundation, founded by Luca Belgiorno-Nettis (www.newdemocracy.com.au/). Some of the deliberative and participatory democratic mechanisms are being trialled to varying extents in legislative frameworks across the globe. There is considerably more information available, including the advantages and disadvantages of each option on the Foundation's website. Among the considerable structural alternatives offered by the Foundation are:

- Citizens Senate[cxxvii] – based on the traditional Greek model where the Senate was comprised of a random selection of the citizen class; in this alternative, citizens would have the right of refusal;
- The Electronic Town Hall[cxxviii] - the core of this concept is to select one fiftieth of the voting age population each year and engage them in discussion, and subsequently an online vote. This voice would constitute an additional house in the parliament. By surveying such an immense sample, there is greater assurance the group is representative of the population as a whole than the elite 'political class';
- Demarchy[cxxix] - while we currently elect a small number of representatives who make decisions on a wide range of issues on behalf of the electorate, demarchy is, by contrast based on a network of numerous decision making groups. Each group deals with a specific function (i.e. transport, land use, parks) in a given area – so it's not a "generalist" system. The membership of each group is chosen randomly each year from all those who nominate they are interested in working on that topic, and specialist expertise or experience can be called in where appropriate to particular topics;
- Citizen Legislature (Sortition)[cxxx] – this alternative recognises the threat of donations and vested interests in politics. The Citizen Legislature is a

logical means of selecting legislators so they will be truly representative, just as the Greeks selected by lottery over more than two centuries. The outcome will be a more descriptively representative legislature, not beholden to special interest donations. A traditionally elected party-based upper house/ senate would remain as house of review;

- The Popular Branch[cxxxi] - western democracies operate three basic branches of government: executive, judicial, and legislative. With parliaments seemingly increasingly unrepresentative of the people they govern, the popular branch concept proposes that a fourth branch should be added, comprised of a randomly drawn group of citizens. The passage of a binding decision would require a supermajority of two thirds of the Popular House as indicative of broad-based popular consent. This is not a consultative group drawn to discuss a single issue: it is proposed The Popular Branch would be institutionalised and permanent with a clear separation of powers. This would include a potential power for judges to send a question to the assembly to settle a matter where the court would otherwise be making new law;
- Consensus Conferences[cxxxii] - similar to a summit, a consensus conference brings together lay people and subject matter experts to identify common ground in topics where there is technological or scientific complexity, and where key aspects of the issue are uncertain, contested or controversial. Generally the ratio of lay citizens (or "Citizen Panellists") to experts is 2:1. In operation, the panel receives appropriate background data and material. The lay panel then questions the experts to its satisfaction, then assembles a report which includes only the elements upon which they can agree;
- Multi-Body Sortition[cxxxiii] - A variation on traditional sortation, this model seeks to divide the activities of lawmaking among several groups with different functions (choose issues, develop and review bills, voting and oversight) and different characteristics. The members of these bodies would be randomly selected rather than being elected. Some bodies would be ongoing (like current legislatures), and others would be temporary (like juries);

Alternatively, the Foundation also offers a series of incremental democratic and voting alternatives:

- Introduce Citizens' Panels to assist Voters in Understanding Policy Specifics[cxxxiv] - this model is now in place in Oregon. Random samples of several hundred voters are drawn by the Electoral Commission to explore individual elements of policy proposed by all parties and independents. The group meets over a period of several months and can hear from experts as agreed to by the group. The requirement is for them to produce a short explanatory consensus paper on a given issue which is then disseminated to the citizenry. In Oregon, it is included in the ballot paper materials handed out at the polling place;
- Optional Preferential Voting[cxxxv] - the major electoral recommendation of the 2009 Citizens' Parliament which assembled 150 randomly selected citizens drawn from every electorate nationally (funded and operated by the Foundation). Optional preferential voting serves to eliminate preference deals which are lightly understood and (as a result) not trusted by the vast majority of voters. There is no longer an 'above the line' vote for Upper House Candidates as voters gain the choice to preference as many or as few candidates as they choose. They gain confidence that a vote for Candidate A does not unknowingly translate into a vote for Candidate B because of a preferencing arrangement that they cannot reasonably be expected to be familiar with;
- Introduce a 'None of the Above' Voting Option[cxxxvi] - the 'none of the above' option better reflects the will and voice of the people, allowing dissatisfied and disengaged citizens to be heard while creating a clear distinction with inadvertent informal votes. This option could be viewed as a 'halfway step' to non-compulsory voting, as it reduces the compulsion on voting to one of attendance at a polling place;
- Executive Appointment[cxxxvii] - the political process results in a number of people with specialist expertise and management talent not making themselves available for senior office. It is often commented that one advantage of the US system is the capacity of the President to draw respected people of achievement and talent and appoint them to senior roles. One example quoted by the New Democracy website, the role of Secretary of Defence is not filled by an elected representative, rather, by nomination by the President – with the recently retired Robert Gates a notable example of an appointment who served both Republican and Democratic presidents and as a result was viewed by many as 'above the politics';

- Eliminate Private Donor Funding[cxxxviii] - similar to the argument in favour of political advertising, parties argue that third party donations are a form of freedom of speech. A contrary view suggests that they significantly reduce public confidence in the motives of our elected representatives due to the perception that donations are only made in expectation of a commercial return, rather than as an altruistic contribution to civic life;
- Cap Political Advertising[cxxxix] - Australian advertising entrepreneur John Singleton described election campaigns as the "ultimate one day sale". Arguments in favour of political advertising centre on the theme that it provides voter information and is a form of freedom of speech, while the contrary view suggests that political advertising provides little in the way of information;
- Increase and Promote Pre-polling[cxl] - there is evidence the pre-poll vote has increased substantially in recent elections as a proportion of the overall vote. Pre-polling is seen as improving the deliberative and comparative component of voting, although parties are resourcing pre-polling places so that the voter is no less subject to sloganeering and pamphleteering than on polling day;
- Lift Legislative Exemptions Applying Solely to Political Advertising[cxli] - Currently, political advertising is not required to adhere to the same guidelines as commercial advertisers under the Competition and Consumer Act or the Privacy Act. Political advertising should adhere to the same test, to "have the intent, or likely effect, to mislead or deceive" as any other advertising, reducing the current advertising partisan emphasis on sensationalised and unsubstantiated claims;
- Tie Party Funding to Diversity Requirements[cxlii] - one (albeit unresearched by the Foundation) concept proposed by recently retired politicians would aim to break the increasing trend toward "career" politicians by proportionally tying the party funding per vote from the AEC to a sliding scale based on the proportion of representatives elected who were previously party staffers or student politicians.

There are undoubtedly opportunities to formulate mechanisms for participatory democracy, such as more inclusive forms of public engagement in committees which offer greater public legitimacy to outcomes and increased democratic effectiveness.

Generally though, while governments at various levels have taken symbolic steps, such as holding 'regional' parliaments, which increase public awareness of the institutional roles and functions of parliament, we are yet to experience the engagement of citizens in meaningful public debate within those meetings. The failure of government to connect with citizens, to enable them to have input to and deliberate about collective decisions on public problems, remains a fundamental legislative disappointment.

Citizens' Juries or Senates have been applied at the local council level already[cxliii]. In December 2013, the City of Sydney in conjunction with the state government employed a novel approach to consultation. A mini-public comprising of 43 people (including a third under 24 years of age) were randomly recruited from a pool of citizens across Sydney. It was Sydney City's first experience with a citizens' jury. They were asked: "How can we ensure we have a vibrant and safe Sydney nightlife?" The jury deliberated in facilitated, robust sessions for more than 50 hours across three months, hearing from individuals, organisations and advocacy groups. The jury maintained a dedicated online discussion forum and, in April 2014 delivered their report with 25 recommendations of which 23 were adopted by the council.

Stephen Mayne, Chair of the Finance Committee for Melbourne City Council (and long time activist) more recently engaged a citizens 'jury' to advise the Council on their $4 billion ten year plan in an effort to develop a plan which has engagement and 'fearless advice' from 'regular, impartial' people. Of 7,000 people invited, the 1,000 who expressed interest were whittled down to a broad demographic group of 43 who meet twice/month to provide advice. The Council is not bound to the recommendations of the citizens jury, although hope remains high that much of what they recommend will be incorporated in the plan.

The Speaker of the House of Commons in the British Parliament, John Bercow, has commissioned a report identifying the potential for increased application of 'digital' democracy in the UK Parliament. He states his objective is nothing less than Parliament version 2.0. The review is considering potential innovations including online voting, e-dialogue between representatives and those they represent, increased interconnectedness in areas including scrutiny, and increasing the flexibility of debate.

The considerable alternative models summarised above have their various advantages and disadvantages, but overall confirm the opportunities available to enhance the current Australian democratic process. The key concern of any alternative model is that they avoid becoming compromised by vested interests.

Becoming a more effective, efficient democracy is the most important emphasis we can have. As Horne expressed it, we need "a new and relevant sense of reorientation and self-definition", "some new sense of identity". Even back when 'The Lucky Country' was written and reprised, Horne recognised the need for process reform[cxliv] "… but combining a pragmatic style with a workable vision of the future now escapes our political leaders even more direly than it did at the end of the Age of Menzies, speaks to framework as much or more than it does to leadership."

While such suggestions are momentous and sweeping, they enable us to place greater emphasis on the long term, which is where our attention should be, and enable government to be more scrupulously held accountable for outcomes.

# 15. A Sustained Focus on Productivity is Vital

*"To be an investor you must be a believer in a better tomorrow." (Benjamin Graham)*

According to an Australian Infrastructure Audit[cxlv], "Australia's multifactor productivity growth – the rate at which the economy turns labour and capital inputs into outputs – has slowed considerably since 2000." Lowe[cxlvi] makes the salient point that on a finite planet, the concept that we can grow forever is delusional, remarking that "the present situation in which decision-makers ignore both the short term problems that are being directly caused by growth (increasing unemployment, reduced equality and environmental damage) and the long-term problem that growth cannot continue forever in a finite system."

The golden era has passed where government-run companies such as Commonwealth Serum Laboratories (now the publicly listed CSL) were spun out of government to begin a new life as innovative market leaders. Our national quest is now to find the next generation of CSL's, to 'mother' them through infancy, and teach and nourish them to thrive and prosper as grown-ups in the big, wide world.

Australia's investor class has not helped to drive productivity or innovation, with a disproportional diet for juicy dividends punishing those companies which instead seek to invest in their futures, choosing to delay gratification of their shareholders. It has instead spread the disease of short-termism to business, a contagion which ignores the need for developing sustainable long term value.

In business, my experience is that, typically any win which is gained relatively easily is more likely to be lost easily, while those gains hard fought for are also those which more often stand the test of time. We are, generally, believers in a better tomorrow; we have to set the stage for it though, and the stage is a return to long term thinking and sustainable productivity improvement, providing a solid foundation for growth.

### 'Think Global, Act Local'

Productivity develops new meaning as we realise that infinite growth in a finite world is a non-sensical proposition. Al Gore and the Pope have variously warned us about the impact we are having on the degradation of the planet. One of the consequences of the human tendency towards self-improvement is that we have come to act as "masters, consumers, ruthless exploiters, unable to set limits to our immediate needs."[cxlvii] "Never have we so hurt and mistreated our common home as we have in the past two hundred years." There are grave consequences to unending growth; therefore as we consider alternatives to growth, productivity takes on new meaning.

As various commentators have noted (including the Deputy Governor of the Reserve Bank)[cxlviii], we need to analyse and absorb the core issues behind what is inhibiting our productivity, and actively address these inhibitors, which include lack of innovation (finding better ways of doing things rather than simply improving technology), encouraging & rewarding 'appropriate' risk (likely through the tax system), increasing levels of competition, education and infrastructure. Much of this review must be considered through the lens of government, which needs to be transformed to meet our requirements in the modern era, and to become 'match fit' to reduce the cost to serve, and improve service to the people of Australia.

Never has the expression 'think global, act local' been more meaningful than in nurturing Australia's exposure on the world stage. The nation is not structured appropriately to empower Australian business to succeed globally, and while it doesn't stop commercial global expansion, it does not help the way it can. Government isn't there when it needs to be, and can't get out of the way when it should. The administrative burden on business continues to be excessive, particularly on small business. At state level, it often seems that our states are competing with each other for business on overseas trade missions. Filtering our commercial agenda globally is best done federally, however leveraging off our strengths is likely best done at the 'local council' level where infrastructure, capabilities, and aggregation are best managed to achieve successful local outcomes. Countries such as Israel have developed a cohesive platform to support the global expansion of

Israeli businesses, highlighting the advantages for global penetration in established and innovative segments by 'localising' their approach to market.

Having said this, it is vital that Australia treads its own path to innovating & commercialising global investment. It is also vital that we develop a pathway to continuous productivity improvement locally, ensuring that we continue to be cost competitive in the areas business and the government can control. While we have no control over currency fluctuations, ensuring absolute cost across the supply chain is competitive ensures we are best placed to guarantee a prosperous future for those companies seeking to expand offshore.

The graph below (refer figure 18) highlights starkly the Australian productivity 'problem'. Income has grown at a higher rate than productivity, highlighting a reduction in global competitiveness. The cost of this graph is jobs, which go offshore where the work can be done more productively. The graph, as does our poor OECD ranking for labour market efficiency, highlights that industrial relations reform is inevitable – it is a matter of what, when and how.

**Productivity is Almost Everything**

Any expert on economics will argue that improving productivity is the basis for improving the standard of living. Progressive unions understand this trend, and are proactively working with similarly progressive employers to maintain competitiveness. Other, more traditional unions, who fail to understand the broader context for their stakeholders, are actively obstructing productivity improvement, which in turn impacts our international competitiveness. A reduction in our international competitiveness will, in time, lead to a deterioration in the standard of living of Australians.

Paul Carvalho[cxlix] also quotes Paul Krugman in outlining the outcomes of the Harper Review into productivity. Bluescope is a recent case study of a company which has tackled the productivity issue head on, with help from its workforce, the unions, and government, to keep the Port Kembla steelworks open, when it appeared destined to close, keeping jobs which would have been exported in Australia.

An investment in innovation should not be seen in isolation as the required medicine for budget repair. As investors will remind us, an investment in innovation or future technology requires patient capital; the road to positive cashflow (and therefore input to tax coffers) from these investments typically takes considerable time. It will not help our current deficit position. It nonetheless needs to be done. Both nationally though, as in organisations, supporting innovation is one thing; establishing a culture of sustained innovation is quite another step.

The Global Innovation Index 2015 concludes, "Countries attempting to achieve national innovation success need to envision a four-level pyramid as the path to prosperity that is based on key framework conditions; these

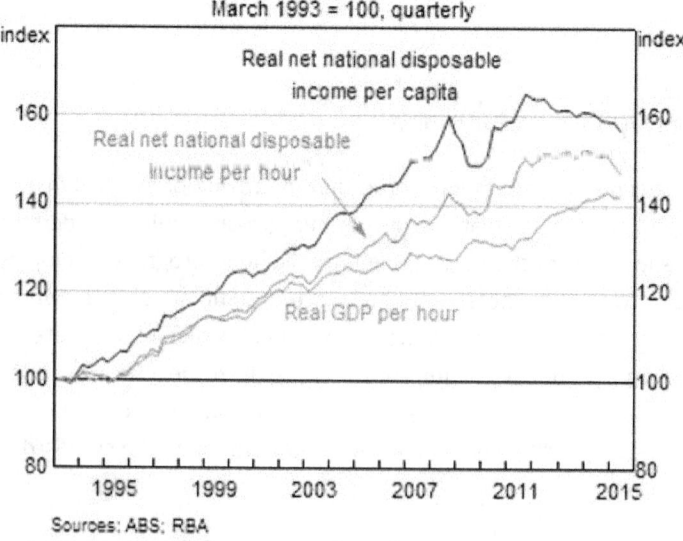

Figure 18 - Graph from 'Aussie Productivity needs to Grow', highlighting that income is growing faster than GDP. Chris Caton, www.livewiremarkets.com

support an effective tax, trade, and investment environment; these in turn support key factor inputs; and finally, at the top of the pyramid, is a group of innovation and productivity policies." While Australia generally performs well across these areas, we have more to do to develop our tax, and investment environments, and require a clear narrative underpinning a culture that is more invested in productivity and innovation, including the development of a more aptly skilled workforce and the development of an 'innovation ecosystem' along the lines of Silicon Valley.

Anecdotal data collated by the McKell Institute for their report into productivity[cl] notes that Australia has lagged OECD 24 nation productivity in every decade since the 1960's with the exception of the 1990's, highlighting that productivity improvement is not the responsibility of government alone, but business as well.

Further analysis across industry sectors between 1995-'96 and 2005-'06 (refer below, figure 19) highlights that some industries outperformed in production gross value terms, with construction, property and communication standing out in terms of growth (contribution to GDP).

Tellingly, the ABS data highlights mining and power as the two poorest areas in terms of GDP improvement. With the benefit of hindsight, had we focused more sharply on improving GDP performance in these two categories, we could well have been better placed to weather the post mining boom period. GDP performance of the power sector is crucial, as it is a core cost input to other industries; US GDP performance in power over the same period was significantly higher, providing an important contribution to improved economic performance in that country, and improved competitiveness as a cost input to production. The energy market is a clear example of a competitive infrastructure services market; the government should be actively seeking to completely exit such markets, allowing the market to more commercially manage the supply/demand dynamic. The national energy market remains a lagging work-in-progress.

Poor productivity is undoubtedly our greatest current barrier to progress. The OECD ranking of nations in terms of global competitiveness ranks Australia 56 from 144 nations in terms of Labour Market Efficiency, far and

## PRODUCTION AND GDP(a)(b)

|  | 1995-96 $m | 2005-06 $m | Change |
|---|---|---|---|
| Agriculture, forestry and fishing | 20,455 | 28,151 | 37.6% |
| Mining | 38,275 | 45,000 | 17.6% |
| Manufacturing | 82,366 | 96,012 | 16.6% |
| Electricity, gas and water supply | 18,271 | 20,549 | 12.5% |
| Construction | 34,829 | 61,644 | 77.0% |
| Wholesale trade | 30,919 | 44,886 | 45.2% |
| Retail trade | 35,891 | 53,242 | 48.3% |
| Accommodation, cafes and restaurants | 13,177 | 20,204 | 53.3% |
| Transport and storage | 28,686 | 42,037 | 46.5% |
| Communication services | 13,700 | 25,331 | 84.9% |
| Finance and insurance | 44,142 | 65,883 | 49.2% |
| Property and business services(c) | 65,735 | 108,434 | 65.0% |
| Government administration and defence | 28,069 | 35,195 | 25.4% |
| Education | 31,732 | 38,556 | 21.5% |
| Health and community services | 37,266 | 55,455 | 48.8% |
| Cultural and recreational services | 9,209 | 13,506 | 46.7% |
| Personal and other services | 12,455 | 17,686 | 42.0% |
| Gross domestic product | 647,660 | 921,747 | 42.3% |

*Figure 19 - Industry Gross Value by Industry Sector (source: Australian Bureau of Statistics (red, below trend; green, above trend added by author)*

away our worst ranking across the 12 pillars rated. In fact, in terms of Flexibility, a sub-header in this category, we were ranked 114 from 144 nations, a sobering perspective when ranked lower than some third world countries included in the OECD rating.

Government has to ensure it is directing support and funding (preferably indirectly or conditionally) towards industries of the future rather than those of the past. Porter's view is that "Government's proper role is as a catalyst and challenger; it is to encourage—or even push—companies to raise their aspirations and move to higher levels of competitive performance", although this is often difficult and counter to the shorter term expectations of stock markets. "Government cannot create competitive industries; only companies can do that", however Government can assist powerfully to expedite global penetration. "Government policies that succeed are those that create an environment in which companies can gain competitive advantage rather than those that involve government directly in the process, except in nations early in the development process. It is an indirect, rather than a direct, role."

**Go for Growth**

If we embark on a growth agenda, that agenda must be carefully targeted to ensure sustainability. Growth for strategic reason, rather than growth for the sake of it. As the papal encyclical notes, "the pace of consumption, waste and environmental change has so stretched the planet's capacity that our contemporary lifestyle, unsustainable as it is, can only precipitate catastrophe."[cli] The type of growth we seek going forward is important to ensure we don't repeat the mistakes of our recent past.

Our key investment therefore has to be spent towards enhancing our growth industries of the future, which will in turn improve productivity, which will in turn underpin further appropriate growth. That is the type of momentum Collins refers to as momentum on the flywheel. Energy, retail shopping hours, coastal shipping – these are areas where a focus on productivity will increase competitiveness, and provide a more immediate return on investment. Appendix 2 outlines the key recommendations coming out of the Harper review into productivity. All are eminently sensible and require a focused effort to implement.

One piece of investment advice imparted on me at some stage seems to apply to the way we manage our economy and investment going forward. When I at one point considered yet another poor investment, I was told, "water your flowers, not your weeds". It seemed like apt advice to me, and it seems an apt approach for governments in their approach to investment. This is, of course, aside from our social obligations, which must be upheld, and subject to the most rigorous governance. Ensuring that the demand for positions is broadly matched to the supply of graduates will ensure we are indeed watering our flowers rather than our weeds.

Deft strategy will outline our engines of growth & prosperity going forward; long term planning will ensure we provide national advantage to those industries of the future. We have to be honest about those industries which will contribute less in future, having spent considerably in the past on propping up dying industries whereas our focus should be on the up & coming growth sectors. You will note automotive production is not amongst this list (much of Ruthven's earlier estimate of $11 billion spent on sunset industries went towards the automotive industry); funding which could have been devoted to developing jobs in the nominated growth industries below.

Our strategy must encourage those businesses reflecting the future with the opportunity to develop the capabilities needed to sustainably compete on the world stage. Australia has, in recent times, devoted excessive resource to its weeds rather than its new growth, the automotive industry being a prime example.

Deloitte has identified the top 25 Industries it believes will pave the way for Australian prosperity in years to come (refer figure 20). While some of these industries are mature industries, and others may be in the 'doghouse' at the moment due to commodity prices and global demand, there is little doubt there are strong, long term opportunities across all these sectors for Australia. While these industries are not a substitute for the wealth provided by mining, they offer significant opportunity for Australia to diversify its industrial base.

Some of the industries above are in their infancy from a market perspective. For example, preventative health and wellness, despite being a relatively new business segment has created enormous growth for Australian businesses based on burgeoning Chinese demand. We need to ensure the sustainability of long run future markets by allocating priority in terms of infrastructure and investment support to enhance those capabilities which underpin these industries.

| | | |
|---|---|---|
| The Current Wave | 1. | Mining |
| The Next Wave – The Fantastic Five | 2. | Agribusiness |
| | 3. | Gas |
| | 4. | Tourism |
| | 5. | International education |
| | 6. | Wealth management |
| Future Waves – Slipstream Stars | 7. | ICT – Gateway to the stars |
| | 8. | Financing the Fantastic Five |
| | 9. | Clean coal |
| | 10. | Gas transport |
| | 11. | Food processing |
| Future Waves – Global Slivers | 12. | Disaster management & preparedness |
| | 13. | Next-gen solar |
| | 14. | Next-gen nuclear |
| | 15. | Medical research |
| | 16. | Ocean resources |
| Future waves – Local Heroes | 17. | Community & personal care |
| | 18. | Retirement living & leisure |
| | 19. | Reskilling an ageing workforce |
| | 20. | Financing the future |
| | 21. | Residential aged care |
| | 22. | Preventative health & wellness |
| | 23. | Digital delivery of health |
| | 24. | Private schooling |
| | 25. | Parcel delivery |

*Figure 20 – The Deloitte top 25 Australian industries of the future. Source: Deloitte Insights – 'Positioning for Prosperity? Catching the Next Wave.'*[clii]

Greater emphasis is required to identify the 'infrastructure' enablers for these industries & invest where we can establish competency & advantage for the nation. The Deloitte report goes on to identify 'Growth Pockets', many of which are aligned with the 'Fantastic Five', including clean coal, gas transport, ICT, food processing, disaster management, next generation energy (solar, nuclear & energy storage), medical research, ocean resources, community & personal care, retirement living & leisure, financing, residential aged care, preventative health & wellness, digital delivery of health, & parcel delivery as industries in which we should seek to compete favourably in the future.

Of course, to increase productivity, a sustained focus on our education system is fundamental. One of the arguable barriers to establishing formal national standards is the choke hold on education maintained by state governments. However, even they must agree that a national uniform system which allows for local differences in curriculum provides the optimal base for an effective system of education. A return to a focus on practical skills, and increased assimilation between high school and TAFE college would also ensure we are preparing our children for careers which match our national skills requirements. The ability to match future vocational supply and demand has been a major failing of our education system.

One of the 'big ideas' to come from the 2020 Summit was that we systemically invest in an Asian education and residency for tens of thousands of young Australians, ensuring that we are more connected within our local region. Improving the multi-lingual and cross-cultural capacity of Australians was seen as integral to our development.

**Advice from Porter – Governing Growth**

Porter queries how certain companies based in certain nations are capable of consistent innovation, ruthlessly pursuing improvement, and seeking an ever more sophisticated source of competitive advantage, able to overcome the substantial barriers to change and innovation that so often accompany success. He concludes that "the answer lies in four broad attributes of a nation, attributes that individually and as a system constitute what he refers to as the 'diamond of national advantage', the playing field that each nation establishes and operates for its industries. Porter nominates these attributes as:

1. *Factor Conditions* – Porter refers here to production, such as skilled labour, natural resources, and infrastructure, and capital which determine trade flows. He notes that "nations succeed in industries where they are particularly good at factor creation", citing the examples of Denmark, which has two hospitals that concentrate in studying and treating diabetes, and hold a world-leading export position in insulin, and Holland, which has premier research institutes in the cultivation,

packaging, and shipping of flowers, maintaining an export leadership position.

2. *Demand Conditions.* The nature of domestic demand for the industry's product or service, including the sophistication of buyers, who provide foresight into advanced customer needs, pressuring companies to meet high standards. Demand conditions provide advantages by forcing companies to respond to tough challenges.

3. *Related and Supporting Industries.* The presence or absence in a nation of supporting industries which are internationally competitive, providing supply chain efficiency.

4. *Firm Strategy, Structure, and Rivalry.* The conditions in the nation governing how companies are created, organized, and managed, as well as the nature of domestic rivalry.

Developing strengths in these factors are the markers of a long term strategy supporting businesses of our future which enable those businesses to compete globally, as is supporting network infrastructure.

The Chinese economy going forward appears to be reflecting the growing pains of transitioning from a corrupt, extractive communist system to a more inclusive, socially conscious oligarchy. This massive change has been managed deftly to date, however stalling growth reinforces the need for restructure of core Chinese institutions. With a focused will, and some luck, China is repositioning itself for a prosperous future, on which Australia can ride, albeit it may well not be in the industries eg. supply of minerals that dominate trade with China today. A shift towards greater democracy in China will unlock the resources devoted to maintaining order, and enable China to take off on its next tailwind of growth, of which Australia will be, if well positioned, a significant beneficiary across a broader range of products and services than the most recent boom.

China's burgeoning middle class, featuring well educated, financially mobile, and philosophical thinkers, will increasingly question their life purpose and goals, in turn pressuring Chinese institutions to reform to meet these higher aims. This development also provides the opportunity to expand our offer to

China to include our growth industries of the future, including services, agribusiness, education, technology, and logistics.

For business, as the world has globalised, competition is now greater than it has ever been. For our nation, the competitive levers are the same. Whether we like it or not, our progress as a nation depends on our ability to simultaneously co-operate and compete with other nations.

Catherine Livingstone, Chair of the Business Council of Australia, suggests that part of our global public relations problem is our institutional system, which sees states competing with each other internationally rather than working together to promote 'Brand Australia'.

While the CSIRO supports innovations getting to market, the Future Fund may consider putting up to 5% of FUM towards investment in 'up and coming' Australian business innovations across the growth industries identified above, to ensure the intellectual property is protected globally, and to enable our businesses to develop appropriate global models, just as Israel (a country with a population equivalent to New South Wales) has done to spark innovation. World class Australian technology in fields as diverse as data encryption, virtualization, battery technology, and social media, to name a few, are developing globally, however we fail to provide the environment needed, creating a vacuum filled by large, more proactive global investors. While it is a strategic mistake for products to enter markets like the US or Europe before they are ready, it is also a national cost for global entry to be delayed, enabling other competitors to develop first mover advantage.

The Australian Institute of Company Directors summarises its blueprint for growth[cliii] as below:

1. "Reforming national governance - Quality, long-term national decision-making is adversely impacted by short and variable federal parliamentary terms, an unrepresentative Senate and an ineffective Council of Australian Governments (COAG) process.
2. Fiscal sustainability - Fiscal sustainability is a vital national priority. Done well, tax reform can improve national prosperity and lift national revenues. The heavy lifting of fiscal repair, however, demands greater

attention on spending and efficiency. We propose both spending and tax reform targets.
3. Innovation and entrepreneurialism - Directors understand that innovation is essential to long-term growth. Policy continuity, consistency in focus, and a change in the regulatory settings that drive risk-aversion will build momentum on the innovation agenda.
4. Human capital - Directors know that an engaged, flexible and productive workforce is essential to drive growth. To meet the demands of a globally competitive workplace, and the changing expectations of working Australians and the community, we call for a national focus on participation, skills investment and more flexible workplace regulation.
5. National infrastructure - Improved infrastructure investment will underpin a more efficient and productive economy. Directors have consistently ranked increased infrastructure investment as the main long-term priority for government action."

As Argus points out, growth is the key to economic prosperity; growth in turn is achieved by new businesses starting up, along with growth in existing businesses. However, the amount of regulation and the complexity of the taxation system are inhibiting new business growth.

**A Call for Integrated Infrastructure Planning**

Jacob Saulwick, writing in October 2015 for the Sydney Morning Herald[cliv], was critical of the Baird government in NSW for not providing appropriate analysis or business cases for planned investment in New South Wales. Again, this seems more an issue of process than it does of government, given the jigsaw of funding sources across government and private enterprise, and the complexity of prioritising projects on a national platform.

The issue with investment, of course, is that there are so many vested interests, which only reassures me, like many Australians, that greater transparency (and accountability) is needed at a national level. What the public are seeking is an integrated national investment plan, with a template approach to analysis and business cases which enables all projects to be developed and evaluated in a uniform manner (as best practicable). This would then enable us to have a national priority list of projects which provides a framework for national debate & decision making.

The development of soli, accurate, uniform data across the nation is integral to integrated planning. While access to transport data has been a major driver of transport innovation in Sydney, anecdotal advice is that other cities (such as Melbourne) are not releasing data for fear of exposing poor performance levels. Vested interests destroy productivity and hinder a national approach.

The lack of an integrated investment plan has resulted in stop/start fiascos, best showcased by projects including Wesconnex (started then stopped at significant wasted cost to the taxpayer), and Brisbane Cross River Rail Tunnel (start, stop, start?), not to mention the opportunity cost lost in projects which didn't make it to the starting line.

The timely appeal by Johnathan Thurston for a new stadium in Townsville following the North Queensland Cowboys inaugural rugby league premiership win in 2015 highlighted the debacle in allocating capital between tiers of government. The Paluszcak government triumphantly got behind the stadium (a pre-election pledge of $100 million), then challenged the federal government to tip in the lion's share of the cost (understood to be approximately $300 million in total) without which the stadium is a white elephant. Without doubt a triumph for politics over rational investment decision making!

Jenny Stewart offers a considered view of our current reality with respect to investment in innovation.[clv] "The situation we are faced with today, with Australia still struggling to commercialise its research, is the result of many years of both policy neglect and policy mistakes. Doing good research is not enough. Without Australian-based firms that can take that research to the next stage, good ideas will either go offshore, or die out." Stewart cites internet businesses as a case in point – "nascent Australian businesses must go offshore to make the contacts, find the investors and recruit the engineers and marketers that they need. The ecosystem of locally-based companies, and the know-how that they nurture and develop over time, is lacking."

It will also require a substantial change in attitude for government to accept that Australian ingenuity can be utilised to improve the service and reduce the cost of service delivery, due to 'a belief (cemented into the public service) that any policy (such as supportive public purchasing) that assists an Australian firm to do anything at all is "protectionist".' If we are to create the factor conditions outlined by Porter, government is integral as an enabler and consumer of the products and services of these 'future' businesses, particularly in technology.

"Treasury is right about incentives. It is silly to think that incentives (such as tax concessions for research and development) will do the trick.' ... 'It is no accident that the two best-known technology-based companies to have originated in Australia – Cochlear and CSL – are in the medical field. There is public interest, a history of flexible government support, and a tradition of working across boundaries. We need these same ingredients in other fields."[clvi] Stewart comments that the focus needs to be on development of appropriate innovation policy and support systems – serious bipartisan commitment, underpinned by the network of contacts, mentoring and support needed to do the hard development and commercialisation yards.

Innovation though is just one plank of the investment requirement. We have to be investing to support our strategy and long term plans. Some of this investment will reap relatively quick dividends while other investments will take considerably longer to provide returns. For this reason, a template is needed to enable such investment to be tracked and assessed, which contributes to improved decisions later.

The imperative to enhance Australia's medium and long-term productivity performance becomes even more urgent if we are to continue to raise living standards in our nation. Strategy must account for a systemic lift in productivity, or our competitiveness will be at risk.

# Part C

# Regaining Momentum on the 'Flywheel' – The 'How'

# 16. Confronting the Brutal Facts

*"There are no facts, only interpretations." (Friedrich Nietzsche)*

For profound national change to occur, change has to happen first at the level of individuals. Ordinary Australians, politicians and voters alike, have to be prepared to change, and feel that change is happening. The power to reform governance in Australia will happen when the voice for change increases and resonates, and people who have determined on the need to change converge, resolute and allied in their desire for that change to occur. For the sustainability of such change to occur, individuality gives way to mutual interdependence.

Australians have proven to be outspoken and yet timid in their approach to high level change. This must change. Australian poet and self-described 'conservative anarchist' Harold Stewart commented that "all Australians are anarchists at heart",[clvii] and while this may be overreaching, it is our character to dive straight in to right a wrong when we see it, although politics and the modification of systems of governance tends to bring out reticent apathy in the electorate.

Reiterating the shortfall in healthcare in 2030 implied by Mike Baird (refer Chapter 6), Baird made the valid point that while our healthcare system is not perfect, we have the lowest spend among OECD nations (9.1% of GDP, compared to 17% in the United States)[clviii], to which Baird concluded "so no effort to manage cost will solve the long term issue. That is the brutal reality and the sort of discussion we have to have ... why are we letting this problem just roll on?"

It is these broad ranging, big subject, brutal reality conversations we have to have in parliament, through the media, and across society.

The notions we'll consider in the following chapters are basic to change management principles. They are, in the context of fundamental governance change, overly simplistic. With great frequency in the past however, such notions and concepts underlying change which are typically foundational to business have not been adequately considered by government to the detriment of good decisions executed poorly.

It is time to have substantive debate about the structure of the institutional systems we demand for the future, ensuring we maintain effective governance and sustainability of our core values of freedom and equality, but to take out the unnecessary 'lard' we've built up since colonisation and through and since federation.

Baird refers to 'the quadrella' as possible – increased revenue, reduced income tax, reduced corporate tax, and equitable outcomes for all. However, it is the conversations before this, aptly summing up our brutal reality, which lead to the development of a national narrative which enables this 'quadrella'.

**The Cathartic Impact of Brutal Honest Appraisal**

For substantive change to occur, a personal honesty and brutal confrontation of the facts will be required. This brutal confrontation will require a rigorous and consistent base of agreed data and evidence. As Tony Featherstone, John Brogden and other credible commentators have proposed, there is a desperate demand for a deeper conversation on the urgent need for reform. This confrontation of necessity includes the prerequisite for changes to our constitution, both at federal and state level.

Political correctness too often gets in the way of brutal honesty. Our Prime Minister is also chief cheerleader, however there needs to be a forum where we can honestly and candidly assess current state and outlook. We are either observing partisan 'sniping' or bad news washed under the carpet; neither is good for the psyche or the balance sheet.

Confronting the brutal facts of our current reality is one of the elements of good to great companies hypothesised by Jim Collins & his team. Our recent political culture has prevented our government from directly (ignoring both factional and partisan boundaries) agreeing the truth of our situation, which typically provides a self-evident platform for decisions which are in the national best interest to be taken. We are a high cost nation – a relatively small population, broadly spread, with high infrastructure and living standards. Unless we overcome the reality of our high cost with low/nil debt, smart infrastructure and productivity standards offsetting our labour cost impost, we cannot expect the windfall of the past to repeat itself.

These deeper conversations aren't happening, because the governance process to support such conversations is not in place. It would require a support framework where politicians were able to express their views freely without fear of retribution or payback; to hold a conscience vote without their views affecting their partisan or political standing. Communities and people have a right to be able to have a say in these conversations; again the governance framework fails to support such engagement currently. We will need to create a communal narrative which enables broad national agreement and engagement to that harsh reality. This agreement and engagement provides the impetus to tackle the issues head-on.

Let's be clear from the outset; this is not a question of competence or blame, but of brutal honesty in the national interest. In so many ways, politically speaking, we punch above our weight. We are a relatively small, geographically spread, young and diverse nation, yet we are constantly on the world stage, helping other nations in times of need. Nor is this about people or personalities. This is a focus on process at the highest, yet most fundamental level. Our current political culture, of partisan conflict, of disproportionate institutional influence, of ignoring 'red flags' don't provide the conditions for this brutal current reality to be assessed.

Change, although necessary, is hard, and will be resisted either by those with a vested interest in the status quo, and those who simply don't like change. And yet, Australians will value leadership which is brutally honest, if they can see perceive that change is in the nation's best interests.

One of the issues our short termism is causing is that we fail to accept that not all investments bear fruit in the short term. If we plant an olive tree or a macadamia tree now, we should not expect any harvest for five years, and optimal harvest a further three years. We cannot expect optimal returns on investment in the short term in many cases, although many such projects are deemed a failure if they don't meet pre-determined, and occasionally unrealistic, hurdles. We have to cut the cloth to fit the suit. Where appropriate, it is important that we take a long term view, which is why a mechanism for long term planning is so important in maintaining the public narrative of the immediate steps and the steps to follow.

## Corralling the Brutal Facts

There are some tenets which 'corral' these brutal facts:

**1. We drive the car; the car should not drive us**

If we view the economy as a car, we need to be clear we are in control even though there are factors which influence performance which are beyond our control. The road is full of good drivers, and not so good drivers. Good drivers are concentrating ahead, aware of situational factors, and taking into account what other drivers may do. Not so good drivers are not driving to the conditions, taking unreasonable risks, and involved in or causing accidents. The economy seems to be a driverless car, and we're not ready for that just yet!

One such example of allowing the car to drive us is our fascination for continuous opinion polling. Opinion polling, unsatisfactorily, rather than measuring opinion, has come to shape opinion. While such sampling provides a snapshot and satisfies the voyeuristic tendency of the electorate, it also drives short term behaviour and inhibits strategic decision making. The poll result, and how leaders respond to the result (there is only one poll that matters has never been less true unfortunately) becomes the news, which then influences future poll outcomes.

We have seen results in the past where a leader's popularity has reached new highs, then any tail-off in popularity (they are still very popular, just not quite as popular, because we don't want our politicians thinking they're popular!) unfairly impacts a still popular leader's ability to implement their agenda.

Polling is not helpful to our ability to implement long term plans through the emotional ebbs and flows in support those plans undoubtedly initiate. Leaders may be leading well, although not leading popularly – there is a difference which has fundamental outcomes for both those leaders and the people they lead.

The cost of polls in terms of leadership stability and the development of 'groupthink' outweigh their benefits. The polling process needs to be reconsidered so that it aids rather than inhibits decision making. Polling should be limited to periods, of say, no less than six months apart, in support of a long term agenda.

Rather than being driven by polling, we have the opportunity to base solid, long term decisions on the considerable data resources of the Australian Bureau of Statistics and the scenario planning capabilities of the Australian Research Council and Academy of Science (refer the Australia 2050 report on the Academy of Science website which identifies benefits and impacts of managing key levers including growth, migration and employment.

Just as we are driven by polling, we are also driven by the short termism of the media. For a long term agenda to be embraced, the media would need to be convinced to report the long game, rather than seek the limelight of media flashes which seem to dominate current headlines.

We need to ensure we are driving the car through better control on expenditure, and a better forecast of demand conditions which help us adjust proactively rather than reactively.

**2. The car is not operating optimally at the moment**

It is important we have a clear view of our current reality. Typically this is hard to do in our two party system, because each party is focused on outfoxing the other rather than confronting the national reality. In addition, both parties are concerned about not upsetting the vested interests which are aligned with them. Productivity is a tough subject for Labor because of its association with the unions; gay marriage is a tough subject for the LNP because of its association with the conservative right. Economic reform and reducing spending is an unpalatable subject for both parties, as their stakeholders will be affected, however it is nonetheless vital. As a result, conversations and decisions which should be straightforward become difficult. We have to diligently and honestly agree our current reality.

We are paying interest we should not have to pay because we have continuously spent more than we earned since Mr Rudd first came to power. It is simply unsustainable for us to expect our standard of living can be maintained while half of all households pay no net tax, while the nation incurs the transaction costs of collecting then returning funds to those same households.

It is sub-optimal that state governments spend beyond their means, place unreasonable demands on local government, and demand more funding from Federal Government – it is akin to driving in forward and reverse simultaneously, as ridiculous as that sounds.

In general terms, decision inertia has overtaken our governance systems in recent years. Every government position or decision is infinitely analysed by the media and vested interest groups, particularly those who lose from such a decision. This has created a stasis in our decision making, the consequences of such decisions becoming too difficult to follow through.

It is vital our governance systems become more inclusive, particularly when difficult decisions are being countenanced, engaging with citizens to provide some buy-in. While there will always be winners and losers, inclusion provides a more proactive forum to ensure decisions are taken, and that the reasons for the choices we make are understood.

We may be surprised by how inclusion will shape decision outcomes.

3. **To survive, a healthy organism evolves with its environment**

Standing still is the equivalent of back pedalling in the current, fast changing world. We have to move forward, to change with the times just to keep up.

Frankly recognising our issues at root cause is the first step. This is about having a desire to be better as a nation, having the confidence in ourselves to enable a direct & frank discussion to enable improvement. Such discussion has to be driven by solid data; Friedrich Nietzsche was insightful in conveying that even facts and data are open to interpretation.

Growth, for example, is being pedalled as a necessary economic outcome, however we have to realise that we cannot grow infinitely in a finite country on a finite planet. Evolving within our environment, directing our energy instead to developing growth in our regional centres and limiting further urbanisation in our major cities is surely more appropriate planning now than when our cities become too big.

When you consider the enormous changes which have occurred in the 115 years since the Constitution was passed, the Constitution needs to reflect our current and future environment, rather than be a relic of the past.

### 4. Simplicity and streamlining should be the standard for process reform

One feature of recent policy development is that the frameworks in which we operate appear to have become more complex and difficult to understand. Our health system is just one such example. Reform has to include a process view of whole of government products and services to minimise the duplication and wasted effort which currently characterises delivery.

What is incontrovertible is that where there is complexity, there is waste. Simplicity is required to deliver processes that are understood, which provide visibility, and avoid dark holes which harbour waste.

### The Peaks and Troughs of Change

The formation of a Governance Committee and Strategy and Long Term Planning Groups would trigger the commencement of this work. To establish strategy, and develop the narrative, and to manage change on a massive scale (as the Chinese are for example doing), the electorate needs to be managed through the stages of change.

The stages of change model (refer figure 21) reinforce the need for a strong strategic narrative, to support the various stages of change the national electorate would undoubtedly go through in such a large scale, long term institutional makeover. Unless we have a strong, direct, truthful narrative that people generally trust, such transformation is nigh on impossible to successfully implement.

The benefit of identifying and going after the 'low hanging fruit' is that it supports the narrative, sets and manages expectations, and braces the electorate for more fundamental reform.

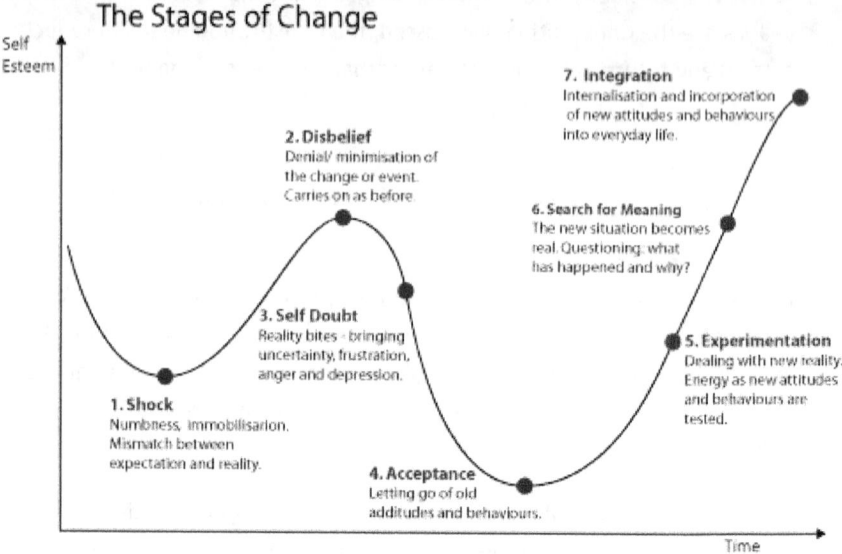

*Figure 21 – The stages of change, as purported by the behavioural change model, taking subjects of change from the point where they are unaware of, or deny the need for change, through doubt that they can embrace the change, to mechanical acceptance, an understanding of the benefits, and commitment to the change, enabling that change to be embedded.*

The stages of change are important because the very nature of such change is rooted in tradition and entrenched barriers. Vested interests, and those who would lose influence in a changed governance environment, those who are safe and protected under the current governance framework will act as barnacles, impeding any change.

### The Role of Government – Set the Scene and Get out of the Way

Porter has identified some simple principles governments should embrace to productively support and enhance international competitiveness:

"encourage change, promote domestic rivalry, stimulate innovation." We need to determine how well we actually follow these principles and where we can improve. Porter underpinned these principles with more specific policy approaches:

a) *'Focus on specialized factor creation.* Government has critical responsibilities for fundamentals like the primary and secondary education systems, basic national infrastructure, and research in areas of broad national concern such as health care.' While he acknowledges these factors do not typically produce competitive advantage, they provide the footing for future advantage. Porter nominates programs such as 'specialized apprenticeship programs, research efforts in universities connected with an industry, trade association activities, and, most important, the private investments of companies ultimately create the factors that will yield competitive advantage.' We would have a very interesting conversation in this country on apprenticeships.

b) *'Avoid intervening in factor and currency markets'*. Australia has wisely taken a 'hands-off' view of such intervention. Of course, a lower dollar supports export at the same time as it makes it more expensive for Australians to travel overseas – there are few winners besides successful currency traders.

c) *'Enforce strict product, safety, and environmental standards'*. Again, Australia has taken a proactive and often anticipatory approach to such standards, which generally stands our export products in high esteem overseas. However, our stance on the environment is seen internationally as an easing of our standards, which Porter labels counterproductive. Of concern here is that strict standards 'must be combined with a rapid and streamlined regulatory process that does not absorb resources and cause delays.'

d) *'Sharply limit direct cooperation among industry rivals'*. Porter notes the most pervasive global fad today is the call for 'cooperative research and industry consortia', based on the premise that rival independent research is wasteful and duplicative and enhances economies of scale. The United States, antitrust laws have been modified to allow more cooperative R&D while Europe is engaged in multi-country mega research and innovation projects.

e) *'Promote goals that lead to sustained investment'*. Government has a vital role in shaping the goals of investors, managers, and employees through policies. Government needs to set the scene for competitive, well governed enterprises, then get out of the way and allow them to flourish. Examples include regulation of capital markets, encouraging sustained investment in human skills, in innovation, and in physical assets, including tax incentives for long term gains being restricted to new investment in corporate equity and long-term capital gains incentives for superannuation and similar funds.

Porter also nominates other principles, including deregulate competition, enforce strong domestic antitrust policies, and reject managed trade'. In these areas, Australian competition policy is widely considered world class.

Australia has adopted an aggressive approach to opening up trade with a broad range of foreign nations. Like any business risk has to be managed by providing a trade footing across a broad range of industries to a broad portfolio of customers, avoiding excessive concentration in a particular segment or nation.

Maintaining impetus in research, innovation, new products and approaches is difficult from a change perspective, unless actively managed, whether by business or nation. We can't simply expect to invest and reap the benefits. Change will always be filtered by those who passively or hostilely resist development and change, so that new ideas can atrophy without the drivers being aware. It is then only a matter of time before aggressive competitors disrupt or overtake this work, such is the pace of change.

It is now just over seven years since the global financial crisis. Whereas before though we had 'money in the bank', higher interest rates and growing Chinese demand to buffer the crisis in Australia, those 'levers' are no longer there. If we were to face another significant world economic shock in coming years, our ability to weather it as a nation is questionable, constrained by higher public debt, less available investment to support stimulus and limited interest rate head room. Other factors, including a lower Australian dollar and reduced financing costs provide some cushion, however our budget position is perilous if we consider the possibility of another 'shock' before we are forecast to return to surplus. We are vulnerable, and typically vulnerability does not support effective decision making.

There are some profound and weighty topics which Parliament can embark on debate, including:

1. Workplace relations needs to be on a par with world's best practice, because it is not our intention to compete on wage rates with developing countries; we have to establish a plan to improve national productivity
2. Address directly a bloated government bureaucracy
3. Establishing a path to return to budget surplus, rather than vague forward numbers; we have no way to fund deficits other than debt or 'selling off the farm'
4. A tax system which imposes too many taxes inefficiently and inequitably. One option, raising the GST and reducing the tax rate would, on face value, provide a lift for business investment, however it is our expenditure which needs to be more assertively managed
5. Identifying priority infrastructure which will underpin growth in the industries we are targeting
6. Protect our inheritance by returning to a situation where developing youth skills and reskilling to meet future demand is valued to support our growth industries eg. apprenticeships
7. Preparing appropriately for an ageing demographic

We have to find structural and meaningful ways of having the community join the debate, not in back room focus groups, but in visible forums which support the development of the narrative.

**Barnacle Removal**

Transformation rather than reform, and on a scale not previously considered. Transformation requires education as the foundation for change. Transformation of foundational historical legacy systems such as party representation is warranted and necessary to develop a process we can have faith in. The development of values provides the basis for education at an individual level, upon which any institutional transformation can occur. The discussion on taxation reform has gone on for too long, with too little done about it, apart from significant noise, and smoothing around the edges. Tax reform in itself is a smaller part of the argument than people realise.

Without reform of the expenditure and budget frameworks, and revenue increase through tax reform will be 'gobbled up' by increased expenditure, because that is what has always happened. Apart from the Future Fund, we've not done enough to 'shock proof' and 'future proof' our economy.

Deep structural reform is needed, and whatever the result, there will be losers. Similarly, expenditure has to be cut, and there will be losers; so long as we are not marginalising groups in the population.

Directly and truthfully staging and holding a discussion with the Australian public early is paramount. While successive recent governments understood this needed to be done, none have done it well, which goes a long way to explaining why many 'big' ideas have fallen flat.

# 17. A True National Debate

*"I love argument, I love debate. I don't expect anyone just to sit there and agree with me, that's not their job." (Margaret Thatcher)*

*"Great leaders are almost always great simplifiers, who can cut through an argument, debate & doubt to offer a solution everybody can understand." (Colin Powell)*

While shareholders in a company have a number of ways of expressing activism, both individually and as a collective, if they disagree with some aspect of governance or performance in that company, it is more difficult for citizens to express their activism against government in a way that government is forced to take that activism into account. The ballot box is one way, however it is usually too late by then, and typically does not resolve the issue. Those wanting change, or to express an opinion can write a letter to the editor, stage a demonstration, or join GetUp!, however the opportunities for those who disagree with policy to air their views are limited for a democracy. We've lost the ability to stage a meaningful citizens' debate.

However, while activism provides a means of protesting the status quo and airing alternative views, it is alignment and unity which provides the most robust platform for change. The purpose of debate is to achieve alignment, and may just sometimes involve sectors of the community 'sucking it up'. Right now, the constant harping and sniping, divisive and pointless argument by minorities, the insistent bark of the media, and the inability to achieve consensus of any type by government, is impacting the effort to change.

Of course, discussion of such high level issues as equality, prosperity, and environment will be by nature highly challenged. Not only is the outcome Australians seek quite diverse, the complex and intersecting means taken to achieve such outcomes will also involve considerable debate. Consensus will take government considerably along the journey away from the current activist stance.

Similarly, long term planning will take on an increasingly global look as the interconnectedness of nations increases; the need to manage social media, environment, global migration and international fiscal levers means that action taken in one country now more than ever impacts other countries.

In the US, activism is being manifested in the positive poll results for Donald Trump and Bernie Sanders. Both are taking advantage of the electorate's desire for real change and political revolution. Whether the brand of change and revolution of either candidate, were they to reach the oval office, reflects what the community is really seeking remains to be seen. It highlights though that democracies require a mechanism to express and receive feedback to activist viewpoints. As Sanders asserted, 'it's time for real change'. It is a message voters relate to, and Australia is no different. The Xenophon Party will be a major upcoming recipient of citizen activism in action in Australia. Although the new party's platform is not entirely clear at this stage given its recent genesis, it will petition some of the middle ground to which the partisan system has failed to declare ownership.

Frank and rigorous debate converts opposition to understanding; from understanding can develop grudging support; from grudging support, advocacy can develop. This is the process of developing consensus. The danger, as Mr Turnbull has found in the first months of 2016 is that debate can be cast as indecision.

Debate ... strategy ... Are they too hard? Is, as Mark Latham poses, social democratic reform insoluble? Or does it simply pave the way for more unnecessary philosophical discussion? Natasha Stott Despoja asserts that 'parliament should be leading these debates, and we're not."[clix]

### Establish an Enduring Citizens' Forum

A lack of inclusion of citizens in the decision making process, particularly for core and difficult decisions, is a foundational failure of the current system. Including citizens in the decision making process offers greater social diversity, and provides a platform for buy-in before the decision is finalised rather than after the fact.

What might a meaningful citizen's debate look like? It could indeed look like the various summits we've held. With strategy development separated from strategy execution in a democratic makeover, the fear that such summits unduly cause politicians to raise then dash the hopes of democratic participants is managed more effectively. Informed opinion is placed ahead of political opinion, and notions raised at a citizens' forum for consideration by a strategy group are fed back to participants as for immediate consideration, deferral, or rejection according to alignment with the national strategy.

Debate has to be taken out of the hands of public servants and become 'politicus' – 'of citizens'. Debate has to lead to verifiable outcomes, not become a 'whingefest' for the disaffected. Debate could be best applied to identify and address some of the 'low hanging fruit' while the narrative and foundation for forum on more structural matters is developed.

Such an ongoing process will do more to capture the public's imagination and engagement, and separate the strategic from the superficial, providing a mechanism for the concerned public to influence government debate.

**Create the Need and Develop the Narrative for Constitutional Change**

A true national debate can only realistically occur if we can remove some of the traditional obstacles to meaningful government change, to create the environment of agility and flexibility to which Leinwand and Mainardi refer (Figure 14). The need for constitutional change is our highest priority. Inevitably, such a proposal raises concerns of the floodgates opening. While New Zealand and other nations without entrenched constitutions have lived in that environment, they have yet to see anarchy prevail. The closest New Zealand came to constitutional crisis was in 1984, following the election of the Fourth Labour Government. The incumbent Prime Minister Sir Rob Muldoon refused to implement the instructions of Prime Minister-elect David Lange to devalue the New Zealand dollar to head off a speculative run on the dollar. Muldoon relented three days later, resolving the crisis, under pressure from his Cabinet which threatened to install Deputy Prime Minister Jim McLay in his place. Following this event, the Constitution was reviewed and the Constitution Act introduced the following year.

New Zealand has since passed the Citizens Initiated Referenda Act (1993), which allows for non-binding referendums on any issue should advocates submit a petition to Parliament signed by 10% of registered electors. In 1999, one such referendum was held, on the question of whether the number of Members of Parliament should be reduced from 120 to 99. Electors overwhelmingly voted in favour of the proposal, however to this day the proposal has never been implemented! The lack of implementation of referenda in New Zealand has led to calls for such referenda to be made binding on the government of the day, similar to the direct democracy seen in Switzerland. However, the Government has been resolutely against this idea.

The concept of seeking a referendum to simplify the mechanism for change is, though problematic and difficult, not without merit. While it is vital to ensure sound governance principles remain, we require decisive action; the presence of such a clamp reduces, and almost immobilises our desire and ability to implement appropriate, substantive change. If we can alter and simplify the mechanism to enact reform without pre-supposing how it might be used, and trust our governance framework to manage subsequent changes responsibly, it is reasonable to consider the merits of such a change in principle. Reducing the grasp the Constitution imposes over reform is the key debate we need to have, as it affects many of the changes proposed here.

An appropriate channel for enabling constitutional change is to develop a planning forum for constitutional change. In 2010, Prime Minister Gillard established a Referendum Panel to advise the nation on the best type of indigenous recognition in the Constitution. The Panel was effectively reconstituted by Prime Minister Turnbull in conjunction with Opposition Leader Bill Shorten in December 2015. The reconstitution of the Council provides a great opportunity for the Australian people to re-engage more generally with the evolution of our 115 year old Constitution. Brown[clx] noted the potential for wider constitutional reform in an article for The Drum in 2010 – "… there is a huge need for the Commonwealth Parliament to map out a larger process for how it plans to progress not just this (indigenous reform), but other reforms", noting specifically for federal government to be able to grant funding directly to local councils. As simple as this motion sounds (the addition of three words to the Constitution), it has failed to pass twice at referendum, due principally to a lack of bipartisan support, although Brown also notes that "Australians were clearly not persuaded that the change was important or worthwhile enough to be tampering with their foundational constitutional document."

Professor Brown reinforces the effort needed to "remind Australians about the role and content of their Constitution, and engage them in the development of the proposed change. There are also other basic changes to the Constitution that might be desirable in the short term - especially changes to promote and require cooperation between our levels of government." It is vital that we establish a system which is transparent and thorough, and ensures engagement, thereby building a level of trust in any potential change process undertaken.

Brown further reminds us of the underlying context "where a majority of Australians believe our federal system should also change much more fundamentally, in the longer term, to deliver a better system of government. So if Australians are presented with changes in the short term, they will presumably want to know that the proposals are not just random band aids for the sake of change, but going in a sensible direction."

A full contextual discussion of the need for constitutional change is timely, however the narrative for this discussion would have to clearly identify the reason, and possibly the urgency for change, while establishing an appropriate structure (perhaps along similar lines to the Referendum Council) with a broader remit and a greater opportunity to engage with interested citizens.

The great barrier to effective change is nearly always related to a failure to engage with an appropriate narrative reflecting the importance of change. Recent leaders have shown themselves to either underestimate the desire of Australians to have a conversation on key issues, or not being truly interested in what they have to say. For whatever reason, recent governments have not been able to converse with constituents, and have paid the price in popularity. The Turnbull government is up front engaging in conversation with the public at a high level in areas such as tax reform and innovation, and is receiving encouraging feedback. However, as the date of writing, they have not yet communicated a narrative to explain why change is necessary.

In a situation where approximately 50% positive to, or is lukewarm supportive of a change & the remaining 50% is lukewarm unsupportive or against change, it is extremely difficult to craft a narrative which provides sufficient impetus to underpin that change. One of the key issues in engineering change in government at the moment is that vested interests, typically representing small minorities protest disproportionately. Vested interests (for example the political faction or sector impacted) impede change, a key factor in the brake they have on productivity. And of course, not all change is popular even though it is often in our best collective interest, or even necessary despite a lack of popular support.

Niccolo Machiavelli[clxi] "believed that only a society in which conflict was allowed, was indeed part of the system ... tend to overshadow more controlled and homogenous nations." It seems though that we've taken the debate too far and allowed it to preclude effective decision making, because the safer road is often to do nothing or make cosmetic change.

Technology provides opportunities in ways beyond a vote every three years & satisfaction polling.

A true debate is one which holistically determines what is in the nation's best interests, and should limit the input of the 'special interest groups' and lobbyists referred to earlier, so that the result is a true national dialogue. Mancur Olson observed that the longer a democracy operated, the greater the likelihood that policy becomes influenced, and even driven by, special interest groups. Those that build their war chests of funding and influence develop even greater sway. The debate has to hear what vested interests have to say, but not preclude it from a different course of action if that action is found to be overwhelmingly in the national interest.

Providing an ongoing mechanism for debate which includes everyday Australians would separate our democracy from any other around the world. Both current and future generations must have the opportunity to openly and candidly debate what works and what does not work, unbridled by the constraints we now have, or a shackled view that we cannot improve. The ABC debate program Q&A has provided such a forum, although we need to do what we can to ensure it remains non-partisan, truly reflective of the populist view, and with a narrative based towards action.

The issue raised by Robert Gottliebsen[clxii] regarding infrastructure is really a structural issue with debate generally. "There is no real debate about infrastructure alternatives. For example, we are going to build a second Sydney airport, which will make Australia's largest city a travel nightmare. We don't consider a Melbourne and Sydney fast train as an energy-efficient alternative. We are talking about massive development in the north, which faces huge infrastructure issues. We don't consider moving the water south where there is infrastructure. We have endless state-federal squabbles over infrastructure. Thousands of public servants are employed in these useless debates."

A true national debate is not politicians seeing as many people in their electorates as possible around election time, or a once-a-year forum. It is an ongoing interactive debate, canvassing a broad range of opinions, distilled into strategies, which can then be translated into consistent policy and meaningful action. Social media provides a wonderful medium for this debate to occur, so long as debate canvasses broadly and not just special interest groups. Involvement also needs to see reward in the form of outcomes.

The disengagement of youth in the electoral system will be somewhat addressed by considering and enabling an earlier entry age for voters. If we are allowing our youth to drive at the age of sixteen for example, they have surely also earned the right at vote at that age.

**Alternative Citizen-Inclusive Models**

The internet and other communications technologies now provide new, formidable means of engaging citizens, and acquiring participation, feedback, and collaboration. Various alternative models of 'participative democracy' have been presented, which highlight the potential for greater mainstream (electorate) input into political decision making[clxiii], some of which have been summarised previously in Chapter 14.

Various models for democratic participation are being shown to be available and to work in other cities and nations. Paul Budde[clxiv] recently reported on an initiative from the Inter-American Development Bank (IADB), which in conjunction with a "well defined smart city process that allows citizens to participate in shaping the budget allocations, local tax revenue collection increases. In this way more funds are channelled to citizens' top priority services, and as a result citizen satisfaction with council services is measurably higher." However, Budde adds that the positive outcomes of such initiatives are "at risk in a silo-based government structure, where there are too many other new civic initiatives competing with the introduction of this holistic process and where implementation of the process may not be adequately supported by training and technical assistance for the staff", affirming that we have to get structure addressed, and the right people on and off the bus to ensure a supportive, learning environment is established.

Referring to the opportunity to resolve urgent economic issues from a 'smart holistic government approach', Budde nominates a number of key high-level elements that are critical for a smart government moving forward, including:

- "Creating a smart government (take down silos, adopt open government). ICT can help to create more horizontal structures, which are essential in the process of social and economic transformation.

- Breaking down these silos requires leadership from the top (the incoming Prime Minister has already indicated that he wants to get this message across to his colleagues and throughout the government departments). These silos result in outcomes including enabling a known paedophile in Western Australia to apply for and receive a blue card in Queensland.

- Establishing a stakeholders group of community and industry leaders (business, healthcare, education, community services, transport, energy, telecoms, etc). These people will have to be champions of the cause.

- Establishing a platform of businesses – they will need to implement the actual smart city services. Opening up more data sets will also increase business participation).

- Engaging with the people of Australia. This won't be too difficult for those people who are already digital natives, but it will be far more difficult to get the people on board who are going to be the losers in these transformation processes. Without equally good policies in place that include this section of the population the policies and strategies will still fail."

Government needs to develop a closer affinity with its stakeholders. Some countries, such as Canada have a Citizens Forum on Canada's Future (also known as the Spicer Commission), a mechanism for feedback and an earpiece for ordinary citizens. A similar forum in Australia was one of the 'ideas' suggested at the 2020 Summit. The Canadian Summit commenced about 25 years ago, a deliberate initiative to reach out to a disaffected electorate. Canadian citizens held the view that their anachronistic Senate should be dispensed with. The view of the Commission Chairman, Keith Spicer remains that the Senate should be replaced with a Constituents Assembly, a forum which the US and France have also used at stages on their road to improved democracy. While the Commission did not see the institutional change it sought, it became a lightning rod for attitudinal change among the electorate.

The 2020 Summit, in hindsight audacious in its timing and extraordinary in its scope, is the closest we have come to such a forum in Australia, albeit this was effectively a unique event, which it probably should not have been. Such a forum has merit in Australia as an ongoing form of democratic participation, so long as we clearly establish the objectives of such forum, their fit in the process of strategy development, and ensure we foster an environment protective of the national interest without vested, local or state parochialism being brought to bear. Attendees at the 2020 summit recall being 'bombarded' by lobbyists once their selection was made known. And, as for Canada, it may change the way we view our leadership and our governance system. Professor Davis noted the frustration that comes with citizenry influence in political debate.

The forum of narrative has to be more formal and scheduled. The budget speech is not sufficient or the most appropriate means of engaging with the community on high level issues, nor is it sufficiently proactive.

It is time the 'sacred cows' are openly debated, and their future questioned. The debate about the contribution of state government going forward has been raised but never pushed, and yet it remains a commonly held view.

The impact of vested interests percolates quietly in the background, but unless there is a controversy, they quietly continue to peddle their influence.

This is where ethics, values and governance play their part. As a nation, it is complex and difficult to achieve consensus. Values, ethics, a transparent governance process provide a platform for unity of sense of purpose. Planning rigour provides the necessary foresight and visibility to our expectations. United, we can achieve consensus on issues which would not be possible within our current institutional framework. Without values and ethics, effort becomes fragmented under stress. Strong, united, values based cultures will circle the wagons under duress, and fight the fight that needs to be fought. Weaker social cultures will be overrun in similar circumstances. This lack of attention to values, and poor modelling of values by politicians forms the basis of our mistrust of government & other large institutions.

**Change Through Politicians or Change Through People?**

Barbara Tuchman wrote, 'government remains the paramount area of folly because it is there that men seek power over others, only to lose it over themselves.'[clxv] Politicians are best placed to end this folly, before it overtakes them, as, for example, demagoguery is overtaking the US presidential elections. A bipartisan focus on reform is the most persuasive and effective means of wresting the political fly wheel forwards.

To enable such reform will require a pragmatism we have not seen in recent times, accompanied by a thawing in the cold relationship between politicians across both major parties. Politicians have in large part effectively lost power over themselves, over their ability to make decisions on conscience. In a change environment of significant complexity, only pragmatic self-analysis, coupled with a determination to break through the barrier of party politics will allow the most resilient of politicians to show the way, rebuilding bipartisan and electoral trust, to lay the foundation for systemic change.

Henry Kissinger conveyed the solitude and adversity involved in such change during a lecture series in Australia in November 1995.[clxvi] "The hardest problem for a leader is to take his society from where it is to where it has never been, and that is a lonely task. If he gets too far ahead of his people, he will be destroyed; if he is too cautious, problems will overwhelm him. How to find that middle ground is the overwhelming problem of politics. It is a problem I do not believe any society that I know has solved."

Should we see no signs of change from those in power, people power will increase in resonance, as people become more openly hostile and angry about the status quo, or blithely seek, America-like, a new 'champion' to rise from the ashes.

# 18. Grass Roots Transformation of our Core Institutions

*"A revolution is not a dinner party, or writing an essay, or painting a picture, or doing embroidery. It cannot be so refined, so leisurely & gentle, so temperate, kind, courteous, restrained & magnanimous." (Mao Zedong)*

Peter Beattie, former Premier of Queensland comments, "Australia now needs to either redefine or forge a new role for the states or abolish them."[clxvii] This is not to say that either a federated or unitary system is more suitable for Australia, rather a hybrid of either. Other former Premiers, such as Bob Carr, John Brumby and Geoff Gallop are defenders of State Governments. Bob Carr's assertion however that it would take a referendum, which would unlikely be unanimous, doesn't seem to provide enough reason not to hold it.

Unfortunately, change on this scale typically requires some galvanising force behind it. Crisis most readily galvanises change. Courageous leadership can galvanise change, as can social impetus, although courage and impetus in extreme measure is typically needed, particularly on the scale and complexity of country-level change.

Adrian Kay illustrates the potential for greater application of multi-level governance (MLG)[clxviii] in the federation, a system of 'continuous negotiation among nested governments'. Although MLG describes the current process, there is an opportunity to use this system to address the strategic relationship rather than tactical issues, thereby moving 'Commonwealth-State relations away from a zero-sum game. However, this is only an option if we come to the conclusion that we cannot govern without a third tier of government.

**First, the Foundations – Establish Urgency and Build an Alliance for Change**

...

We will not proceed beyond the first step unless there is a passionate and profound aspiration from a significant representative constituency for change to take place. Alternatively, profound change will be brought on by a crisis, be that another significant recession or a foundational constitutional or social crisis.

A 2014 survey of constitutional values conducted by Griffith University[clxix] found that only 63% of respondents believe the three tiered system of government works well, and 69% believe that democracy works well in Australia (compared with 82% satisfaction in 2010). 50% of respondents believed that intergovernmental collaboration does not work well. In surveying preferences for government structure twenty years out, only 25% preferred to retain the status quo (compared to 31% in 2008) while 72% of respondents suggested change was necessary. 41% of respondents were in favour of the establishment of a regional government structure.

Such figures support the view that a passionate aspiration for change can be established.

Returning to the simple principles outlined in Chapter 14, with a focus on performance and simplicity, a quiet, but profound, resilient & tough minded reform of our core institutions is required. Revolution, as implied by Mao, offers a new beginning. The downside cost of change is instability. Business has adapted to a competitive marketplace in a way that our core institutions have not been subjected to, managing this instability along the journey. While I am not promoting competition in our legal institutions for example, the imperative for business is to improve the quality and timeliness of service delivery while managing costs down, all in an environment of accountability. This imperative needs to be applied to our core institutions.

An alliance for change of this scale would comprise the engagement of a significant confederation of people and interests aligned for the national interest. This group provides the impetus for transformation, setting the stage, and influencing the growth of this 'coalition' (a different coalition!). This group would build the case for what needs to be done, and review the risks of proceeding, and not proceeding. They are the 'momentum leaders'.

However, given that political cycles are typically significantly longer than business cycles, getting the appropriate political infrastructure in place early is important. The Chinese revaluation of the yuan is, for example, a deliberate effort to improve the global competitiveness of Chinese products.

Four year terms for government, particularly federally, should be a high priority. Three years does not enable a political agenda to be sensibly implemented. Four years provides additional time for the sitting government to be proactive rather than responding to short deadlines. The saving of this extra year is one less election is one less election every 12 years, not to mention the boost to business. It is estimated that business investment decreases by approximately 5% in the year of an election due to uncertainty associated with a potential change of government.

However, four year terms is a band aid solution to the undeniable and formidable truth that a partisan approach to democratic government is not providing the direction that a dynamic modern society needs to ensure the stability of its plans to survive and align with the future. Now, more than ever, we need more to provide a prosperous path to the future. We must read and discern the signs of increasing electoral volatility, the increasing popularity of policy light demagogue electoral candidates, and the increasing and unreasonable demands being placed on leaders – the democratic framework is letting us down.

There is no better example than the inability to align key national systems, including education and health, which is directly created by the excessive influence of state systems on our national agenda. There is no reason we cannot continue to have local differences to meet local needs, however a national framework remains the simplest, most effective way of influencing both national education and health standards.

The critics of 'big', centralised government are ignoring how 'big' our government has become. It remains one of the major professions of growth in this country. Others will agree the benefits of devolving greater responsibility to a community council, rather than that power being dissipated by state governments as it is at present. Whatever the view of experts, there is undoubtedly a way of altering the balance of power to achieve more effective, more efficient government, with Federal government setting the strategy, key policy, and long term plans, and local government 'customising' these high level 'rules' to best effect locally, providing more decentralised local action where it is needed to deliver stronger, more inclusive societies.

Don Argus points out that the wheels of national effectiveness rely on efficiency in our social & justice systems. Any change to be agreed has to be considerate of this.

**Get Some Wins on the Board ...**

It sounds trite to contemplate getting some 'smallish' wins on the board, however building support and momentum is vital, and this comes with proven results and outcomes. Setting some short term objectives and meeting those objectives engenders trust, and prepares people for the longer journey ahead.

**... while Setting up to Tackle the Big Issues**

Not to suggest it is, but if Australia was a business, it would have undergone substantial transformation to reposition it for market changes. Layers of management would be cut, processes altered & enhanced, and departments restructured to manage service & cost. While this has been done, it is not the 'root & branch' reform that is needed to reposition our country to embark on the next generation of change, to take our place in the world as the confident (in fact cocky!) disruptive upstart we protest to be.

Just as security was a foundation for Federation, we now face a significant security threat which again requires us to look at how we are organised. A uniform national policing system, database, and threat alert processes are vital, but difficult to achieve with current technological infrastructure. Fundamentalist terrorism is here for the foreseeable future; we must enable ourselves the tools to fight this battle as effectively as we can. Unlike previous wars, this war is not country, race or even belief specific; it is therefore harder to battle than any previous war we have faced.

Many large corporations maintain internal continuous improvement teams. It would be worthwhile to discuss whether the government warrants a Productivity Office, which is responsible for driving change, reform, and innovation to achieve productivity improvement. I for one am sick of talking about the jargon of productivity improvement; unless we have a clear agenda to achieve and measure outcomes, we will continue, as Don Watson remarks, to treat "'productivity' much as we used to treat religious observance"[clxx].

# 19. Regaining Momentum on the 'Flywheel' – Discipline and the Dashboard

*"Greatness is not a function of circumstance. Greatness, it turns out, is largely a matter of conscious choice, and discipline." (Jim Collins)*

I understand it was former American football coach Leo 'Lou' Holtz who said, 'if you're not growing, you're dying'. This has been expressed alternatively, 'if you're not getting better, you're getting worse'. While I've always considered these sayings to be somewhat overstated in a commercial context, there is a lesson there for us as people, in business, and even possibly as a nation.

Terminology coined by Jim Collins has been unashamedly applied throughout this book, as it best describes the 'hard grind' needed, as opposed to the flashiness often associated with transformation. Collins extensively analysed and compared the characteristics of what he called 'Good to Great' companies with 'Comparison' companies. As stated previously, this is not intended to be a critique but rather a call to arms to become better as a nation; to go from 'good' to 'great'. The core skills needed in government to go from good to great is to establish a simple, clear agenda or strategy (make some conscious choices), and to maintain a disciplined focus on achieving it. Discipline, as Collins points out is not simply about disciplined action, it is disciplined thought preceding disciplined action.

Collins drafted a model to explain how great enterprises build-up, then break through. The 'flywheel' of change starts slowly, almost imperceptibly, builds momentum as the right people are put on the bus and initiate change, and alignment is created as people understand the need for change. Momentum builds over time as results become visible, and people become more engaged and energised (refer Figure 22).

This is not rocket science, although it is extremely complex in the scale of which we are discussing. This approach will yield far more reformative and productive results than the 'flip-flop' policy changes of the past. Collins describes going from good to great as appearing 'boring and pedestrian', which is a mark of the diligence and intensity which addresses risks before they are sensationalised by the media.

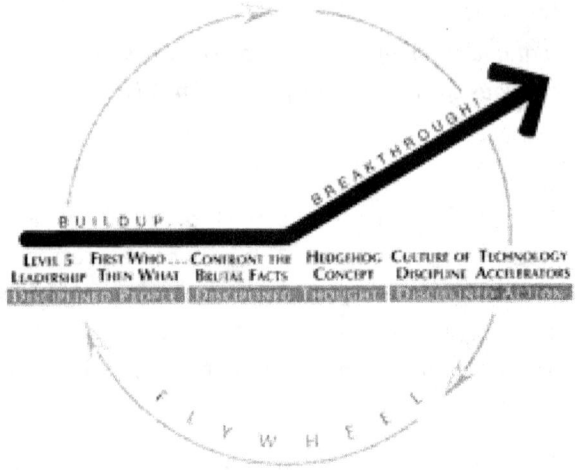

Figure 22 – Jim Collins 'Flywheel' model from 'Good to Great', illustrating that change is typically slow and grinding to start, momentum builds with persistence and a focus on discipline in the enterprise across these areas, which at some point reaches break through, where momentum becomes almost self-propelling.

The issue for Australia is regaining and maintaining momentum, which is one major reason why strategy development is separated from government. Handover of government though is a key inflection point for change of this scale. We are, it can be said, in a 'doom loop' for the moment, a trough in momentum, and the Australian challenge is to regain that momentum for our nation.

A targeted lift in performance, particularly on this scale, is years in the making; to be sustained, it has to be deliberately and carefully structured. There is a risk in trying to do too much, or in hastening quickly. This is where the development of a Strategy Group can provide the formulation and oversee the development of strategy.

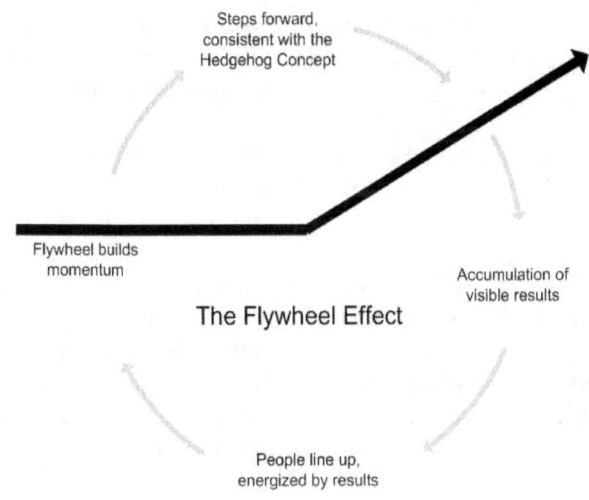

*Figure 23 – The momentum of the 'flywheel'. Momentum reaches the point where it becomes self-perpetuating; the strategy becomes less important as people become more aligned with the narrative for change. Source: 'Good to Great', Jim Collins*

Government's role would be to implement, and their re-election success would depend on their capability to contribute to strategy development and to execute strategy.

| Signs That You're on the Flywheel (Good to Great Companies) | Signs That You're in the Doom Loop (Comparison Companies) |
|---|---|
| Follow a pattern of build-up, leading to break through | Skip build-up and jump right to break through |
| Reach break through by an accumulation of steps, one after the other, turn by turn of the flywheel; feels like an organic evolutionary process | Implement big programs, radical change efforts, dramatic revolutions; chronic restructuring – always looking for a miracle moment or new saviour |

| | |
|---|---|
| Confront the brutal facts to see clearly what steps *must* be taken to build momentum | Embrace fads and engage in management hoopla, rather than confront the brutal facts |
| Attain *consistency* with a clear Hedgehog Concept, resolutely staying within the three circles | Demonstrate chronic *inconsistency* – lurching back and forth and straying far outside the three circles |
| Follow the pattern of disciplined people, disciplined thought, disciplined action | Jump right to action, without disciplined thought and without first getting the right people on the bus |
| Harness appropriate technologies to your Hedgehog Concept, to accelerate momentum | Run about like Chicken Little in reaction to technology change, fearful of being left behind |
| Maintain consistency over time; each generation builds on the work of previous generations; the flywheel continues to build momentum | Demonstrate inconsistency over time; each new leader brings a radical new path; the flywheel grinds to a halt, and the doom loop begins anew |

*Figure 24 – How to tell if you're on the flywheel or in the doom loop, as it applies to companies. Any institution, such as Government, has momentum and can be considered in the same way We require disciplined thought (strategy) and action (implementation of strategy) to regain momentum as a nation on the 'flywheel'. Source: 'Good to Great', Jim Collins*

The Harvard Business Review[clxxi] has identified the major reasons why transformation efforts fail:

1. 'Not establishing a great enough sense of urgency' – those people who have had involvement with government, and share concern about the status quo say we'll need a disaster or an emergency to create the urgency needed for change; let's aspire to this not being so;
2. 'Not creating a powerful enough guiding coalition' – partisanship has made agreement in the national interest more difficult to achieve. Bipartite agreement to constitutional change and reform would be necessary for change to proceed;

3. 'Lacking a vision' – self-evident, as is the sustainability of that vision;
4. 'Under-communicating the vision by a factor of ten' – an inability to design, prepare and cogently argue the narrative must be resolved; the economic imperative is apparent, but is being lost in the discussion of what type of change needs to occur. On their own, changes to GST, capital gains or family subsidies will not repair the budget black hole. A more encompassing narrative is needed;
5. 'Not removing obstacles to the new vision' – this reason accentuates the argument for constitutional change; it provides failing politicians with 'something to blame;
6. 'Not systematically planning for and creating short term wins' – the need for short term wins is either being lost in broader discussion, or not being communicated effectively. Even if we are slowing the burn rate through defined action, or making symbolic savings, this action needs to be communicated continually. How often do we hear a government claiming astronomical 'savings' without understanding the notional context to such statements;
7. 'Declaring victory too soon' – this is not a fight where victory can ever be declared, although declaring our conquests along the way is essential;
8. 'Not anchoring changes in the culture of the organisation' – institutional reforms such as a leadership development structure within parties and government which are anchored in a modern constitution will provide an improved foundation to have the 'right people on the bus' going forward.

Understanding and communicating these reasons will enable a transformation of government to be navigated with greater purpose, and preserve 'flywheel' momentum.

The August 2015 National Reform Summit identified four key take-outs, which, if progressed, would start the flywheel and significantly contribute to our national interest, while forming the basis of a national strategy:

- Higher quality national governance
- Tax reform
- National infrastructure plan
- Increased productivity & workplace participation

At a level or two below would be a clear plan of actionable steps, timings and responsibilities.  Again, this is oversimplifying the process of change, particularly on this scale, however our error in the past has been to create complexity as a deterrent to change.

We could have saved an enormous amount of creative energy and revisiting past ideas if, prior to the 2015 Summit, we had audited the ideas from the Rudd 2020 Summit, identified which of the 900 ideas had merit, and the stage of implementation of those ideas which had been determined to have merit, prioritised them, and accorded accountability to delegate and measure. Ah, but I forget – the 2020 Summit was an initiative of the Labor Party, whereas now the Liberal Party were holding the 2015 Summit! Again, counter-intuitive to common sense and reflecting the doom loop approach referred to by Collins.

Perhaps a Summit shouldn't be scheduled without the outcomes of past summits first being presented.  A regular strategy forum with the electorate would enable such 'indicators' to be aired and performance explained.


**Communicate Continually**

Peter Cosgrove summarises that "leadership uncommunicated is leadership unrequited".  Strong, effective narrative is vital in considering a change of such consequence.

Behind such institutional developments, a strategy & planning framework would measure and honestly appraise strategy status, and would include:

- At least annual review of actual v plan performance
- Rolling strategies & plans across 12 month, and 3 x 5 year (total 15 year) timeframes
- A scorecard highlighting performance

Simplifying the structure of government has benefits for the reporting of government activity and performance.  The bi-play between levels and functions of government reduces the accountability for performance of government across the board.  Just as many large organisations fail to structure to ensure accountability, government structure is a dis-enabler for performance.

Were we able to transform government to two levels, with (say) 145 national electorates, we would have a more credible platform to compare performance, even allowing for the regional and social differences. Picture the benefits of a clear set of performance reports for each electorate across an agreed range of financial, service, productivity, people and social indicators, produced regularly, which provides tangible and transparent data, which reinforces accountability and identifies performance issues.

Such devices reduce the mystique of government performance, and enable better decisions on a foundation of solid, clear data. We don't have that foundation in place at the moment to the extent we need to.

**A Non-partisan National Scorecard**

Again, simple is boring. One of the 'ideas' from the 2020 Summit was to develop a mechanism which allows the electorate to follow and understand progress, a 'national dashboard' of key performance indicators which would be published on a regular basis. This makes perfect sense to a businessperson who wants clarity of performance. Of course, numbers, and especially government numbers can be manipulated, and so it is important that the base is visible and stable. We have to look to measures that reflect our core goals and with which ordinary Australians have empathy.

The development of benchmarks or performance indicators though comes with a note of caution. Some years back, while consulting to a significant global company to enhance their cashflow, we were proudly shown a bonus system implemented to ensure 30 day payments were made on time to promise. In doing so, employees were paid a bonus if for 100% achievement of on time payment. What employees were doing however was paying some accounts as early as 25 days prior to scheduled payment to ensure their KPI was met. The KPI set inappropriate behaviour in place, and was in fact costing the company significantly. Benchmarks and performance indicators can be deceptive; the types of indicators and calculating mechanisms need to be thought through.

What would be helpful in uncovering some of the mystique of politics for the average Australian voter would be the establishment of a performance dashboard which highlights performance in an operational sense rather than a financial sense, and enables ordinary Australians to understand the trends which influence Australian society, and frames discussions around infrastructure, social support, etc. For one, I was surprised and disturbed to read in the papers recently that 800,000 Australian are on a disability pension. A further statistic is that only one in ten Australians uses public transport to get to work; more people walk to work than catch a bus. Melbourne's iconic trams carry four times as many people to work as Sydney's iconic ferries. Finally, despite a supposedly massive increase in education spending, Australia is now well behind for 15 year olds relative to other OECD nations ten years ago. Finally, three decades ago the median age of an Australian was 30.5, today it is 37.3 and in 2044 it is projected to be 40. These are 'indicators' which affect our way of life.

In the past, these have been or become political statements; Australians are looking for clear, untainted facts to understand trends and drive decisions. Published in a verifiable way, untainted by partisan politicking, where trends are clear. Having them in one place, published rather than simply available on an obscure website, will assist direct conversations based on facts.

# Part D

# Where to from Here – A Call to Disciplined Thought and Action

# 20. Where to from Here – A Call to Disciplined Thought and Action

*"Every journey starts with the first step" (Chinese proverb)*

*"Take time to deliberate, but when the time for action comes, stop thinking and go in." (Napoléon Bonaparte)*

The outcome of the 2016 Federal election is yet another sign that we cannot afford to ignore the potential leadership crisis developing. Voters don't know what they want and don't appear confident with the main alternatives, and are therefore voting in hope that the secondary tier of parties will fulfil their needs.

Prior to each Federal election, each government department prepares an incoming Government brief for both the Coalition (Blue book) and the ALP (Red book), offering candid advice on the challenges facing the nation, and some views on the impact of known priorities of the new government. The party that forms government receives their book; the other book is destroyed. Given the outcome at the 2016 which hung in the balance for some time afterwards, the make up of both books would have indeed made interesting reading.

Geoff Gallop, former Premier of Western Australia has fought the fight of the radical progressives for many years, having served in politics and understanding its limitations. Writing for the Griffith Review[clxxii], he cites the need to seek balance in reform, substantive but moderate. "We need a new radicalism that moves away from majoritarianism and centralism to one that emphasises the balance between individual rights, and state and federal power." In pressing for a national charter of rights, he states, "instead of aspirational nationalism, we need co-operative federalism".

To develop a specific approach in this book would be naïve, presumptuous, and contrary to the process view forwarded. We have to avoid the desire towards what Kim Williams refers to as 'slavish absolutism'. While this results in cries of indecisiveness from the opposition and the media, it is an inexorable part of the process of building engagement while gathering data, both of which are crucial to good decision making.

Nobody has the answers, and that's the point. The governance process we develop has to draw on the talent and diversity of our political class and, more importantly, our citizen class to engineer the best possible national outcome.

Fifteen years on, social commentator Hugh Mackay's research still rings true. He points to a communal disappointment, and even despair that the nation is falling short of its potential and failing to deal with serious issues. His greatest fear is "of division and fragmentation, breeding hostility, violence, anger and envy", a scenario he does not regard as impossible. Strategy and identity are the glue needed to avoid such an outcome.

The official closing statement of the National Reform Summit (NRS) held in August 2015 is that 'Reform is now urgent'. More urgent still is a clear pathway to reform. Our performance as a nation is the elephant in the room we don't seem to be able to discuss objectively and address comprehensively. A clear, deliberate, non-partisan path to achieving the phases of reform is necessary if we are to indeed manage a change of this magnitude, and clearly show that progress to the stakeholders, the Australian community. The NRS is indeed a first and small (but necessary) step "sought to build a consensus for reform and break the political deadlock that has increasingly frustrated policy change" (Gina Rushton, The Australian). Reform is, just as Nick Cater suggests, not just about improving national prosperity, but improving lives. Reform though is systemic.

While it would be simpler to formulate and argue in favour of big plans to fix what we have, it will be a series of boring, grinding strategies and actions which will facilitate budget repair and return our national flywheel to the momentum needed. It will require stability of strategic leadership, and the development of frameworks which ensure the most capable are developed for the mantle of leadership.

As Nick Cater observes[clxxiii], "The next steps are daunting. First, we must try to cut through the confusion to agree not just on the need for reform, but what reform might actually look like.

As ever in politics, such change relies on mature discussion and compromise. Our political leaders must re-engineer their approach to the art of politics, which, as Robert Menzies once said, is the art of persuasion. That doesn't change – it is the art of persuasion in the unified national interest, rather than partisan or other vested interests which must change. Such reform also relies on a more constructive and strategic media, and a more inclusive and informed electorate.

Of course, an agenda of this magnitude would take considerable time, perhaps ten years, likely more. It would require a capable Governor General, experienced in long term strategy and planning, and without a political agenda, to lead such a momentous programme. Handily, we have a wonderfully talented incumbent with substantial leadership and strategic skills. Are we game to consider the constitutional change required to initiate such a step change? Is Sir Peter Cosgrove, our current Governor General, one of our most inspiring and highly regarded leaders, who has commanded some of our greatest conflicts and crises with distinction up for this battle? More to the point, is our Parliament up to it?

Determining the decision process for large and tough decisions is a key step. The need for constitutional change to enable much of this reform is a key step. We then need to decide which brutal facts need to be confronted, which core premises we can find national, non-partisan or bi-partisan alliance on, and hold public debate to understand the rationale and implications of any views and decisions we may wish to take to forum.

One of the greatest issues is to ensure we can maintain a cohesive implementation agenda through governmental change; at election time, this may be as simple (although it never is!) as a statement from the incumbent government of the status of proposed reformist action, and a public debate resulting in joint commitment about how the reform plan will be continued if a change of government were to occur.

There are some simple rules which apply to change; they apply to change on this scale just as they do change of any scale. They're just a little more complex in change of this magnitude.

Progress is motivating and provides transparency. It enables effort and investment to be evaluated and shifted when necessary. The mechanism though needs to be visual data, charts and pictures; words provide hiding places.

Don't try to do too much at once. Pick some relatively easy projects, get them done, show they're done and the benefits gained, thereby building momentum for the next step. Better to do three things well than ten things badly.

**Anchoring Change**

Develop an ongoing narrative which supports the journey towards the values and strategy. Too much of our public communications and media reporting is disjointed. An interested electorate will appreciate simple, streamlined, integrated reporting aligned with key objectives.

Change itself works simultaneously from the top down and bottom up. If we were to move towards a simplified national structure, we need to be developing impetus at the local level, to build our local culture, identify what we are good at, and create still more social, integrated and prosperous local environments.

Australia has a lot to be thankful for; we have an enviable standard of living, we are (generally) considered well in the global pantheon as a stable, mature nation, a reasonable place to visit and invest.

The risks are huge, and are being related to us by journalists and other market commentators almost daily. They are being expressed by people in conversations in the street. The government can no longer afford to shrug its shoulders, continuing to work hard, but not coming to grips with the substantive structural change our country needs.

An agenda for change, regardless of whether it includes some or all of these ideas and initiatives, not to mention the many not considered here, is a momentous program which requires time. Ignoring the need for change in perpetuity, to establish agreed values, a forum for long term bipartisan planning, etc. will take as much as ten years, and will require leadership which can provide continuity and penetration over this extended period.

So what will it take? Firstly, it would require a non-partisan discussion devoid of politics to have a forthright discussion, to agree the brutal reality of our current situation – running low on cash, foreign investors nibbling away at our core assets, and a partisan system which doesn't allow us to move forward as we'd like. We need to agree we are in the 'doom loop'.

Once we've agreed as a nation, we are in the 'doom loop', we can start to plot a way out. This may involve some 'quick' fixes, some unpopular decisions, and some short term pain, however if we can develop momentum from disciplined, well considered action, we will start to build momentum.

We've not seen momentum in our economy, or indeed our nation, aside from the momentary 'sugar hit' to business when Turnbull was appointed Prime Minister, for quite a few years.

We need to specifically establish a structure which enables strategy and long term planning. If both major parties weren't so aggressively partisan, this could be structured as a tripartite process, however a nonpartisan process is likely more appropriate, at least in the short term.

Separately, we need to determine the collective benefit of agreeing our values and what we stand for as a country, and a process to continually review these principles so that they remain current.

If we are to undertake changes of national consequence, it will need to be resourced with the appropriate skill sets to enable the change and ensure governance is maintained. We will need the best and brightest involved from an oversight perspective, and utilise core skills and expertise in change management, governance, communications and organisational design.

We don't appear, to the outsider looking in, to have a review & continuous improvement process which can be applied to our core institutions. As former Queensland Premier, Campbell Newman will attest, a process to engineer institutional change which is not carefully considered will result in mishap. Continuous improvement needs to become an institutional mindset, as it is now a commercial mindset, whether it is applied to retention of intellectual property, improvement in process resulting in improved turnarounds or institutional outcomes, or in reduced cost and therefore lower imposition on our taxation base.

To reiterate at the risk of reader boredom, a change of this magnitude requires a disciplined, focused initiative. It is not a sudden change, but a grinding, continuous forward motion. We can ill afford to be apathetically indifferent or disconnected.

Australians are not shy of reform, but as several summit contributors noted, they need to know why reform is necessary, the consequences of not proceeding, and what form it may take. They need to be confident that it is being conducted in the national interest, and is not merely a sop to sectional interests. Reform is not just about fixing numbers, but improving the quality of our lives.

**Being the Lucky Country**

Kevin Rudd's election night victory speech was more notable than his concession speech some years later – optimistic in victory rather than chastened in defeat. He said, "Australia's long-term challenges demand a new consensus across our country. I want to put aside the old battles of the past … between business and unions … between growth and the environment … between federal and state, between public and private."

We need to find consensus in how we can, as a nation, 'put aside the old battles of the past'.

Phil Ruthven[clxxiv] notes that 2016 "… is an important year to start addressing the long malaise in our economy of nearly 10 years as a result of poor leadership, lack of reforms in industrial relations and taxation, insufficient innovation and patchy productivity. Nearly everybody knows this; it is a case of getting on with it."

The Pope though perhaps best contextualises the road we need to take; a concern for our fellow humans and the planet on which we live, rather than a single minded focus on prosperity - "A sense of deep communion with the rest of nature cannot be real if our hearts lack tenderness, compassion and concern for our fellow human beings."[clxxv]

But we've heard this all before. Liz Byrski made note some sixteen years ago that "to ignore the opportunities for review and enrichment offered by a new century would be a tragedy of neglect."[clxxvi] That tragedy continues to play itself out, sixteen years on.

Again, we should contemplate, what happens if we do nothing? Doing nothing (or not doing enough) is simply no longer a palatable option. We indeed need to throw open the windows of our democracy, and let a little fresh air in, to echo the words of Kevin Rudd at the opening of the 2020 Summit.

Our greatest fear, if we do nothing, is that we continue to evolve towards a more fragmented, more materialistic, less communal society. Mackay notes, "there is a sense of mutual obligation that lies at the heart of any coherent moral or ethical system. It evolves out of community experience'[clxxvii]. We are not, generally, 'functioning as the kinds of communities to which we actually want to belong; the kinds that develop the moral sense you get from living and working together, working out the tensions which always exist between, say, what I want and what you want.'

We also have to be easier on our politicians. They are overwhelmingly there for the public good rather than personal power. We are creating a risk averse leadership cadre through our inherent lack of trust. This in turn breeds politicians permanently on the defensive, when the best politicians are arguably those willing to take calculated risks for the greater good.

We have to overcome our fundamental dislike of our Prime Ministers. They have a tough job to do, and it is not best done trying to keep everyone happy. New Zealand has enjoyed the benefits of stability and economic reform despite a Prime Minister they are not in love with leading a minority government since 2008. We need to grow up and understand and accept what is truly in the national interest.

We are undeniably the lucky country, however we are equally at a significant junction in our development. We are prosperous, near the top of many global scorecards, and the envy of most other nations.

Our past counts correspondingly for much and for nothing as we navigate forward - it is what we do from here that matters. Australia has to position itself for its future, rather than allow the future to shape us, as has been occurring. We need to design the democracy of the future. It will require true introspection, bold ideas, disciplined debate, strong leadership, and intrepid, even audacious action to demand, design and instigate a progressive democratic framework. The cost is high, and the correct path arguable; what is indisputable is the legacy it delivers for generations to follow if we get it right.

Replete with symbolism, Australia must develop its competitive moat, develop momentum on the fly wheel, and actively return to the idealism of 'the lucky country' from which we have imperceptibly wavered, to deliver a nation which is better led, more caring and communal, focused with consensus on better outcomes for all Australians.

So … are we lions or lambs?

# 21. Summary of Some Suggested Ideas and Actions

*"However beautiful the strategy, you should occasionally look at the results."*
*(Winston Churchill)*

A true action plan, assigning timing and responsibilities would be not only presumptuous but impractical at this point. During my research for this book, I read from the many Summits held over recent years which uncovered many brilliant and effective ideas; it is almost impossible to decipher whether these notions and opinions became something more.

Having said that, there are some notions expressed here which may or may not reiterate ideas raised at these or other forums, which need to be further considered, and rejected or debated further. They are loosely headed to satisfy my need for organisation, but not in any specific execution order.

Among the tactical items discussed in this book:

| Values and Accountability | Develop a 'state of the union' style format for the PM to review progress and communicate planning priorities on at least an annual basis |
|---|---|
| | Review use of polling costs relative to benefits, and what polling is in the public interest |
| | Increase the level of education on citizenship and the Constitution in national schools |
| Strategy & Planning | Develop a long term non-partisan strategy and planning framework which enables public input and feedback, including separating strategy and long term planning from the government role of implementation |
| | Develop a training environment for politicians and 'would be' politicians |
| | Each portfolio to develop a 'strategy on a page' annually, which is publicly presented at the start of the year, and reviewed at the end of the year |
| | Implement a 'stakeholder management process, be it annual, bi-annual – what we've done well, what we need to do better, etc. |

|  |  |
|---|---|
| | A clear agenda & timeframe for tax reform |
| | Conduct an ongoing audit of summit outcomes to assess action taken to implement agreed 'good ideas' |
| | Establish future summits as a citizens' forum with input to the development of national strategy |
| | A clear plan for sustainable productivity improvement |
| | Develop a plan which empowers indigenous Australians to regain pride & self-esteem |
| | Develop & implement a national framework to support innovation |
| Institutional Reform | Broaden the remit of the Referendum Council to enable discussion across a range of constitutional change issues |
| | Aggregate councils in number & electoral boundaries to conform with federal seats |
| | A regular, transparent accounting an audit of political party funding |
| | Implement a government 'report card' |
| | Parliamentary reform (4 year terms is a (relatively) quick fix) |
| | Classify investments in terms of strategic contribution (per Chapter 6) |
| | Develop the same superannuation platform for public servants as the rest of the country |
| | A revised, updated expense process to be develop where all expenses are justified |
| | Convert to voting to a computerised process |
| | Tighten requirements for formation of political parties so that only those best suited to influence the public agenda, with appropriate governance in place have the opportunity to vie for our vote |
| | Transform towards an integrated national policing system |
| | Refining and digitising institutional processes, with particular focus on creating more uniform operating platforms, which increase digital security and institutional productivity |
| Measurement | Audit findings of previous summits to determine how many ideas have been implemented, and which others should be implemented or ignored |
| | Develop a comparative scorecard for regional councils, reported regularly, which records performance across a range of financial, social, service and people indicators |

# Appendix 1

World Economic Forum – Global Competitiveness Index 2014-'15 – Australia's Rankings by Sub-Category

| Category & Sub-Category | Global Ranking/144 | Score/7 |
|---|---|---|
| **Institutions** | 19 | 5.1 |
| Public Institutions | 20 | 5.0 |
| Private Institutions | 16 | 5.4 |
| **Infrastructure** | 20 | 5.6 |
| Transport Infrastructure | 19 | 5.2 |
| Energy & Telephony Infrastructure | 20 | 6.0 |
| **Macroeconomic Environment** | 30 | 5.6 |
| Government Budget Balance (% GDP) | 86 | -3.7 |
| Gross National Savings (% GDP) | 42 | 24.7 |
| Inflation (annual % change) | 1 | 2.5 |
| Government Debt (% GDP) | 31 | 28.8 |
| **Health & Primary Education** | 17 | 6.5 |
| Health | 12 | 6.9 |
| Primary Education | 18 | 6.0 |
| **Higher Education & Training** | 11 | 5.7 |
| Quantity of Education | 1 | 7.0 |
| Quality of Education | 19 | 5.2 |
| On-the-job training | 25 | 4.9 |
| **Goods Market Efficiency** | 29 | 4.8 |
| Competition | 29 | 5.0 |
| Quality of Demand Conditions[2] | 42 | 4.3 |
| **Labour Market Efficiency** | 56 | 4.3 |
| Flexibility[3] | 114 | 4.1 |
| Efficient Use of Talent[4] | 32 | 4.5 |

---

[2] Quality of Demand Conditions separately assessed by scoring Degree of customer orientation & Buyer sophistication

[3] Flexibility separately assessed by scoring Co-operation in labour/employer relations, Flexibility of wage determination, Hiring & firing practices, Redundancy costs & Effect of taxation on incentives to work. Australia ranked lowest v global peers on Flexibility of wage determination (132/144) & Hiring & firing practices (136/144)

[4] Efficient Use of Talent separately assessed by scoring Pay & productivity (125/144),

| | | |
|---|---|---|
| **Financial Market Development** | **6** | **5.4** |
| Efficiency | 20 | 4.5 |
| Trustworthiness & Confidence | 4 | 6.4 |
| **Technological Readiness** | **19** | **5.6** |
| Technological Adoption | 22 | 5.6 |
| ICT Use | 21 | 5.7 |
| **Market Size** | **18** | **5.1** |
| Domestic Market Size | 17 | 5.1 |
| Foreign Market Size | 32 | 5.4 |
| **Business Sophistication** | **28** | **4.7** |
| Local Supplier Quantity | 39 | 4.8 |
| Local Supplier Quality | 21 | 5.3 |
| State of Cluster Development | 43 | 4.2 |
| Nature of Competitive Advantage | 28 | 4.6 |
| Value Chain Breadth | 95 | 3.6 |
| Control of International Distribution | 56 | 4.1 |
| Production Process Sophistication | 29 | 4.9 |
| Extent of Marketing | 16 | 5.4 |
| Willingness to Delegate Authority | 17 | 4.9 |
| **Innovation** | **25** | **4.4** |
| Capacity for Innovation | 27 | 4.6 |
| Quality of Scientific Research Institutions | 9 | 5.8 |
| Company Spending on R&D | 39 | 3.6 |
| University-Industry Collaboration on R&D | 21 | 4.8 |
| Government Procurement of Advanced Technology Products | 73 | 3.4 |
| Availability of Scientists & Engineers | 27 | 4.7 |
| PCT Patent Applications (applications/million pop.) | 21 | 78.4 |

Notes: Rankings (some subjective) are applied (1-7) unless other specific measures have been specified.

# Appendix 2

Outcomes of the Harper Review (from Harper review: The key recommendations, Sydney Morning Herald, March 31, 2015)

| Area | Panel's view | Recommendations |
|---|---|---|
| Taxis & ride sharing | "Reform of taxi regulation in most jurisdictions is long overdue. Regulation limiting the number of taxi licences and preventing other services from competing with taxis has raised costs...and hindered the emergence of innovative passenger transport services." | Deregulating the limit on taxi licences and regulating to ensure "minimum standards" rather than hinder competition in the form of new ride-sharing services like Uber |
| Retail trading hours | "The growing use of the internet for retail purchases is undermining the original intent of restrictions on retail trading hours...deregulation of retail trading hours is overdue" | Immediately remove remaining restrictions on retail trading hours (with alcohol and gambling services treated separately) and limiting any restrictions to Good Friday, Christmas Day and ANZAC Day morning |
| Misuse of market power | "An effective provision to deal with unilateral anti-competitive conduct is a necessary part of the competition law." | Empowering smaller businesses to effectively combat, through legal avenues, large companies unfairly undermining competition |
| Pharmacies | "...ongoing regulation of pharmacy is justified and needs to remain in place. However, current regulations...impose costs on consumers." | Remove restrictions on where pharmacies can open and who can own them, replaced with rules ensuring access to quality medicines and advice |
| Parallel imports | "Parallel import restrictions are similar to other import restrictions (such as tariffs) in that they benefit local producers by shielding them from international competition. They are effectively an implicit tax on Australian consumers and businesses." | Restrictions should be immediately removed, making it easier for individuals or retailers to import certain products without needing to go through an authorised distributor or IP owner. This would see a dramatic drop in the price of some goods, including books and second-hand cars |

| Intellectual property | "an appropriate balance must be struck between encouraging widespread adoption of new productivity-enhancing techniques, processes and systems on the one hand, and fostering ideas and innovation on the other." | Productivity Commission to undertake a review of IP looking at technology and market developments and how IP should be considered in international trade agreements |
|---|---|---|
| Roads | "Reform of road pricing and provision should be a priority. Road reform is the least advanced of all transport modes and holds the greatest prospect for efficiency improvements..." | Governments should co-operate to implement more "cost-reflective" tolls and charges with new technologies, subject to independent oversight. Fuel tax and registration fees should be eased |
| Liquor & gambling | "Liquor retailing and gambling are two heavily regulated sectors of the economy. The risk of harm to individuals, families and communities from problem drinking and gambling is a clear justification for regulation...Reviews of these regulations should draw on evidence, including comparing competition and harm reduction outcomes" | The government review restrictions on supermarkets selling liquor |
| Planning & zoning | "Planning and zoning requirements can restrict competition by creating unnecessary barriers to entry. The regulations should encourage competition and not act to limit entry into a market." | Subject planning and zoning restrictions to a public interest test, making it easier for newer, smaller entrants. Make business zones as broad as possible |
| Coastal shipping | "reform of coastal shipping and aviation cabotage regulation should be a priority" | Restrictions on coastal shipping should be removed, unless it can be demonstrated that the benefits outweigh the costs and can only be achieved with regulation |
| Electricity & gas | "Energy sector reform remains important, since energy is a critical input to other sectors of | State and territory governments should apply the National Energy Retail Law, deregulate energy |

| | | |
|---|---|---|
| | the economy. Increasing competition in energy will help place downward pressure on energy prices to the benefit of consumers." | prices, transfer responsibility for reliability standards to a national framework and regulator |
| New competition policy body | "reinvigorating competition policy requires leadership from an institution specifically constituted for the purpose". | A new body called the Australian Council for Competition Policy should be established to advocate and drive reform and perform reviews of policy |

Read more: http://www.smh.com.au/federal-politics/political-news/harper-review-the-key-recommendations-20150331-1mc1x2.html#ixzz3sTK8zw1S

# Appendices, References and Endnotes

## References

'50 Political Classics', Tom Butler-Bowdon, Nicholas Brealey Publishing, 2015

'A Comparison of the Australian, British, and American Political Systems', R. (John) Kilcullen, Macquarie University, 1995, 2000

'A Conga Line of Suckholes', Mark Latham, 2006, Melbourne University Press

'An Open Letter to the New Prime Minister', Don Argus, The Australian, 19 September 2015

'Australia 2020 Summit Final Report, Department of Prime Minister and Cabinet, 2008

'Australia's Competitiveness – from Lucky Country to Competitive Country', Michael Enright & Richard Petty, John Wiley & Sons, 2013

'A Very Australian Conversation', General Peter Cosgrove, Boyer Lecture series, Harper Collins, 2009

'Battlelines', Tony Abbott, Melbourne University Publishing, 2009

'Beyond the Nadir of Political Leadership', Dr. Anne Tiernan, Griffith Review 51, Jan 2016

'Connecting Citizens to Legislative Deliberations: Public Engagement in Committees', Carolyn Hendriks and Adrian Kay, The Crawford School of Public Policy (ANU), Paper presented at 2015 Australian Political Studies Association (ASPA) Annual Conference, Canberra September 2015

'Creating a Strategy That Works', Paul Leinwand and Cesare Mainardi, strategy+business, February 3, 2016 / Spring 2016/ Issue 82, http://www.strategy-business.com/article/Creating-a-Strategy-That-Works

'Good to Great', Jim Collins, Random House, 2001

'Governance of the Nation: A Blueprint for Growth', Australian Institute of Company Directors, March 2016

'Great by Choice', Jim Collins & Morten T. Hansen, Random House Business Books, 2011

'Harvard Business Review on Change', President and Fellows of Harvard College, Harvard Business School Press, 1996

'In Our Time, The Issues and the People of our Century', Geoffrey Blainey, Information Australia, 1999

'In Search of Good Government', Phil Ruthven, Company Director Magazine, April 2015, p34-5

'Laudato Si': A Political Reading', Robert Manne, The Monthly, July 2015, www.themonthly.com.au/blog/robert-manne/2015/01/2015/1435708320/laudato-si-political-reading

'Lazarus Rising', John Howard, Harper Collins, 2013

'Liberty, equality, fraternity: redefining 'French' values in the wake of Charlie Hebdo', The Conversation, Ian Coller, January 13, 2015

'Negotiating our Future: Living Scenarios for Australia to 2050' Australian Academy of Science, science.org.au/Australia-2050, reprinted 2015

'Passion, People, Risk and Opportunity. The Case for Public Service leadership in Reforming the Federation', edited excerpt from the Garran Oration by The Hon. Mike Baird, Australian Journal of Public Administration, Vol 74, Issue 4, December 2015, Wiley

'Positioning for Prosperity? Catching the Next Wave', Deloitte, 2014

'Reforming Australia's Federal Framework: Priorities and Prospects', Anne Tiernan, Griffith University, Australian Journal of Public Administration, Vol 74, Issue 4, December 2015, Wiley

'Reform of the Federation: White Paper', Department of Prime Minister & Cabinet, Issues Paper 1, September 2014

'Ruling the Void: The Hollowing of Western Democracy', Peter Mair, Verso, 2013

https://stakeholdermanagement.wordpress.com/2015/10/10/governance-and-ethics/, Stakeholder Management Blog, Dr Lynda Bourne

'Ten Reasons Global Investors are Petrified of Australia', Robert Gottliebsen, The Australian, 30 September 2015

'The Adolescent Country, A Lowy Institute Paper', Peter Hartcher, Penguin

'The Australian Century; Political Struggle in the Building of a Nation', Robert Manne, Text Publishing, 1999

'The Australian Moment', George Megalogenis, Penguin Australia, February 2012

'The Best Australian Political Writing', edited by Tony Jones, Melbourne University Press, 2008

'The Best Australian Political Writing', edited by Eric Beecher, Melbourne University Press, 2009

'The Competitive Advantage of Nations', Michael E. Porter, Harvard Business Review, March 1990

'The Federal Budget is Hard to Fix but here are some Solutions', John Wanna, The Conversation, 11 November 2015

'The Global Innovation Index 2015: Effective Innovation Policies for Development', 2015, Cornell University, INSEAD, and WIPO, www.globalinnovationindex.org

'The Latham Diaries', Mark Latham, 2005, Melbourne University Press

'The Lucky Country? Reinventing Australia' Ian Lowe, UQ Press, 2016

'The Lucky Culture, The Rise of an Australian Ruling Class', Nick Cater, Harper Collins, 2013

'The Making of Australia', David Hill, Random House, 2014

'The Rise & Fall of Australia', Nick Bryant, Random House Australia, July 2014

'The Way Ahead', Liz Byrski, New Holland Publishers, 1998

'The Words that Made Australia', Robert Manne and Chris Feik, Black Inc. Agenda, 2012

'The World's 10 Best Governments', Forbes, 29 November 2012

'Time for Action', John Brogden, Company Director Magazine, August 2015, p4

'Understanding Productivity: Australia's Choice', Roy Green, Phillip Toner, Renu Argawal, The McKell Institute, November 2012

'United States: Where's the Strategy?', Andy Zelleke and Justin Talbot Zorn, The Diplomat, 5 February 2014

'Where is constitutional reform in Australia going?', Prof. A J Brown, Updated 9 Nov 2010, http://www.abc.net.au/news/2010-11-09/where_is_constitutional_reform_in_australia_going

'Why Nations Fail', Daron Acemoglu and James Robinson, Crown Publishing, 2012

## Endnotes

[i] from 'Crazy or Brave', Kate Legge, The Weekend Australian Magazine, April 2, 2016
[ii] per the AICD brochure 'Governance of the Nation: A Blueprint for Growth'
[iii] Introduction to 'The Best Political Writing', 2008
[iv] 'Politics', Aristotle 350BC
[v] 'The Lucky Culture and the Rise of an Australian Ruling Class', Nick Cater
[vi] 'Battlelines', Tony Abbott, 20??, p152
[vii] per the 2009 Boyer Lecture series
[viii] 'The Lowy Institute Poll 2015', Alex Oliver, http://www.lowyinstitute.org/files/final_2015_lowy_institute_poll
[ix] 'Vested Interests are Killing our Capitalist Democracy', Ross Garnaut, May 23 2016, The Australian Financial Review
[x] Comment from Professor Glyn Davis on ABC Radio National, 'Looking back at the 2020 summit', 25 August 2011, http://www.abc.net.au/radionational/programs/futuretense/2011-08-

25/2933372

[xi] per the 2009 Boyer Lecture series

[xii] 'An Open Letter to the New Prime Minister', Don Argus, The Australian, 19 September 2015

[xiii] per Cater 'The Lucky Culture and the Rise of an Australian Ruling Class'

[xiv] 'The Rise and Fall of Australia', Nick Bowen (57% on Kindle??)

[xv] 'Time for a 21st century system of government to go with our 21st century cabinet', John Brogden, Sydney Morning Herald, September 22, 2015

[xvi] 'Great Expectations: Government, Entitlement and an Angry Nation', Laura Tingle, Quarterly Essay 46, 2012

[xvii] '50 Political Classics', Tom Butler-Bowdon, p179

[xviii] '50 Politics Classics', Tom Butler-Bowdon, Nicholas Brealey Publishing, 2015, p9

[xix] 'Reforming Australia's Federal Framework: Priorities and Prospects'

[xx] 'Conversations with the Constitution: not just a piece of paper', Craven G., UNSW Press, Sydney, 2004, per 'Reform of the Federation: White Paper', PM&C, September 2014, https://federation.dpmc.gov.au/sites/default/files/issues-paper/issues_paper1_a_federation_for_our_future.pdf

[xxi] per Boyer Lecture series, 2009

[xxii] ' Triumph and Demise: The Broken promise of a Labor Generation', Paul Kelly, Melbourne University press, 2014

[xxiii] 'The Rise and Fall of Australia'

[xxiv] 'The Rise & Decline of Nations', Mancur Olson, as summarised in '50 Political Classics' p228

[xxv] 'In Search of Good Government', Phil Ruthven, Company Director, April 2015, p34

[xxvi] 2006, per Tiernan, 'Reforming Australia's Federal Framework: Priorities and Prospects'

[xxvii] http://lgam.wikidot.com/council-populations

[xxviii] 'The Rise and Fall of Australia'

[xxix] 'Fixing Funding in the Australian Federation: Issues and Options for State Tax Reform', Richard Eccleston and Helen Smith, University of Tasmania, Australian journal of Public Administration, Vol 74, Issue 4, December 2015

[xxx] Locke J., 'Two Treatises of Government and a Letter Concerning Toleration', Yale University Press, 2003

[xxxi] 'The Adolescent Country, A Lowy Institute Paper', Peter Hartcher, Penguin

[xxxii] Opening remark from Prime Minister Rudd at the 2020 Summit

[xxxiii] PM&C 2014:20, https://federation.dpmc.gov.au/issues-paper-1-federation-our-future, per Tiernan, 'Reforming Australia's Federal Framework: Priorities and Prospects'

[xxxiv] Australia 2020 Summit Final Report, Department of Prime Minister and

Cabinet, http://apo.org.au/files/Resource/2020_summit_report_full, page 1

[xxxv] Per 'The Best Australian Political Writing', 2008

[xxxvi] 'Diary', George Brandis, Spectator Australia, 9 January 2016, p5

[xxxvii] Dr Anne Tiernan, 'Reforming Australia's Federal Framework: Priorities and Prospects'

[xxxviii] 'The Competitive Advantage of Nations', Michael E Porter, Harvard Business Review, March 1990

[xxxix] Per ABC Radio 'National Citizen juries - leadership for a new democracy', 3 January 2016, http://www.abc.net.au/radionational/programs/bigideas/citizen-juries---leadership-for-a-new-democracy/6755314

[xl] 'How Labor Governs', 1923 per 'A Conga Line of Suckholes'

[xli] 'The Latham Diaries', Mark Latham, 2005, Melbourne University Press

[xlii] By Theodore White, describing Lyndon Johnson's instinct for power, per Latham, 'A Conga Line of Suckholes'

[xliii] As summarised in & quoted from '50 Political Classics', Tom Butler Bowdon, p68

[xliv] 'Lazarus Rising', John Howard

[xlv] 'Club Sensible is casting its eye over Julia and Tony', Christopher Pearson, The Australian, 24 April 2010

[xlvi] The Lucky Country, Donald Horne, Penguin, 2009

[xlvii] From 'Learning Lessons from History', David Stephens, Canberra Times, 23 December 2013, http://www.canberratimes.com.au/comment/learning-lessons-of-history-20131222-2zstr.html

[xlviii] Interview with Sabra Lane, 7·30 report, ABC Television, 17 March 2016

[xlix] 'The Lucky Country', Donald Horne, Penguin, 2009

[l] 'Why we're Groping in the dark on Political Donations', Bernard Keane, 2 Feb 2016, http://www.crikey.com.au/2016/02/02/why-were-groping-in-the-dark-on-political-donations/

[li] 'Ruling the Void: The Hollowing of Western Democracy', Peter Mair, Verso, 2013

[lii] The Australian Financial Review, 2008, per 'The Best Australian Political Writing', 2009

[liii] 'The Lucky Country? Reinventing Australia' Ian Lowe

[liv] 'The Fourth Revolution', John Micklethwait and Adrian Wooldridge, as summarised in '50 Political Classics, Tom Butler-Bowdon, p197

[lv] 'The Post-American World', Fareed Zakaria, as summarised in '50 Political Classics', p314

[lvi] 'Why Nations Fail', Daron Acemoglu and James Robinson, 2012

[lvii] 'The Downside of Protectionism',Phil Ruthven, Company Director, March 2014, p56

[lviii] 'A Call to Action', Phil Ruthven, Company Director, May 2015, p32

[lix] http://www.gnhbhutan.org/about/
[lx] http://monocle.com/film/affairs/soft-power-survey-2015-16
[lxi] https://neo.ubs.com/shared/d11PQx5T84/?off_id=AC201510E72070370W343592219&ma=X47536B674A685951&camp_id=EM:UNKW:2015-10:29:U
[lxii] http://www.indexmundi.com/agriculture/?commodity=orange-juice
[lxiii] 'The Rise and Fall of the Great Powers', Paul Kennedy, as summarised in '50 Political Classics', Tom Butler-Bowdon, p148
[lxiv] https://www.globalinnovationindex.org/content/page/data-analysis/
[lxv] 'The World's 10 Best Governments', Forbes, 29 November 2012
[lxvi] http://reports.weforum.org/global-competitiveness-report-2014-2015/rankings/
[lxvii] http://www.countryranker.com/worlds-top-20-countries-with-best-government
[lxviii] 'United States: Where's the Strategy?', Andy Zelleke and Justin Talbot Zorn, The Diplomat, 5 February 2014
[lxix] 'The Costello Memoirs, The Age of Prosperity', Peter Costello with Peter Coleman, Melbourne University Press, 2008, p374
[lxx] 'Reigniting the Economy', Phil Ruthven, Company Director, pg30-31, Vol 31, Issue 9, October 2015
[lxxi] per 'Lazarus Rising'
[lxxii] 'Beyond the Nadir of Political Leadership', Dr. Anne Tiernan, Griffith Review 51, Jan 2016
[lxxiii] 'A Call to Action', Phil Ruthven, Company Director, May 2015, p33
[lxxiv] 'The Downside of Protectionism', Phil Ruthven, Company Director, March 2014, p56
[lxxv] From the Garran Oration 'Passion, People, Risk and Opportunity'
[lxxvi] 'Three things must change for a healthier democracy', Tim Dunlop, The Drum, 17 Oct 2014, http://www.abc.net.au/news/2014-10-17/dunlop-three-things-must-change-for-a-healthier-democracy/5820612
[lxxvii] per 'The Best Australian Political Writing', 2009
[lxxviii] 'The new road to ruin is paved with disaffection', Chris Kenny, The Australian, 12 March 2016
[lxxix] 'Beyond the Nadir of Political Leadership', Dr Anne Tiernan, Griffith Review 51, Jan 2016
[lxxx] 'Ten Reasons Global Investors are Petrified of Australia', Robert Gottliebsen, The Australian, 30 September 2015
[lxxxi] Interview with Gary Gray and Ian MacFarlane by Sabra Lane, 7:30 Report, ABC Television, 17 March 2016
[lxxxii] 'The Federal Budget is Hard to Fix but here are some Solutions', John Wanna, 11 November 2015, http://theconversation.com/the-federal-budget-is-hard-to-fix-but-here-are-some-solutions-50309

[lxxxiii] 'Right Path to recognition', Noel Pearson, The Australian, 12 March 2016
[lxxxiv] 'Battlelines', p.133
[lxxxv] 'What Australia needs is a genuine house of review', Joff Lelliott, The Drum, 3 Jan 2014
[lxxxvi] 'Taylor eyeing $27bn dividend from digital', Joe Kelly, The Australian, 20 February 2016, p6
[lxxxvii] "A Little Rebellion Now and Then is a Good Thing: A Letter from Thomas Jefferson to James Madison." Early America Review 1, no 1 (1996).
[lxxxviii] 'Beyond the Nadir of Political Leadership', Dr. Anne Tiernan, Griffith Review 51, Jan 2016
[lxxxix] per Tiernan, as per endnote above
[xc] The Six Functions of Governance, Dr. Lynda Bourne, PM World Journal, Vol. III, Issue XI, November 2014
[xci] per xlvi
[xcii] quote from Morgan Guerin at Museum Of Anthropology exhibit (January 2016)
[xciii] from 'Australian Political Culture', Rodney Smith, Pearson Education Australia, 2001
[xciv] 'The Way Ahead'
[xcv] Lowitja O'Donoghue, as cited in George Williams, Human Rights in the Australian Constitution, Oxford University Press, Melbourne, 1999, page 16.
[xcvi] 'Liberty, equality, fraternity: redefining 'French' values in the wake of Charlie Hebdo', The Conversation, Ian Coller, January 13, 2015
[xcvii] 'Creating a Strategy That Works', Paul Leinwand and Cesare Mainardi, strategy+business
[xcviii] 'Navigating Business Ethics', an interview with Dr Simon Longstaff, Company Director, Vol 32, Issue 1, February 2016, pg60
[xcix] 'An Open Letter to the New Prime Minister', Don Argus, The Australian, 19 September 2015
[c] 'The Rise and Fall Of Australia', Nick Bowen
[ci] Term used by Brendan O'Neill, 'Think Like an Elite or Quit Public Life', The Weekend Australian, 19-20 September, 2015
[cii] per Latham
[ciii] http://strategicawarenessessentials.com/blog/2015/11/18/6666, Steve Bowman, Strategic Awareness Essentials, 30 November 2015
[civ] The Australian, 2008, per 'The Best Australian political Writing', 2009
[cv] 'We 'don't have the luxury' to prolong leadership deficit', John Lyons, The Australian, 26 September 2015
[cvi] 'America Needs a Chief Strategy Officer', Andy Zelleke, Justin Talbot Zorn, Foreign Policy, November 2012
[cvii] per Parliamentary Education Office website http://www.peo.gov.au/learning/fact-sheets/cabinet.html

[cviii] 'How to fix our dysfunctional federal budget', businessspectator.com.au, John Wanna, 11 November 2015 (originally published in The Conversation)
[cix] 'I am not blind to the flaws that ended my prime ministership', Tony Abbott, The Australian, 23 April 2016
[cx] 'Familiar Studies of Man and Books', Robert Louis Stevenson, 1882, per Latham
[cxi] From 'The Autobiography', Margaret Thatcher, as quoted in '50 Political Classics' p278
[cxii] From 'Learning Lessons from History', David Stephens, Canberra Times, 23 December 2013, http://www.canberratimes.com.au/comment/learning-lessons-of-history-20131222-2zstr.html
[cxiii] 'Beyond the Nadir of Political Leadership', Dr. Anne Tiernan, Griffith Review 51, Jan 2016
[cxiv] http://ipsos.com.au/fairfaxipsos-polls-3/
[cxv] per 'The Best Australian political Writing', 2008
[cxvi] 'The Making of Australia', p96
[cxvii] Nicholas Barry, commenting on 'Political Amnesia – How We Forgot How To Govern', by Laura Tingle, Quarterly Essay, The Conversation, 2 December 2015, http://theconversation.com/review-political-amnesia-how-we-forgot-how-to-govern-50596
[cxviii] 'The Rise and Fall of Australia'
[cxix] per Latham, 'A Conga Line of Suckholes'
[cxx] 'Why Nations Fail', Daron Acemoglu and James Robinson, 2012
[cxxi] https://pirateparty.org.au/
[cxxii] per 'The Best Australian political Writing', 2009
[cxxiii] 'On the Abolition of Question Time', Patrick Allingham, Griffith Review 51, Jan 2016
[cxxiv] 'The Rise and Fall of Australia'
[cxxv] 'The Way Ahead'
[cxxvi] per Latham
[cxxvii] Based on a paper by Alex Zakaras, reproduced on the New Democracy website
[cxxviii] Based on the work of Marcus Schmidt, reproduced on the New Democracy website
[cxxix] Based on selective excerpts by Brian Martin, University of Wollongong, reproduced on the New Democracy website
[cxxx] Based on selective excerpts from 'A Citizen Legislature' by E. Callenbach and M Phillips, reproduced on the New Democracy website
[cxxxi] Based on the work of Prof. Ethan Leib, University of California, reproduced on the New Democracy website
[cxxxii] Reproduced based on information on the New Democracy website
[cxxxiii] Based on the paper 'Democracy Through Multi-Body Sortition' (Terry

Bouricius), published to the Journal of Public Deliberation (Vol.9 Iss. 1, Article 11, reproduced on the New Democracy website

[cxxxiv] Concept originated by Ned Crosby and Pat Benn, reproduced on the New Democracy website

[cxxxv] New Democracy website

[cxxxvi] New Democracy website

[cxxxvii] New Democracy website

[cxxxviii] New Democracy website

[cxxxix] New Democracy website

[cxl] As suggested in Rethinking the Vote, reproduced on the New Democracy website

[cxli] New Democracy website

[cxlii] New Democracy website

[cxliii] 'Citizens Juries – Leadership for a New Democracy', ABC Radio National, 3 January 2016, http://www.abc.net.au/radionational/programs/bigideas/citizen-juries---leadership-for-a-new-democracy/6755314

[cxliv] 'The Lucky Country' Introduction to the Fifth Edition by Donald Horne

[cxlv] Audit conducted by Infrastructure Australia. Quote from Australian Infrastructure Plan, February 2016, http://infrastructureaustralia.gov.au/policy-publications/publications/files/Australian_Infrastructure_Plan.pdf

[cxlvi] 'The Lucky Country? Reinventing Australia' Ian Lowe, UQ Press, 2016

[cxlvii] Laudato Si', the papal encyclical, per Robert Manne

[cxlviii] 'Fundamentals & Flexibility', Philip Lowe, speech to CFA Institute of Australia, 13 October 2015, www.rba.gov.au/speeches/2015/sp-dg-2015-10-13.html

[cxlix] 'The long legislative road to competitive markets', Paul Carvalho, 25 Nov 2015, http://www.businessspectator.com.au/article/2015/11/25/national-affairs/long-legislative-road-competitive-markets?utm_source=exact&utm_medium=email&utm_content=1696929&utm_campaign=kgb&modapt=

[cl] 'Understanding Productivity: Australia's Choice', Roy Green, Phillip Toner, Renu Argawal

[cli] per Robert Manne

[clii] Deloitte Insights, 'Positioning for Prosperity? Catching the Next Wave,' 2015

[cliii] 'Governance of the Nation: A Blueprint for Growth', Australian Institute of Company Directors. Note point 4 of the blueprint (Partnership with not-for-profits) excluded as it was considered outside the scope of this book.

[cliv] 'Baird is Big on Promises but light on Business Cases', Jacob Saulwick, Sydney Morning Herald, 3 October 2015

[clv] 'It will take more than being 'bouncy' to fix Australia's innovation system', Jenny Stewart, businessspectator.com.au, 9 Nov 2015

[clvi] 'It will take more than being 'bouncy' to fix Australia's innovation system', Jenny Stewart, businessspectator.com.au, 9 Nov 2015

[clvii] 1989, per Latham, 'A Conga Line of Suckholes'

[clviii] per Garran Oration per 'Passion, People, Risk and Opportunity'

[clix] per 'The Way Ahead'

[clx] 'Where is constitutional reform in Australia going?', A J Brown

[clxi] As per '50 Political Classics' p15

[clxii] 'Ten Reasons Global Investors are Petrified of Australia', Robert Gottliebsen, The Australian, 30 September 2015

[clxiii] An example being 'Connecting Citizens to Legislative Deliberations', Hendriks and Kay as referenced

[clxiv] 'Our high tech PM gets some things right', Paul Budde, October 2015 http://www.buddeblog.com.au/frompaulsdesk/our-hi-tech-prime-minister-moving-towards-smart-government/

[clxv] 'The March of Folly', Barbara Tuchman, 1984, per Latham, 'A Conga Line of Suckholes'

[clxvi] per Latham

[clxvii] per 'Why we need state governments in Australia', Sid Maher, The Australian, 5 January 2013

[clxviii] The concept of multi-level governance was first proposed by Marks (1993); Kay's reference is taken from Australian Journal of Public Administration, Vol 74, Issue 4, December 2015

[clxix] 'Australian Constitutional Values Survey 2014, Newspoll Limited, Professor AJ Brown, Griffith University, October 2014

[clxx] 'Worst Words', Don Watson, The Guardian, 2015, p4

[clxxi] 'Harvard Business Review on Change', Harvard Business School Press, 1996

[clxxii] 'A Radical Legacy', Geoff Gallop, Griffith Review 19

[clxxiii] 'National Reform Summit: we need to agree on what reform is for', Nick Cater, The Australian, 26 August 2015

[clxxiv] 'Beyond 2016', Phil Ruthven, Company Director, December 2015, p31

[clxxv] per Robert Manne

[clxxvi] 'The Way Ahead', Liz Byrski

[clxxvii] 'The Way Ahead'

www.ingramcontent.com/pod-product-compliance
Lightning Source LLC
Chambersburg PA
CBHW070225190526
45169CB00001B/78